# The

# Gobbledygook

# Book

D0775767

# The

# Gobbledygook

# Book

Dictionary of Acronyms

Abbreviations

Initializations

&

Esoteric Terminology

Compiled by Franklin W. Fox, III

Momentum Books, Ltd.
Troy, Michigan

Manufactured in the United States of America

ISBN: 1-879094-50-9
1998   1997   1996   1995        5  4  3  2


Published by Momentum Books, Ltd.
6964 Crooks Road, Suite #1
Troy, Michigan 48098
USA

# *Table of Contents*

# INTRODUCTION

As our complex world grows even more complex, simplification of communication becomes a necessity. Instead, the opposite seems true. Every day we are besieged by new acronyms, abbreviations and esoteric terms that merely add to the confusion.

Worst offenders are those whose help we need most: police, government, military, doctors and lawyers. Even our kids are growing up speaking a language filled with acronyms that most adults can't comprehend. And, in a steadfast attempt to imitate reality, our movies and television programs are sacrificing understanding on the altar of illusion. They would rather say "MI" than "heart attack" because that's the enigmatic way real doctors speak.

There are also those institutions that are secretive on purpose, making even their simplest designations difficult to understand. The CIA director of clandestine services is called the DDP, which is also the name for the department he runs. And today's new military is even more arcane than the old, using MRI's instead of K rations, and BDU's instead of fatigues.

This modest little volume may not simplify your existence, and it certainly won't give away any national secrets. But it could help remove some of life's unnecessary mysteries of which there are already too many.

As we say on the cover, the entries are not all-inclusive—just the ones we believe most people will stumble across sooner or later. And in the case of multiple definitions, the most common are usually listed first.

Special thanks are due Anna Aydt Doyle and Mark Haney. Without their valuable assistance, *Buzzwords from Cyberspace* would have remained UFO's in an alien environment.

# *General Acronyms*

# *Abbreviations*
# *&*
# *Initializations*

**A** = atomic, as in A-bomb
    = answer
    = away (sports)
    = assist (sports)
    = excellent, scholastic grade
    = battery size
    = USDA grade for dairy products and eggs
    = stock and bond rating
    = blood type (also B, AB and O)
    = adultery; the infamous scarlet letter
    = adenine; one of four DNA building blocks (see C, G, T)
    = Austria (international car index mark)
**A's** = Oakland Athletics baseball team
**A-1** = excellent; originated by Lloyd's of London to rate ships
**A4** = international paper size closest to US letter size; 210mm x 297mm or 8.27" x 11.69"
**AA** = Alcoholics Anonymous
    = Alzheimer's Association
    = antiaircraft
    = American Airlines
    = battery size
    = USDA grade for dairy products and eggs
    = All-American
    = stock and bond rating
**AAA** = American Automobile Association
    = Amateur Athletics Association
    = American Accounting Association
    = American Arbitration Association
    = American Anthropological Association
    = antiaircraft artillery; "triple A"
    = battery size
    = Agricultural Adjustment Administration
    = stock and bond rating

**AAAA** = American Association of Advertising Agencies
    = American Association for Affirmative Action
**AAAC** = Affirmative Action Advisory Committee
**AAAI** = American Academy of Allergy and Immunology
**AAAL** = American Academy of Arts and Letters
**AAAS** = American Association for the Advancement of Science
**AABB** = American Association of Blood Banks
**AACA** = Antique Automobile Club of America
**AACC** = American Association for Contamination Control
**AACS** = Airways and Air Communications Service
**AAD** = American Academy of Dermatologists
**AAF** = American Advertising Federation
    = American Association of Florists
    = Amateur Athletic Foundation
    = Allied Armed Forces (WW II)
**AAFES** = Army and Air Force Exchange Service; the PX or BX
**AAFP** = American Academy of Family Physicians
**AAFS** = American Academy of Forensic Sciences
**AAGP** = American Academy of General Practice
**AAI** = Allied Armies in Italy (WW II)
**AAIA** = Association on American Indian Affairs
**AAM** = American Association of Museums
**AAMA** = American Automobile Manufacturers Association
**AAMH** = Association for Advancement of Mental Health
**AAN** = American Academy of Neurology
**A&M** = agricultural and mechanical
**A&P** = Atlantic and Pacific supermarkets
**A&R** = artists and repertory
**AAO** = American Academy of Ophthalmology
    = American Academy of Optometry
    = American Academy of Osteopathy
**AAOM** = American Academy of Oral Medicine

**AAP** = American Academy of Pediatrics
  = American Association of Pathologists
  = affirmative action program
**AAPBC** = American Association of Professional Baseball Clubs
**AAPG** = American Association of Petroleum Geologists
**AAPM** = American Association ofPhysicists in Medicine
**AAPS** = Association of American Physicians and Surgeons
**AAR** = against all risks
  = Association of American Railroads
**AARP** = American Association of Retired Persons
**AAS** = American Astronautical Society
  = American Astronomical Society
  = American Association of Suicidology
**AASHTO** = American Association of State Highway and Transportation Officials
**AAU** = Amateur Athletic Union
  = Association of American Universities
**AAUN** = American Association for the United Nations
**AAUP** = American Association of University Presses
**AAUP** = American Association of University Professors
**AAVSO** = American Association of Variable Star Observers
**AAUW** = American Association of University Women
**AAVS** = American Anti-Vivisection Society
**AAZK** = American Association of Zoo Keepers
**AB** = Alberta (postal symbol)
  = bachelor of arts (Latin: *artium baccalaureus*)
  = at bat
  = blood type (also A,B and O)
  = air base
**A/B** = airborne (military)

**ABA** = American Bar Association
    = American Burn Association
    = American Booksellers Association
    = American Boxing Association
**ABBR** = abbreviation
**ABC** = American Broadcasting Company
    = American Bowling Congress
    = already been chewed, as in ABC gum
**ABC's** = the alphabet
**ABCC** = Atomic Bomb Casualty Commission
**ABM** = anti-ballistic missile
**ABN** = airborne
**ABNCP** = airborne command post
**A-BOMB** = atomic bomb
**ABP** = American Board of Pathology
**ABQ** = Albuquerque, New Mexico, airport
**ABR** = abridged
**ABS** = anti-lock brake system
    = abdominal muscles
    = absolute
    = American Bureau of Shipping
**ABT** = American Ballet Theater
**ABWA** = American Business Women's Association
**AC** = alternating current (see DC)
    = air conditioning
    = athletic club
    = Air Canada
    = Albert Champion
    = British car made by Autocarriers, Ltd.
**Ac** = actinium; a chemical element
**A/C** = air conditioning

**ACA** = American Chiropractic Association
     = Adult Children of Alcoholics (also ACOA)
     = American Composers Alliance
     = American Council for the Arts
     = Arms Control Association
     = Acapulco, Mexico, airport
**ACAD** = academy
**ACB** = American Council of the Blind
**ACCT** = account
**ACD** = automatic call distributor
**ACDA** = US Arms Control and Disarmament Agency
**AC/DC** = bisexual
**AC-DELCO** = GM acronym: Albert Champion - Dayton Electronics Company
**ACDE** = American Council for Drug Education
**ACDF** = Adult Children of Dysfunctional Families
**ACE** = American Council on Education
     = Active Corps of Executives (SBA)
     = Association of Conservation Engineers
     = Allied Command in Europe; NATO HQ
**ACHP** = Advisory Council on Historic Preservation
**ACIR** = Advisory Commission on Intergovernmental Relations
**ACLANT** = Allied Command Atlantic HQ (NATO)
**ACLU** = American Civil Liberties Union
**ACNP** = American College of Nuclear Physicians
**ACNW** = Advisory Committee on Nuclear Waste
**ACOG** = American College of Obstetrics and Gynecology
**ACORN** = Association of Community Organizations for Reform Now
**ACP** = American College of Physicians
**ACRI** = Air Conditioning and Refrigeration Institute
**ACRONYM** = word formed from the first letter or let-

ters of each of the successive parts or major parts of a compound term

**ACS** = American College of Surgeons

= American Cancer Society

= American Chemical Society

= Army Community Service

**ACSH** = American Council on Science and Health

**ACSM** = American Congress of Surveying and Mapping

**ACT** = American College Testing program

= Action for Children's Television

**ACTF** = American College Theatre Festival

**ACTWU** = Amalgamated Clothing and Textile Workers Union

**ACWM** = Americans for Customary Weights and Measures

**ACY** = Atlantic City, NJ, International Airport

**ACYF** = Administration for Children, Youth and Families (DHHS)

**AD** = advertisement

= anno Domini (Latin: in the year of our Lord)

= assistant director

= art director

**ADA** = American Dental Association

= American Dairy Association

= American Diabetes Association

= assistant district attorney

= Americans for Democratic Action

= air defense artillery

**ADAM** = American Divorce Association of Men

**ADAMHA** = Alcohol, Drug Abuse, and Mental Health Administration

**ADC** = Aid to Dependent Children (see AFDC)

= aide-de-camp

**ADD** = attention deficit disorder (also ADHD)

= Administration of Developmental Disabilities (DHHS)

**ADEA** = Age Discrimination in Employment Act
**ADF** = automatic direction finder
**ADH** = anti-diuretic hormone
**ADHA** = American Dental Hygienists' Association
**ADHC** = adult day health care (VA)
**ADHD** = attention deficit hyperactive disorder
**ADI** = area of dominant influence (of advertising)
**ADIZ** = air defense identification zone
**ADJ** = adjective
**ADL** = Anti-Defamation League
**ad lib** = improvise (Latin: *ad libitum*, for at pleasure)
**ADM** = admiral
    = administrative
**ADMIN** = administration
**ADMIRAL Q** = WWII code name used by FDR
**ADP** = asteroid discovery project (space)
**ADPA** = American Defense Preparedness Association
**ADR** = American Depository Receipts (stock exchange)
**ADRDA** = Alzheimer's Disease and Related Disorders Association
**ADRMP** = auto-dial recorded message player; "ad-ramp"
**ADRS** = automated data retrieval system
**ADS** = Agent Distributor Service, abroad (DOC)
**ADSA** = American Dream Savings Account
**ADV** = advance
    = advertising or advertisement
    = adverb
**AEA** = Atomic Energy Agency, International (UN)
    = Atomic Energy Authority
    = Actors' Equity Association
    = Artists Equity Association
    = American Economic Association
**AEAF** = Allied Expeditionary Air Force (WW II)

**AEC** = Atomic Energy Commission
  = Alternative Energy Coalition
**AEE** = Association of Energy Engineers
**AEF** = American Expeditionary Forces (WW I)
  = Allied Expeditionary Force (WW II)
**AER** = Army Emergency Relief
**AES** = American Epilepsy Society
**AET** = automotive emissions test
**AF** = Air Force
  = audio frequencies
  = Air France airlines
**AFA** = Air Force Association
  = American Federation of Astrologers
  = American Forensic Association
**AFAM** = Ancient Free and Accepted Masons
**AFB** = Air Force Base
  = American Foundation for the Blind
**AFBF** = American Farm Bureau Federation
**AFC** = American Football Conference
  = automatic frequency control
**AFCC** = Air Force Communications Command
**AFCS** = Active Federal Commissioned Service
**AFDB** = Alternative Fuel Data Bank
**AFDC** = Aid to Families with Dependent Children (see ADC)
**AFGE** = American Federation of Government Employees
**AFI** = American Film Institute
  = American Fur Industry
  = Association of Federal Investigators
**AFIO** = Association of Former Intelligence Officers
**AFL-CIO** = American Federation of Labor and
Congress of Industrial Organizations
**AFM** = American Federation of Musicians
**AFMC** = Association of Former Members of Congress

**AFN** = Armed Forces Network
**AFND** = Armed Forces News Division
**AFNE** = Americans For Nuclear Energy
**AFP** = American Federation of Police
    = Agence France Presse
**AFPI** = American Foreign Policy Institute
**AFPVD** = American Federation for the Prevention of Venereal Disease
**AFR** = African
**AFRO** = Afro-American
      = Afro-American hairdo
**AFS** = American Floral Society
**AFSATCOM** = Air Force satellite communications system
**AFSC** = Armed Forces Staff College
**AFSCME** = American Federation of State, County and Municipal Employees
**AFT** = American Federation of Teachers
    = afternoon·
**AFTRA** = American Federation of Television and Radio Artists
**AFV** = armored fighting vehicle
**AG** = attorney general
    = adjutant general
    = agricultural
    = army green
**Ag** = silver (Latin: *argentum*); a chemical element
**AGA** = American Gas Association
     = American Gastroenterological Association
     = American Genetic Association
**AGC** = Association of General Contractors
**AGCY** = agency
**AGF** = US Army Ground Forces
**AGI** = adjusted gross income (as in tax forms)

**AGMA** = American Guild of Musical Artists
= American Gear Manufacturers Association
**AGNET** = Agriculture and Home Management On-Line Network (USDA)
**AGRIC** = agriculture or agricultural
**AGRICOLA** = General Agriculture Database (USDA)
**AGS** = American Geographical Society
= American Geriatrics Society
**AGU** = American Geophysical Union
**AGZ** = actual ground zero
**AH** = anno hegira; in the year of Muhammad's flight from Mecca, AD 622
= ampere-hour
**AHA** = American Heart Association
= American Historical Association
= American Hospital Association
**AHF** = American Health Foundation
**AHL** = American Hockey League
**AHMA** = American Hardware Manufacturers Association
**AHPA** = American Horse Protection Association
**AHS** = American Horticultural Society
**AHSA** = American Horse Shows Association
**AI** = artificial intelligence
= Air India
**AIA** = The American Institute of Architects
**AIAA** = Aerospace Industries Association of America
**AIC** = Address Information Center (US Postal Service)
= The American Institute of Chemists
**AIChE** = American Institute of Chemical Engineers
**AICPA** = American Institute of Certified Public Accountants
**AICR** = American Institute of Cancer Research
**AID** = Agency for International Development (DOS)
= artificial insemination by donor (see AIH)

**AIDS** = acquired immune deficiency syndrome
**AIEE** = American Institute of Electrical Engineers
**AIFD** = American Institute of Floral Designers
**AIH** = artificial insemination by husband (see AID)
**AIHA** = American Industrial Hygiene Association
**AIMM&PE** = The American Institute of Mining, Metal-
lurgical, and Petroleum Engineers
**AIP** = American Institute of Physics
**AIRCAV** = Airborne Cavalry (US Army)
**AIR EVAC** = evacuation by aircraft
**AIVF** = Association of Independent Video and Filmmakers
**AJ** = Air Belgium
**AJA** = American Judges Association
**AJC** = American Jewish Congress
**AJGA** = American Junior Golf Association
**AJM** = American Journal of Medicine
**AJPH** = American Journal of Public Health
**AK** = Alaska (postal code)
**AKA** = also known as; alias
**AKC** = American Kennel Club
**AK-47** = Soviet assault rifle
**AL** = Alabama (postal code)
    = American League (baseball)
    = Arab League
**Al** = aluminum; a chemical element
**ALA** = American Library Association
    = American Lung Association
    = Alabama
**ALAM** = Association of Licensed Automobile Manufacturers
**AL-ANON** = alcoholics anonymous, support group for
families of alcoholics (not part of AA)
**ALAS** = Alaska
**ALCAN** = Alaska-Canada, as in Alcan Highway

**ALCM** = air-launched cruise missile
**ALCOA** = Aluminum Company of America
**ALEC** = American Legislative Exchange Council
**ALG** = algebra
**ALO** = authorized level of organization
**ALOE** = A Lady of England; pseudonym of Charlotte Maria Tucker, author of children's tales
**ALPA** = Air Line Pilots Association
**ALR** = American Law Reports
**ALS** = American Lupus Society
    = autograph letter signed
**ALT** = alternate
    = altitude
**ALTA** = Alberta
**AM** = ante meridiem (before noon; see PM)
    = amplitude modulation band (radio; see FM)
    = American
    = Aeromexico
    = anno mundi (Latin for year of the world); 3761 BC, year of creation according to the Jewish Calendar
**Am** = americium; a chemical element
**AMA** = American Medical Association
    = Automobile Manufacturers Association
    = American Motorcycle Association
    = American Management Association
**AMB** = ambassador
    = Antarctic Meteorite Bibliography (NASA)
**AMBBA** = Associated Master Barbers and Beauticians of America
**AMBUCS** = National Association of American Business Clubs
**AMC** = Association of Management Consultants
    = Air Mobility Command (military)
**AMCCOM** = Armament, Munitions and Chemical Command (US Army)

13

**AME** = African Methodist Episcopal Church
**AMEDD** = US Army Medical Department
**AMER** = America or American
**AMERIND** = American Indian
**AMEX** = American Stock Exchange
       = American Express
**AMF** = American Machine and Foundry
**AmFAR** = American Foundation for AIDS Research
**AM/FM** = radio with both bands
**AMG** = American Military Government
**AMI** = American Meat Institute
**AMP** = ampere
**AMPAS** = Academy of Motion Picture Arts & Sciences
**AMP HR** = ampere-hour
**AMPTP** = Alliance of Motion Picture and Television Producers
**AMS** = American Meteorological Society
       = American Mathematical Society
       = Agricultural Marketing Service
**AMT** = alternative minimum tax
       = amount
**AMTRACK** = National Railroad Passenger Corporation
**AMU** = atomic mass unit
**AMVETS** = American Veterans of World War II
**ANA** = American Nurses' Association
       = American Numismatic Association
       = Association of National Advertisers
**ANARC** = Association of North American Radio Clubs
**ANAT** = anatomy or anatomical
**ANC** = African National Congress
       = Anchorage, Alaska, airport
       = ancient
**ANEC** = American Nuclear Energy Council

**ANG** = Air National Guard
**ANGB** = Air National Guard Base
**ANGLO** = Anglo-American
       = Caucasian
**ANL** = Argonne National Laboratory
**ANMCC** = Alternate National Military Command Center, Raven Rock, PA
**ANNCR** = announcer
**ANON** = anonymous
**ANP** = aircraft nuclear propulsion
**ANPA** = American Newspaper Publishers Association
**ANS** = American Nuclear Society
     = American Numismatic Society
**ANSI** = American National Standards Institute
**ANT** = antonym
    = antenna
**ANTILOG** = antilogarithm
**ANZAC** = Australian and New Zealand Army Corps (WW I)
**ANZUS** = Council of Australia, New Zealand and the United States
**AOA** = American Optometric Association
     = American Osteopathic Association
     = Administration on Aging (DHHS)
**AOC** = area of concentration
**AOH** = Ancient Order of Hibernians
**AOK** = all okay (aerospace)
**AOL** = America Online
**AOPA** = Aircraft Owners and Pilots Association
**AORN** = Association of Operating Room Nurses
**AOU** = American Ornithologists' Union
**AP** = Associated Press
   = air police (Air Force MP)
   = aiming point (military)
   = armor piercing

**APA** = American Psychiatric Association
　　　 = American Pharmaceutical Association
　　　 = American Psychoanalytic Association
　　　 = American Psychological Association
　　　 = American Philological Association
　　　 = American Planning Association
**APAA** = Automotive Parts and Accessories Association
**APC** = all purpose capsule; aspirin, phenacetin and caffeine
　　　 = American Plastics Council
　　　 = armored personnel carrier
**APCA** = Air Pollution Control Association
**APCO** = Association of Public Safety Communications Officials
**APHA** = American Public Health Association
**APHIS** = Animal and Plant Health Inspection Service (USDA)
**API** = American Petroleum Institute
　　　 = American Paper Institute
　　　 = American Press Institute
**APO** = army and air force post office
**APP** = application
　　　 = appendix
**APPA** = American Public Power Association
**APR** = annual percentage rate, of interest
　　　 = April
**APS** = accident-prone situation
　　　 = atomic power station
　　　 = American Physics Society
　　　 = American Philatelic Society
**APT** = apartment
　　　 = Associated Pharmacologists and Toxicologists
**APTA** = American Physical Therapy Association
**APU** = auxiliary power unit (aircraft)
**APV** = all-purpose vehicle

**APWA** = American Public Welfare Association
**APWU** = American Postal Workers Union
**APXS** = alpha-proton-x-ray spectrometer; for taking close-ups of Martian rocks
**APY** = annual percentage yield
**AQ** = Aloha Airlines, Hawaii
**AQHA** = American Quarter Horse Association
**AR** = Arkansas (postal code)
    = artificial respiration
    = aspect ratio
    = Aerolineas Argentinas
    = army regulation
**Ar** = argon; a chemical element
**ARAB** = Arabian
**ARAMCO** = Arabian-American Oil Company
**ARCC** = American Rivers Conservation Council
**ARCH** = architecture
**ARCO** = Atlantic-Richfield Company
**ARDA** = Atomic Research Development Authority
**ARDC** = American Racing Drivers Club
    = Army Armament Research and Development Center
**AREA 51** = Groom Dry Lake; Air Force secret test facility in Nevada
**ARIZ** = Arizona
**ARK** = Arkansas
**ARL** = Air Resources Laboratory (NOAA)
**ARM** = adjustable rate mortgage
**ARN** = Animal Rights Network
**ARNG** = Army National Guard
**ARP** = Arp Catalog of peculiar galaxies (astronomy)
**ARR** = arrive or arrival
**ARS** = Agricultural Research Service
    = American Rose Society

**ARSA** = American Reye's Syndrome Association
**ARTY** = artillery
**ARVN** = Army of Vietnam (US Army designation)
**AS** = American Samoa (postal code)
 = Alaska Airlines
**As** = arsenic; a chemical element
**ASA** = American Society of Appraisers
 = American Standards Association
 = Amateur Swimming Association
 = Amateur Softball Association
 = American Statistical Association
 = American Sugar Alliance
**ASADA** = Atomic Space and Development Authority
**ASA NUMBER** = film sensitivity rating
**ASAP** = as soon as possible
**ASAT** = anti-satellite weapon
**ASC** = American Society of Cinematographers
**ASCAP** = American Society of Composers, Authors, and Publishers
**ASCE** = American Society of Civil Engineers
**ASCLD** = American Society of Crime Laboratory Directors
**ASCMS** = American Society of Contemporary Medicine and Surgery
**ASCOB** = assorted colors other than black (used by dog breeders)
**ASCP** = American Society of Clinical Pathologists
**ASD** = American Society of Dowsers
**ASDIC** = Anti-Submarine Detection and Investigation Committee (WW II)
**ASE** = American Society of Employers
 = American Society of Editors (movies)
 = American Stock Exchange; also AMEX
 = Automotive Service Excellence

**ASEAN** = Association of South-East Asian Nations
**ASES** = American Solar Energy Society
**ASGCA** = American Society of Golf Course Architects
**ASH** = American Society of Hematology
**ASHG** = American Society of Human Genetics
**ASHRAE** = American Society of Heating, Refrigerating & Air Conditioning Engineers
**ASI** = airspeed indicator
**ASID** = American Society of Interior Designers
**ASIH** = American Society of Ichthyologists and Herpetologists
**ASIL** = American Society of International Law
**ASIM** = American Society of Internal Medicine
**ASIP** = American Society for Investigative Pathology
**ASIS** = American Society for Industrial Security
**ASJA** = American Society of Journalists and Authors
**ASL** = American sign language
= Atmospheric Sciences Laboratory (US Army)
**ASLA** = American Society of Landscape Architects
**ASLB** = Atomic Safety and Licensing Board
**ASM** = American Society for Metals
= air-to-surface missile
**ASMA** = American Society of Music Arrangers
**ASME** = American Society of Mechanical Engineers
**ASN** = American Society of Notaries
**ASNE** = American Society of Naval Engineers
**ASNPE** = American Society of Newspaper Editors
**ASOL** = American Symphony Orchestra League
**ASPA** = American Society for Public Administration
**ASPAC** = Asian and Pacific Council
**ASPCA** = American Society for the Prevention of Cruelty to Animals

**ASPCC** = American Society for the Prevention of
Cruelty to Children
**ASPRS** = American Society of Plastic and
Reconstructive Surgeons
**ASQC** = American Society for Quality Control
**ASR** = airport surveillance radar
= air-sea rescue
**ASRC** = Atmospheric Sciences Research Center
**ASROC** = anti submarine rocket
**ASSE** = American Society of Safety Engineers
**ASSN** = association
**ASSOC** = associate
**ASSR** = Autonomous Soviet Socialist Republic
**ASST** = assistant
**ASSY** = assembly
**AST** = apparent solar time; sundial time
**ASTA** = American Society of Travel Agents
**ASTM** = American Society for Testing and Materials
**ASTP** = army specialized training program
**ASTR** = astronomy
**ASV** = advanced safety vehicle
= American Standard Version, of the Bible
**ASW** = anti submarine warfare
**ASZ** = American Society of Zoologists
**AT** = antitank
**At** = astatine; a chemical element
**ATA** = American Trucking Associations
= American Translators Association
**AT&SF** = Atchison, Topeka and Santa Fe (railroad)
**AT&T** = American Telephone and Telegraph
**ATC** = air traffic control
= automatic temperature control (automotive)
**ATCA** = Air Traffic Control Association

**ATF** = Bureau of Alcohol, Tobacco and Firearms; also BATF (US)

= automatic transmission fluid

**ATIS** = Automatic Transcribed Information Service, of airport flight conditions (USAF)

**ATL** = Atlantic

**ATLA** = Association of Trial Lawyers of America

**ATLAS** = early US missile

**ATM** = automated-teller machine

**ATP** = Association of Tennis Professionals

**ATT** = attached

**ATTN** = attention

**ATTY** = attorney

**ATU** = Amalgamated Transit Union

**ATV** = all-terrain vehicle

**AT WT** = atomic weight

**AU** = astronomical unit; mean radius of earth's orbit or 93 million miles

**Au** = gold (Latin: *aurum*); a chemical element

**AUA** = American Urological Association

= Aruba airport

**AUG** = August

= augment

**AURORA** = secret Mach 5 Lockheed recon plane

**AUS** = Australia

= Army of the United States

**AUSA** = Association of the US Army

**AUTH** = author

= authentic

= authorized

**AUTO** = automobile

= automatic

= automatic pistol

**AUTODIN** = automatic digital network
**AUTOVON** = automatic voice network
**AUW** = advanced underwater weapons; nuclear depth bombs
**AUX** = auxiliary
**AV** = audio-visual
   = Authorized Version, of the Bible
**AVC** = American Veterans Committee
**AVDP** = avoirdupois; system of weights as opposed to metric or Troy
**AVE** = avenue
**AVG** = American Volunteer Group in WWII China; "Flying Tigers"
      = average
**AVI** = automatic vehicle identification, by license-plate bar code; not here yet but it's coming
**AVL** = automatic vehicle location (mobile communications)
**AVMA** = American Veterinary Medical Association
**AVN** = aviation
**AVS** = Association for Voluntary Sterilization
**AWA** = American Wine Association
**AWACS** = airborne warning and control system (military radar aircraft)
**AWC** = Army War College
**AWD** = all-wheel drive
**AWF** = American Wrestling Federation
**AWMA** = Air & Waste Management Association
**AWOL** = absent without leave
**AWWA** = American Water Works Association
**AX** = American Express
**AXAF** = Advanced X-ray Astrophysics Facility, proposed for space
**AY** = Finnair airline

**AYH** = American Youth Hostels
**AZ** = Arizona (postal code)
    = Al Italia airline
**AZA** = American Zoo and Aquarium Association
**AZT** = azidothymine; treatment for AIDS

**B** = born
    = blood type (also A, AB and O)
    = good, scholastic grade
    = lower-budget movie
    = bishop (chess)
    = bomber (USAF)
    = boron; a chemical element
    = Belgium (international car index mark)
    = stock and bond rating
    = bid price (stock exchange)
**B-1** = low-level supersonic penetration bomber, by Rockwell International
**B-1B** = stealth version of the B-1
**B-17** = WW II 4-prop heavy bomber; "Flying Fortress"
**B-24** = WW II 4-prop heavy bomber; Consolidated "Liberator"
**B-25** = WW II twin-prop fighter-bomber; North American "Mitchell"
**B-29** = WW II 4-prop heavy bomber dropped first A-bombs on Japan; Boeing "Super Fortress"
**B-36** = 6 pusher-prop heavy strategic bomber by Convair; first plane big enough to carry the first H-bomb (see MARK 17)
**B-47** = six-jet sweptwing medium bomber; Boeing "Stratojet"
**B-52** = long-range nuclear bomber; Boeing "Stratofortress" or "BUFF"
**B-53** = gravity bomb; 12-ft. long, nine-megaton "silo buster"

**B-58** = delta-wing bomber; Convair "Hustler"

**BA** = bachelor of arts

    = Batterers Anonymous

    = batting average (baseball)

    = Buenos Aires

    = British Airways

    = British-American

**Ba** = barium; a chemical element

**BAA** = Bureau of African Affairs

**BACAS** = Business Analysis and Customer Approval System (computers)

**B&B** = bed and breakfast

**B&O** = Baltimore and Ohio (railroad)

**B&W** = black and white

**BAR** = Browning automatic rifle

    = barometer or barometric

**BART** = Blacks in Advertising, Radio and Television

    = Bay Area Rapid Transit, in San Francisco

    = baronet

**BATEA** = best available technology economically available

**BATF** = Bureau of Alcohol, Tobacco and Firearms; also ATF (US)

**BB** = bases on balls, given up by a pitcher (baseball)

    = shot used in an air rifle or pistol (.18 inch)

    = standard shot-size designation

    = stock and bond rating

    = US Navy designation for battleships

**BBB** = Better Business Bureau

    = standard shot-size designation (.19 inch)

    = stock and bond rating

**BBC** = British Broadcasting Corporation

**BBER** = Bureau of Business and Economic Research

**BB-GUN** = air pistol or rifle firing BB shot

24

**BBL** = barrel or barrels
**BBQ** = barbecue
**BC** = before Christ (calendar)
    = British Columbia
    = boat club
    = popular comic strip by Johnny Hart
**BCA** = Balloon Club of America
**BCCA** = Beer Can Collectors of America
**BCD** = binary coded decimal
**BChE** = bachelor of chemical engineering
**BCS** = bar-code sorter
**BCTWIU** = Bakery, Confectionery, and Tobacco Workers International Union
**BD** = board
    = bound
    = barrels per day
    = bomb disposal
**BDA** = Bermuda airport
**BD FT** = board foot or board feet
**BDU** = battle dress uniform
**BE** = bachelor of engineering
**Be** = beryllium; a chemical element
**BEA** = Bureau of Economic Analysis
**BEBA** = Bureau of Economic and Business Affairs
**BEC** = Bureau of Employment Compensation
**BEd** = bachelor of education
**BEEMER** = variation of Bimmer, for BMW
**BEF** = British Expeditionary Force
    = before
**BELG** = Belgium or Belgian
**BEM** = British Empire Medal
**BENELUX** = Belgium, Netherlands and Luxembourg
**BETA** = videotape format largely superseded by VHS

25

**BEV** = billion electron volts
= Black English vernacular
**BF** = black female
= boldface
**Bf 109** = WW II German pursuit plane, by Messerschmitt; also Me 109
**BFA** = bachelor of fine arts
= black female American
= Balloon Federation of America
**BFOQ** = bona fide occupational qualifications
**BGN** = Branch of Geographic Names (DOD)
**BGR** = Bangor, Maine, airport
**BHE** = Bureau of Health Education
**BHEP** = basic human error probability
**BHI** = Better Hearing Institute
**BHM** = Birmingham, Alabama, airport
**BHP** = brake horsepower
**BHSP** = basic human success probability
**Bi** = bisexual
= bismuth; a chemical element
**BIA** = Bureau of Indian Affairs
**BIB** = biblical
**BiBF** = bisexual black female
**BIBL** = Bibliographic Information File (LC)
**BiBM** = bisexual black male
**BID** = Business Improvement District
= twice a day (Latin: *bis in die*)
**BIE** = Bureau of Industrial Economics (DOC)
**BiF** = bisexual female
**BIG 3** = General Motors, Ford and Chrysler
**BIG 10** = midwestern college athletic conference
**BIG BOARD** = New York Stock Exchange; NYSE
**BIG SKY** = northwestern athletic conference

**BIKE** = bicycle
**BIL** = Billings, Montana, airport
**BiM** = bisexual male
**BIM** = Bimini, Bahamas, airport
**BIMMER** = BMW
**BIO** = biological
    = biography
**BIO-HAZARD** = biologically hazardous
**BIOPIC** = biographical movie
**BIS** = Bismarck, North Dakota, airport
    = Bank for International Settlements
**BIW** = body in white; automotive prototype in unpainted metal
**BiWF** = bisexual white female
**BiWM** = bisexual white male
**BIZ** = business
**BJ** = bachelor of journalism
**BK** = Burger King
    = book
    = bank
    = balk (baseball)
**Bk** = berkelium; a chemical element
**BL** = block (basketball)
**BLA** = Brown Lung Association
**BLDG** = building
**BLDR** = builder
**BLit** = bachelor of literature
**BLK** = black
    = block
**BLM** = Bureau of Land Management
**BLS** = Bureau of Labor Statistics
**BLT** = sandwich of bacon, lettuce and tomato
**BLVD** = boulevard

BM = basal metabolism
    = black male
    = bowel movement
BMA = Black Music Association
    = black male American
BMAA = Bicycle Manufacturers Association of America
BMC = British Motor Corporation
BMCS = Bureau of Motor Carrier Safety
BMDO = Ballistic Missile Defense Organization
BMEP = brake mean effective pressure
BMEWS = ballistic missile early warning system
BMI = Broadcast Music Incorporated
    = Book Manufacturers Institute
BMOC = big man on campus
BMP = Soviet armored fighting vehicle
BMR = basal metabolic rate
BMW = *Bayerische Motoren Werke*; German automobile company
BMX = bicycle motocross; cross-country race
BN = battalion
BNA = Nashville, Tennessee, airport
BO = body odor
    = box office
BOAC = British Overseas Airways Corporation
BOAUS = Boat Owners Association of the United States
BOCK'S CAR = nickname of B-29 that dropped A-bomb on Nagasaki; after the plane's usual but not acting pilot
BOD = biochemical oxygen demand
BOI = Boise, Idaho, airport
BOISA = Bureau of Oceans and International and Scientific Affairs
BOMC = Book of the Month Club
BOQ = bachelor officers' quarters (military)

**BOS** = Boston, Massachusetts, airport
**BOSOX** = Boston Red Sox baseball team
**BOT** = botany or botanical
**BP** = blood pressure
    = boiling point
    = beautiful people
    = British Petroleum
    = bishop
**B/P** = blueprint
**BPA** = Baseball Players Association
**BPAA** = Bowling Proprietors' Association of America
**BPD** = barrels per day
**BPH** = benign prostate hyperplasia (or hypertrophy); enlarged prostate
**BPOE** = Benevolent and Protective Order of Elks
      = best people on earth
**BPR** = Bureau of Public Roads; old cover for CIA HQ
**BPW** = Business and Professional Women's Clubs
**BR** = brown
    = bedroom
    = brass
    = British
**Br** = bromine; a chemical element
**BR&C** = base realignment and closure (military)
**BRAZ** = Brazil or Brazilian
**BREN GUN** = British light machine gun; after Brno (Czechoslovakia) and Enfield (England) where made
**BRG** = British racing green; car color
**BRI** = Behavioral Research Institute
    = Business Research Institute
**BRIG** = brigade
     = brigadier
**BRIG GEN** = brigadier general

**BRIT** = Britisher or British
    = Britain
**BRM** = British Racing Motor; British race cars
**BRO** = brother
**BROS** = brothers
**BRWM** = Board on Radioactive Waste Management
**BS** = bachelor of science
    = bull manure
**BSA** = Boy Scouts of America
    = Botanical Society of America
**BSC** = British Society of Cinematographers
**BSE** = breast self-examination
**BSO** = blue stellar objects; possibly aged quasars
**BSR** = buzz, squeak, rattle; also NVH (automotive)
**BTM** = Butte, Montana, airport
**BTR** = Baton Rouge, Louisiana, airport
**BTRY** = battery
**BTU** = British thermal unit; measure of heat
**BU** = bushel or bushels
**BUF** = Buffalo, NY, airport
**BUFF** = big ugly fat fornicator; B-52 bomber
**BUPERS** = Bureau of Personnel (USN)
**BUR** = bureau
    = Burbank, California, airport
**BURBS** = suburbs
**BUS** = business
**BVD's** = men's shorts, after BVD brand
**BVI** = Better Vision Institute
**BVT** = brevet
**BW** = black wall tires
    = black and white
    = Borg-Warner
**BWI** = British West Indies
    = Baltimore, Maryland, airport

**BX** = base exchange
**BZ** = experimental drug that blocks nerve impulses and causes death

**C** = Celsius or centigrade
    = copyright
    = cent
    = color
    = century
    = cycle
    = carat; unit of weight for precious stones, equal to 200 milligrams
    = cancer, as in "the big C"
    = center (sports)
    = catcher (baseball)
    = carbon; a chemical element
    = speed of light
    = 100 in Roman numerals
    = battery size
    = cup
    = satisfactory, scholastic grade
    = code name for head of Britain's MI6, from CSS
    = circa (Latin for about)
    = stock and bond rating
    = cytosine; one of four DNA building blocks (see A, G, T)
**$C^3$** = command, control and communication (military)
**C-4** = plastic explosive
**C-5A** = largest cargo aircraft in the world; Lockheed "Galaxy"
**C-47** = WW II twin-prop cargo plane; military version of the DC-3; "Skytrain"
**C-54** = WW II 4-prop cargo plane; military version of the DC-4; "Skymaster"
**C-119** = WW II twin-prop cargo plane; Fairchild "Flying Boxcar"

**CA** = California (postal code)

= about (Latin: *circa*)

= Air China

= US Navy designation for heavy cruisers

= covert action

**Ca** = calcium; a chemical element

**CAA** = Clean Air Act

**CAB** = Civil Aeronautics Board

**CAD** = computer aided design

= computer aided dispatching (mobile communications)

= Cadillac

**CADDY** = Cadillac

**CAD/CAM** = computer aided design/computer aided manufacturing

**CADO** = Central Air Documents Office

**CAFE** = corporate average fuel economy (automotive)

**CAL** = California

= calendar

= caliber

= calorie

**CALC** = calculated

**CALIF** = California

**CALTECH** = California Institute of Technology

**CAM** = computer aided manufacturing

= common area maintenance (real estate)

**CAMI** = Civil Aeronautical-Medical Institute

**CAN** = Canada

**CANW** = Citizens Against Nuclear War

**CAO** = chief administrative officer

**CAP** = capital

= Civil Air Patrol

= College of American Pathologists

= Community Access Programming

**CAPT** = captain
**CARB** = California Air Resources Board
       = carburetor
**CARD** = cardinal
**CARDS** = St. Louis Cardinals baseball team
**CARE** = Cooperative for American Remittances to Everywhere
**CARICOM** = Caribbean Community and Common Market
**CART** = Championship Automobile Racing Teams
**CAS** = The Children's Aid Society
**CASCOM** = Combined Arms Support Command (military)
**CASE** = Council for Advancement and Support of Education
**CASMS** = computer-controlled area sterilization multi-sensor system; bugging devices dropped by plane to pick up troop movements
**CASSIS** = Classification and Search Support Information System
**CAT** = catalog
**CATH** = cathedral
**CATV** = cable TV
**CAV** = cavalry
**CAVU** = ceiling and visibility unlimited
**CB** = citizens' band radio
       = corner back (football)
       = confined to barracks
**CB's** = US Navy Construction Battalions; SEABEES
**Cb** = columbium; a chemical element
**CBA** = Christian Booksellers Association
**CBBB** = Council of Better Business Bureaus

**CBC** = complete blood count
= Congressional Black Caucus
= Canadian Broadcasting Company
**CBD** = cash before delivery
**CBE** = Commander of the (Order of the) British Empire
**CBEO** = colorblind equal opportunity
**CBO** = Congressional Budget Office
**CBOE** = Chicago Board Options Exchange
**CBS** = Columbia Broadcasting System
**CC** = community college
= cubic centimeters
= carbon copy
= country club
= chamber of commerce
= Christian Coalition
= stock and bond rating
**CCB** = Common Carrier Bureau
**CCC** = Civilian Conservation Corps
= Commodity Credit Corporation
= stock and bond rating
**CCCA** = Classic Car Club of America
**CCCO** = Central Committee for Conscientious Objectors
**CCCP** = USSR in Russian
**CCF** = common-cause failure
**CCNB** = Concerned Citizens for the Nuclear Breeder
**CCR** = camera cassette recorder
**CCTV** = closed-circuit television
**CCW** = carrying a concealed weapon
= counterclockwise
**CD** = compact disc
= certificate of deposit
= Civil Defense

**Cd** = coefficient of drag
    = cadmium; a chemical element
**CDA** = Commercial Development Association
**CDC** = Centers for Disease Control and Prevention
**CDE** = Conference on Disarmament in Europe
**CDI** = Center for Defense Information
**CDN** = Canadian
**CDPA** = Civil Defense Preparedness Agency
**CDR** = commander
**CDT** = central daylight time
**CE** = counterespionage
    = Chemical Engineer
    = Civil Engineer
    = Corps of Engineers, US Army; also USACE
**Ce** = cerium; a chemical element
**CEA** = Council of Economic Advisors
**CED** = Committee for Economic Development
**CEEB** = College Entrance Examination Board
**CELEB** = celebrity
**CEM** = cement
**CEMF** = counter electromotive force
**CEN** = center or central
**CENES** = *Centre National d'Études Spatials*; French Space Agency
**CENT** = century
    = centigrade
**CENY** = Commodities Exchange of New York
**CEO** = chief executive officer
**CEQ** = Council on Environmental Quality
**CERCLA** = Comprehensive Environmental Response, Compensation and Liability Act; the Superfund
**CERN** = *Conseil Européen pour la Recherche Nucléaire* (French); now the European Organization for Nuclear Research

**CERT** = certified
= certificate
**CETA** = Comprehensive Employment Training (DOL)
**CEV** = Contemporary English Version, of the Bible
**CF** = cystic fibrosis; disease which destroys lung tissue
= center field (baseball)
= centrifugal force
**Cf** = californium; a chemical element
**cf** = compare (Latin: *confer*)
**CFA** = Consumer Federation of America
**CFC** = chlorofluorocarbon; refrigerant implicated in depletion of earth's ozone layer
**CFE** = Conventional Forces in Europe treaty
**CFF** = Cystic Fibrosis Foundation
**CFM** = cubic feet per minute
**CFO** = chief financial officer
**CFR** = Code of Federal Regulations
= Council on Foreign Relations
**CFS** = chronic fatigue syndrome
= cubic feet per second
**CFTC** = Commodity Futures Trading Commission
**CG** = Coast Guard
= centigram
= center of gravity
= complete games pitched (baseball)
= commanding general
**CGO** = Committee on Government Operations (US Congress)
**CGR** = Center for Governmental Research
**CGSC** = Command and General Staff College (US)
**CGT** = capital gains tax
**CGW** = chemical and germ warfare
**CGX** = Chicago, Illinois, Meigs airport

**CH** = chapter
= champion
= chaplain
= children
= church
= check (chess)
= Switzerland (international car index mark)
**CHAN** = channel
**CHAP** = chapter
**CHAPTER 7** = US bankruptcy law; court-appointed trustee sells assets and debtor is discharged of debts
**CHAPTER 11** = company reorganizes under court supervision
**CHAPTER 12** = farm reorganization bankruptcy
**CHAPTER 13** = debtor arranges to repay debt
**CHEKA** = first Soviet security organization
**CHEM** = chemistry
= chemical
= chemist
**CHEMO** = chemotherapy; chemical therapy
**CHEV** = Chevrolet
**CHEVY** = Chevrolet
**CHG** = charge
**CHI** = Chicago
**CHIN** = Chinese
**CHM** = chairman
**CHMSL** = center high-mounted stoplight; "chim-sul" (automotive)
**CHOPPER** = helicopter; also "HELO"
**CHP** = California Highway Patrol
**CHRB** = Community Housing Resource Board
**CHRON** = chronological
**CHS** = Charleston, South Carolina, airport

37

**CI** = counterintelligence
= cubic inches
**CIA** = Central Intelligence Agency
**CIB** = combat infantryman badge
**CIC** = Counter Intelligence Corps (military)
**CID** = criminal investigation division or department
**CIE** = *compagnie* (French for company)
**CIEP** = Council on International Economic Policy
**CIGS** = Chief of the Imperial General Staff (British)
**C-in-C** = commander-in-chief
**CINC** = commander-in-chief
**CINCHAN** = Commander-In-Chief, Channel (NATO)
**CINCLANT** = Commander-in-Chief Atlantic fleet
**CINCMED** = Commander-in-Chief Mediterranean
**CINCPAC** = Commander-in-Chief Pacific fleet
**CINCPOA** = Commander-in-Chief Pacific Ocean Areas
**CINCSAC** = Commander-in-Chief Strategic Air Command
**CINCSWPA** = Commander-in-Chief Southwest Pacific Area
**CINDAS** = Center for Information and Numerical Data Analysis and Synthesis (NBS through Purdue)
**CIR** = circle
**CIRC** = circular
**CIP** = cataloging in publication (LC)
**CIT** = citation
= citizen
**CIV** = civil
= civilian
**CJ** = chief justice
**CJCS** = Chairman of the Joint Chiefs of Staff (military)
**CK** = check
**CL** = center line
= centiliter
= US Navy designation for light cruisers

Cl = chlorine; a chemical element
CLA = Children's Literature Association
CLE = Cleveland, Ohio, airport
CLIS = Criminalistics Laboratory Information System (DOJ)
CLR = clear
CLT = Charlotte, North Carolina, airport
CM = centimeter
Cm = curium; a chemical element
CMA = Chemical Manufacturers Association
= Country Music Association
= cash management account
CMD = command
CMDG = commanding
CMDR = commander; also CDR
CMF = Country Music Foundation
CMG = Companion of (the Order of) St. Michael and St. George (British)
= Color Marketing Group
CMH = Columbus, Ohio, airport
CMO = chief medical officer
CMP = current market price
CN = Canadian National (also CNR)
= Cosa Nostra
CNA = Certified Nursing Assistant
= customer name and address
CNG = compressed natural gas
CNN = Cable Network News
CNO = Chief of Naval Operations
C-NOTE = hundred-dollar bill; from the Roman numeral C for 100
CNPPDP = Cooperative National Plant Pest Survey and Detection Program (USDA)

**CNR** = Canadian National Railway
**CNS** = central nervous system
    = Corporation for National Service
**CO** = Colorado (postal code)
    = commanding officer
    = carbon monoxide
    = company
    = conscientious objector
    = county
    = Continental Airlines
**Co** = cobalt; a chemical element
**C/O** = care of
**$CO_2$** = carbon dioxide
**COA** = Crude Oil Analysis Data Bank; world's largest collection
**COAX** = coaxial cable
**COBOL** = common business-oriented language for programming computers
**COBRA** = Consolidated Omnibus Budget Reconciliation Act
**COC** = combat operations center
**COD** = collect on delivery
    = cash on delivery
**CODASYL** = Conference of Data Systems Languages (computers)
**COED** = coeducational
    = female college student
**C of C** = Chamber of Commerce
**C of S** = chief of staff
**COG** = Continuation of Government plan; disperses key members of government in case of attack; code name "STRANGELOVE"
**COIN** = counterinsurgency
**COINTELPRO** = FBI counterintelligence program directed at radicals

**COKE** = Coca-Cola
       = cocaine
**COL** = colonel
     = Colorado
     = college
     = colored
**COLA** = cost-of-living allowance
**COLO** = Colorado
**COM** = commander
     = comedy
     = common
     = communist
     = communication
     = common stock (stock exchange)
**COMB** = combining
       = combination
**COMECON** = Council for Mutual Economic Assistance
**COMET** = computer-operated management evaluation technique
**COMGENPOA** = Commanding General of the Pacific Ocean Areas
**COMINT** = communications intelligence
**COMM** = commission
      = communication
**COMMIE** = communist
**COMMO** = commodore
**COMP** = complimentary
     = composer
     = composition
     = comprehensive
     = thoroughly executed advertising layout
**COMPD** = compound
**COMSAT** = communications satellite

**COMSEC** = communications security
**COMSUBLANT** = Commander Submarine Fleet, Atlantic
**COMSUBPAC** = Commander Submarine Fleet, Pacific
**CON** = convict; prisoner
    = swindle (from confidence man or scheme)
    = confidence
**CONC** = concentrate
    = concrete
**CONF** = Confederate
    = conference
**CONFED** = Confederate
**CONG** = congress
**CONN** = Connecticut
**CONOCO** = Continental Oil Company
**CONST** = constant
    = constitution or constitutional
**CONSTR** = construction
**CONT** = control
    = continental
    = continued
**CONTD** = continued
**CONTR** = contractor
**CONTRIB** = contribution
    = contributor
**CONTU** = National Commission on New Technological
Uses of Copyrighted Works
**CONUS** = Continental US (military)
**CONUSA** = Continental US Army
**CONV** = convertible
    = convention
    = conversion (football)
**COO** = chief operating officer
**COP** = Copyrights Act (US)

**CORE** = Congress of Racial Equality
**CORP** = corporation
    = corporal; also CPL
**CORR** = correction
    = correspondence
**COS** = chief of staff
    = chief of station
    = companies
    = counties
    = Colorado Springs, Colorado, airport
**COSMIC** = Computer Software Management and Information Center (NASA)
**COSWORTH** = automotive engineering firm, after founders Mike Costin and Keith Duckworth
**CP** = cerebral palsy
    = command post (military)
    = candlepower
    = Communist Party
    = Canadian Pacific (also CPR)
    = Canadian Airlines International
**CPA** = Certified Public Accountant
**CPB** = Corporation for Public Broadcasting
**CPC** = Commerce Productivity Center (DOC)
**CPE** = coupe
**CPFF** = cost plus fixed fee
**CPI** = consumer price index
    = characters per inch
**CPIF** = cost plus incentive fee
**CPL** = corporal
**CPM** = cost per thousand
    = cycles per minute
    = count per minute
    = critical path method

**CPO** = chief petty officer
= Community Post Office
**CPP** = Center for Plutonium Production
**CPR** = cardiopulmonary resuscitation
= Canadian Pacific Railway
= critical power ratio
**CPS** = characters per second
= count per second
**CPSC** = Consumer Product Safety Commission
**CPSU** = Communist Party of the Soviet Union
**CPU** = central processing unit (computers)
**CPUSA** = Communist Party of the USA
**CPW** = Central Park West, New York City
**CPX** = command post exercise (military)
**CQ** = call to quarters; message to follow (preceding radio signal)
= charge of quarters (military)
= spell as is (proofreading)
**CQD** = call to quarters—distress; forerunner of sos
**Cr** = chromium; a chemical element
**CRA** = Community Reinvestment Act (us)
**CRAF** = comet rendezvous asteroid flyby (aerospace)
**C RATIONS** = US Army field rations; one meal in two cans
**CRB** = Commodity Research Bureau
**CREEP** = Committee for the Re-Election of the President (Nixon)
**CREF** = College Retirement Equities Fund
**CRESC** = crescendo
**CRIM** = criminology
= criminal
**CRIM CON** = criminal conversation
**CRISP** = Computer Retrieval of Information on Scientific Projects (NIH)

**CRIT** = critical
**CRM** = crumb rubber modifier; ground-up used automobile tires
**CRS** = Congressional Research Service (LC)
    = can't remember [anything]
**CRT** = cathode ray tube; the computer screen
**CRYPTO** = cryptography; encoding and decoding
**CS** = chief of staff
    = civil service
    = clandestine services
    = caught stealing (baseball)
**Cs** = cesium; a chemical element
**CSA** = Confederate States of America
    = Controlled Substances Act (US)
    = Chief of Staff, Army
**CSAP** = Center for Substance Abuse and Prevention
**CSC** = Civil Service Commission
**CSF** = cerebrospinal fluid
**CSG** = Council of State Governments
**C-SPAN** = Cable-Satellite Public Affairs Network
**CSS** = Chief, Secret Service or MI6; "C" (British)
**CST** = central standard time
**CT** = cent
    = central time
    = court
    = count
    = combat team
    = carat
    = Connecticut (postal code)
**CTBT** = Comprehensive Test Ban Treaty
**CTCSS** = continuous tone coded squelch system (mobile communications)

**CTIAC** = Concrete Technology Information Analysis Center (USACE)
**CTIO** = Cerro Tololo Inter-American Observatory in Chile
**CTN** = carton
**CTR** = center
**CTRL** = control
**CU** = close-up
    = cubic
    = Consumers Union
    = credit union
**Cu** = copper (Latin: *cuprum*); a chemical element
**CUME** = cumulative
**CUN** = Cancun, Mexico, airport
**CUR** = current
**CURE** = Citizens United for Responsible Energy
**CUT** = coordinated universal time, based on Greenwich, England; see GMT
**CV** = cardiovascular
    = curriculum vitae; resumé
    = US Navy designation for aircraft carriers
**CVA** = cerebrovascular accident; a stroke
**CVC** = combat vehicle crewman
**CVG** = Cincinnati, Ohio, airport
**CV JOINT** = continuous velocity universal joint (automotive)
**CVS** = Commercial Vessel Safety (USCG)
**CVW** = aircraft carrier air wing; see CV
**CW** = chemical warfare
    = continuous wave, for transmission of Morse code
    = clockwise
**CWA** = Clean Water Act
    = Communications Workers of America
**CWLA** = Child Welfare League of America
**CWO** = chief warrant officer

**CWPS** = Council on Wage and Price Stability
**CWS** = Chemical Warfare Service
**CWT** = hundredweight; 100 lbs.; from C for 100 in Roman numerals
**CX** = Cathay Pacific Airways, Hong Kong
**CXH** = Vancouver, BC, airport
**CY** = calendar year
**CYA** = cover your ass, as in CYA memo
**CYL** = Communist Youth League
**CYL** = cylinder
**CYO** = Catholic Youth Organization
**CYS** = Cheyenne, Wyoming, airport
**CYTD** = calendar year to date
**CZ** = Canal Zone
**CZM** = Cozumel, Mexico, airport

**D** = Democrat
   = depth
   = died
   = date
   = defense (sports)
   = defense man (hockey)
   = director
   = stock and bond rating
   = derivative (mathematics)
   = delta
   = unsatisfactory, scholastic grade
   = battery size
   = 500 in Roman numerals
   = Germany (international car index mark and aircraft code)
   = deuterium (heavy water)
**d** = penny or pence; British designation, also used in US for construction nails

**DA** = district attorney

= duck's rear end; young men's haircut style from the sixties

= delayed action

= Department of the Army

**DACS** = Data and Analysis Center for Software (USAF)

**DACWITS** = Defense Advisory Committee on Women in the Service

**DAL** = Dallas, Texas, Love airport

**D&B** = Dun and Bradstreet

= financial report by Dun and Bradstreet

**D&H** = delivery and handling

**DAR** = Daughters of the American Revolution

**DARCOM** = Army Materiel Development and Readiness Command

**DARE** = Drug Abuse, Resistance, Education

**DARPA** = Defense Advanced Research Project Agency

**DAU** = daughter

**DAV** = Disabled American Veterans

**DAWN** = Drug Abuse Warning Network (DOJ)

**dB** = decibel

**DBA** = doing business as; assumed name

**DBASE** = data base (computers)

**DBD** = Don't Bait Deer

**DBDU** = desert battle dress uniform

**DBE** = disadvantaged business enterprise (US)

= Dame Commander of the (Order of the) British Empire

**DBF** = divorced black female

**DBL** = double

**DBL CH** = double check (chess)

**DBM** = divorced black male

**DBMS** = database management system

**DBQ** = Dubuque, Iowa, airport
**DBS** = direct broadcast from satellite
**DC** = District of Columbia, as in Washington, DC (postal code)
    = direct current (see AC)
    = Diner's Club credit card
    = developed countries
    = Daughters of the Confederacy
**DC-3** = twin-prop Douglas passenger plane introduced in 1934 and still flying
**DCA** = Defense Communications Agency
    = Washington DC, National Airport
**DCAA** = Defense Contract Audit Agency
**DCAS** = Defense Contract Administration Service
**DCI** = Director of Central Intelligence
**DCL** = Direct Communications Link; Washington-Moscow hot line
**DCMG** = Dame Commander Grand Cross of (the Order of) St. Michael and St. George (British)
**DCO** = Defense Coordinating Officer (military)
**DCS** = deputy chief of staff
    = defense communications system
**DC-X** = Delta Clipper Experimental; reusable single-stage VTOL rocket
**DD** = US Navy designation for destroyers
**D-DAY** = the designated day
    = allied invasion of Normandy on June 6, 1944
**DDE** = Dwight David Eisenhower, 34th US president
**DDP** = Deputy Director (or Directorate), Plans (CIA clandestine services)
**DDR** = *Deutsche Demokratische Republik*; German Democratic Republic; former East Germany; also GDR
**DDS** = Doctor of Dental Surgery
    = Doctor of Dental Science

**DDT** = dichlorodiphenyltrichloroethane; insecticide
**DE** = Delaware (postal code)
   = US Navy designation for destroyer escorts
**DEA** = US Drug Enforcement Administration
**DEB** = debutante
   = debenture
   = commander who commits his troops after the threat is over; after French General Marie Eugene Debeney (WW II)
**DEC** = deceased
   = December
   = declination
   = Digital Equipment Corporation
**DECON** = decontaminate
**DEF** = defense
   = definite
   = defeated (sports)
   = defendant
**DEFCON** = defense condition; state of alert (Pentagon)
**DEG** = degree
**DEL** = delete
   = delegate or delegation
   = Delaware
**DELCO** = Dayton Electronics Company (GM)
**DEM** = Democrat or Democratic
**DEMA** = Diesel Engine Manufacturers Association
**DEN** = Denmark
   = Denver, Colorado, airport
**DEP** = deputy
   = deposit
   = departure
   = depot
**DEPT** = department

**DER** = Department of Environmental Research
= Department of Environmental Resources
**DES** = data encryption standard; an NSA code, considered unbreakable
= digital encryption systems, for mobile communications
= Department of Emergency Services
**DET** = Detroit, Michigan, city airport
= detective
= detachment
**DETOX** = detoxify; eliminate poisons or drugs
**DEW** = distant early warning
**DF** = direction finder
**DFA** = doctor of fine arts
**DFC** = distinguished flying cross
**DFM** = distinguished flying medal
**DFW** = Dallas-Fort Worth airport
**DFWA** = Drug-Free Work Place Act
**DG** = Dramatists Guild
= director general
**DGA** = Directors Guild of America
**DGSE** = *Direction Général de la Sécurité Extérieure*; French CIA (see SDECE)
**DH** = designated hitter (baseball)
**DHB** = defense halfback (football)
**DHC** = drophead coupe; British convertible
**DHHS** = Department of Health and Human Services; also HHS
**DI** = drill instructor
**DI5** = new name for British MI5
**DI6** = new name for British MI6
**DIA** = Defense Intelligence Agency
= diameter
**DIAG** = diagonal
**DIAL** = dialect

**DIAM** = diameter
**DICT** = dictionary
**DID** = defense in depth
**DIFF** = difference
        = differential (automotive)
**DIM** = dimension
        = diminutive
**DIMPLE** = Deuterium Moderated Pile Low Energy Reactor
**DIPSO** = dipsomaniac; addicted to alcohol
**DIR** = director
        = directory
**DISC** = discount
        = discovered
**DIS CH** = discovered check (chess)
**DISP** = dispose or disposal
        = dispensary
**DISS** = to show disrespect
**DIST** = distance
        = district
**DISTR** = distribute or distribution
**DIV** = divorced
        = Defense Investigative Service
        = division (military)
        = dividend
**DIY** = do it yourself
**DJ** = disc jockey
        = dust jacket
        = Dow Jones
**DJIA** = Dow Jones Industrial Averages
**DK** = Denmark (international car index mark)
**DL** = disabled list (sports)
        = Delta Airlines
        = international envelope size closest to #10; 110mm x 220mm or 4.33" x 8.66"

**DLA** = Defense Logistics Agency
**DLH** = Duluth, Minnesota, airport
**DLIFLC** = Defense Language Institute Foreign Language Center
**DLit** = doctor of literature
**DLO** = dead letter office
**DM** = *Deutsche mark* (German currency)
**DMA** = Direct Marketing Association
    = Defense Mapping Agency
**DMD** = digital micro-mirror device; computer chip that converts digital broadcast signals to TV images
**DMF INDEX** = decayed, missing and filled teeth
**DMV** = department of motor vehicles
**DMZ** = demilitarized zone
**DN** = down
**DNA** = deoxyribonucleic acid; double helix molecule in the nucleus of every cell
    = does not apply
    = Defense Nuclear Agency
**DNC** = Democratic National Committee
**DNF** = did not finish (sports)
**DNQ** = did not qualify (sports)
**DNR** = do not resuscitate
    = Department of Natural Resources
**DO** = hairdo
    = duty officer
    = ditto
    = doctor of osteopathy
**DOA** = dead on arrival
**DOB** = date of birth
**DOC** = document
    = US Department of Commerce
**DOD** = US Department of Defense
    = Domestic Operations Division (CIA)

**DOE** = US Department of Energy
**DOHC** = double overhead camshafts, in an engine
**DOI** = US Department of the Interior
**DOJ** = US Department of Justice
**DOL** = dollar
    = US Department of Labor
**DOM** = dominion
    = domestic
**DOOSY** = Duesenberg automobile; also "DUESY"
**DOS** = disk operating system (computers)
    = US Department of State
**DOT** = US Department of Transportation
    = directly observed therapy
    = Dictionary of Occupational Titles
**DOZ** = dozen
**DP** = double play (baseball)
    = displaced person
**DPMIAC** = Defense Pest Management Information Analysis Center
**DPS** = department of public safety
**DPW** = department of public works
**DQ** = Dairy Queen
    = disqualify (automobile racing)
**DR** = doctor
    = drive
    = dead reckoning
    = dining room
**DRB** = Division Ready Brigade; airborne brigade on constant alert (US Army)
**DRL** = daytime running lights (automotive)
**DSC** = distinguished service cross
**DSc** = doctor of science
**DSCS** = Defense Communications Satellite System

**DSM** = distinguished service medal
    = Des Moines, Iowa, airport
**DSN** = Deep Space Network (NASA)
**DSP** = Defense Support Program satellites
**DSRV** = deep submergence rescue vehicle
**DSS** = department of social services
**DST** = daylight saving time
**DT** = double time
**DT's** = delirium tremens; the shakes associated with alcoholism
**DTH** = Dance Theatre of Harlem
**DTIC** = Defense Technical Information Center
**DTMF** = dual tone multi-frequency (mobile communications)
**DTP** = desk-top publishing
**DTW** = Detroit, Michigan, Metropolitan Airport
**DU** = Ducks Unlimited
**DUESY** = Duesenberg automobile; also "DOOSY"
**DUPE** = duplicate
**DV** = Douay Version, of the Bible
**DVA** = Department of Veterans Affairs
**DVD** = digital video disk
**DVM** = doctor of veterinary medicine
**DW** = dishwasher
    = dead weight
**DWF** = divorced white female
**DWM** = divorced white male
**DWR** = Department of Waste Resources
**DX** = distance
    = double exposure
**Dy** = dysprosium; a chemical element
**DZ** = dozen

E = east
  = estimate
  = energy
  = erg; measurement of a unit of work
  = error (baseball)
  = effort
  = failing, scholastic grade
  = Spain (international car index mark)
EA = each
EAA = Experimental Aircraft Association
EAC = European Atomic Commission
EACRP = European-American Committee on Reactor Physics
E&E = escape and evasion
E&OE = errors and omissions excepted
EAP = employee assistance program
EASTLANT = East Atlantic Command HQ (NATO)
EB = eastbound
EBS = Emergency Broadcast System
EC = European Communities
  = electrochromic; automotive mirrors that dim
  = Spain (aircraft registration code)
ECA = Economic Commission for Africa (UN)
ECCL = ecclesiastical
ECCM = electronic counter-countermeasures
ECE = Economic Commission for Europe (UN)
ECG = electrocardiogram; tracking of electrical impulses of the heart (also EKG)
ECLAC = Economic Commission for Latin America and the Caribbean (UN)
ECM = electronic counter measures
  = European Common Market
ECNP = Environmental Coalition on Nuclear Power
ECO = ecology

**E COLI** = *Escherichia coli*; common intestinal bacteria which can cause infections in other body systems
**ECON** = economics
= economy
**ECPA** = Electronic Communications Privacy Act
**ECU** = extreme close-up
= engine control unit
= European Currency Unit
**ED** = US Department of Education
= education
= editor
= edition
= extra duty
**EDF** = Environmental Defense Fund
**EdM** = master of education
**EDS** = Electronic Data Services
**EDT** = eastern daylight time
**EDUC** = education
**EE** = electrical engineer
= errors excepted
**EEAC** = Equal Employment Advisory Council
**EEC** = European Economic Community
**EEDB** = Energy and Environment Data Base (DOE)
**EEG** = electroencephalogram; tracking of electrical impulses of the brain
**EENT** = eyes, ears, nose and throat
**EEOC** = Equal Employment Opportunity Commission
**E=MC$^2$** = energy is equal to mass times the speed of light squared
**EES** = emergency exhaust system
**EEVC** = European Experimental Vehicle Committee
**EFD** = Houston, Texas, Ellington airport
**EFF** = efficiency
**EFI** = electronic fuel injection

EFS = electronic funds services
EFTA = European Free Trade Association
EFX = effects (movies)
**eg** = for example (Latin: *exempli gratia*; for the sake of example)
EGADS = electronic ground automatic destruct system (military)
EGR = exhaust gas recirculation (automotive)
EHF = extremely high frequency
EHP = effective horsepower
    = electric horsepower
EHV = extra-high voltage
EI = exposure index
EIA = Energy Information Administration
    = environmental impact appraisal
EIB = Export-Import Bank of the US
EIS = environmental impact statement
EITC = earned income tax credit
EKG = electrocardiogram; tracking of electrical impulses of the heart (also ECG)
EL = elevated train
EL AL = El Al Israel Airlines
ELDO = Eldorado; Cadillac nameplate
ELEC = electric
    = electorate
ELEM = elementary
ELEV = elevator
    = elevation
ELF = extremely low frequency (for communicating with deeply submerged submarines)
ELINT = electronic intelligence
ELP = El Paso, Texas, airport

**EM** = enlisted man
    = electromagnetic
    = engineer of mines
**EMA** = emergency management agency
**E-MAIL** = electronic mail or messages via computer
**EMC** = emergency management coordinator
**EMCT** = Environmental Mutagen, Carcinogen and Teratogen Information Department (DOE)
**EMER** = emergency
      = emeritus
**EMF** = electromotive force
    = electromagnetic field
**EMF/ELF** = electromagnetic field/extra-low frequency
**EMILY'S LIST** = Early Money Is Like Yeast—It Rises; PAC for Democratic women candidates
**EMP** = electromagnetic pulse
    = empire
    = emperor or empress
**EMR** = electromagnetic radiation
**EMS** = emergency medical service
    = European Monetary System
**EMT** = emergency medical technician
**EMU** = electromagnetic unit
**ENC** = enclosure
**ENG** = England
    = English
    = engineer
    = engine
**ENIAC** = Electronic Numerical Integrator and Computer; first electronic computer containing 19,000 vacuum tubes, taking up 1500 square feet and weighing 30 tons; built during WW II
**ENIGMA** = German enciphering machine in WW II

**ENOLA GAY** = nickname of B-29 that dropped A-bomb on Hiroshima; after the pilot's mother

**EO** = executive order

= equal opportunity

**EOB** = Executive Office Building in Washington, DC

**EOC** = emergency operations center

= end of cycle

**EOD** = explosives ordnance disposal

**EOM** = end of message

= end of month

**EOR** = Earth Orbit Rendezvous (NASA)

**EOY** = end of year

**EP** = extended play

= en passant (chess)

**EPA** = Environmental Protection Agency

**EPIC** = Emergency Programs Information Center (USDA)

**EPPA** = Employee Polygraph Protection Act

**EPRI** = Electric Power Research Institute

**EPROM** = electronically programmable read-only memory module

**EPS** = earnings per share

**EPT** = early pregnancy test

**EQ** = educational quotient

= equation

**EQUIP** = equipment

**EQUIV** = equivalent

**ER** = emergency room

= earned runs (baseball)

**Er** = erbium; a chemical element

**ERA** = Equal Rights Amendment

= Economic Regulatory Administration

= earned run average (baseball)

**ERBS** = emergency radio broadcast system
**ERC** = Engineering Research Council
**ERDA** = Energy Research and Development Administration
**ERIC** = Educational Reference and Information Center of NIE; world's largest educational database
**ERISA** = Employee Retirement Income Security Act
**EROS** = Earth Resources Observation System (DOI)
**ERS** = Economic Research Service
**Es** = einsteinium; a chemical element
**ESA** = Endangered Species Act
    = European Space Agency
**ESC** = escape
    = Energy Resources Council
**ESCAP** = Economic and Social Commission for Asia and Pacific (UN)
**ESCWA** = Economic and Social Commission for Western Asia (UN)
**ESF** = Economic Support Funds (international aid)
**ESK** = Eskimo
**ESL** = English as a second language
**ESO** = European Southern Observatory in Chile, South America
**ESP** = extrasensory perception
    = especially
**ESPN** = Entertainment and Sports Network
**ESQ** = esquire
**ESSO** = Standard Oil
**EST** = eastern standard time
    = estimate
    = established
**ESU** = emergency service unit

**ET** = eastern time
    = extra terrestrial
    = Egypt (international car index mark)
**ETA** = estimated time of arrival
**et al** = and others (Latin: *et alii*)
**etc** = and so forth (Latin: *et cetera*)
**ETD** = estimated time of departure
**ETO** = European Theater of Operations (WW II)
**ETOPS** = extended twin-engine operations; FAA safety and reliability rules
**EU** = European Union of 15 countries
**Eu** = europium; a chemical element
**EUR** = European
**EURATOM** = European Atomic Energy Community
**EV** = electron volt
**EVA** = extra vehicular activity (NASA)
**EVAC** = evacuation
**EVAP** = evaporate
**EVE** = evening
**EWO** = emergency war order
**EWR** = Newark, NJ/New York City airport
**EX** = former spouse
    = former
    = without
**EXAM** = examination
**EXC** = excellent
    = exception
**EX-CON** = former convict
**EX DIV** = without dividend
**EXEC** = executive
      = executive officer; also XO (military)
**EXEC PROD** = executive producer
**EX-IM** = US Export-Import Bank

**EXP** = experimental
    = express
    = expense
    = export
    = expires
**EXPO** = exposition
**EXT** = exterior
    = external
    = extra
    = extension
    = extract
**EZ** = easy

**F** = female
  = feminine
  = Fahrenheit
  = France (international car index mark and aircraft code)
  = franc (French currency)
  = focal length, of a lens
  = forward (sports)
  = found
  = failing, scholastic grade
  = forte (music: loud)
  = fighter (USAF)
  = formula
  = fluorine; a chemical element
**F1** = Formula One; races for cars or boats having certain specs; also F2, F3 etc.
**F4U** = WW II carrier pursuit plane; Chance Vought "Corsair"
**F6F** = WW II carrier pursuit plane; Grumman "Hellcat"
**F-51** = WW II pursuit plane (originally designated P-51); North American "Mustang"

**F-80** = first US jet pursuit plane, flown in January, 1944; Lockheed "Shooting Star" (changed from P-80 in 1948)
**FA** = Families Anonymous
    = field artillery
**FAA** = Federal Aviation Administration
**FAB** = fabulous
**FAC** = faculty
    = facsimile
    = forward air controller (USAF)
**FACD** = Fellow of the American College of Dentists
**FACP** = Fellow of the American College of Physicians
**FACS** = Fellow of the American College of Surgeons
**FACT** = Foundation for Alternative Cancer Therapies
**FAF** = Financial Aid Form
**FAGS** = Fellow of the American Geographical Society
**FAHR** = Fahrenheit
**FAI** = fail as is
    = Fairbanks, Alaska, airport
    = *Fédération Aéronautique International* (French)
**FAIA** = Fellow of the American Institute of Architects
**FAM** = familiar
    = family
**FAN** = fanatic
**F&G** = folded and gathered (book publishing)
    = fish and game
**F&G's** = unbound books (book publishing)
**F&I** = finance and insurance
    = Fire & Ice mission to explore the sun and Pluto (aerospace)
**FANDIC** = Families in Action National Drug Information Center
**F&S** = Flaps and Seals; CIA mail surveillance
**FANNY MAE** = Federal National Mortgage Association; FNMA

**FAO** = Food and Agriculture Organization (UN)

**FAPRS** = Federal Assistance Programs Retrieval System (USDA)

**FAQ** = frequently asked question
= fair average quality

**FAR** = Fargo, North Dakota, airport

**FARS** = Fatal Accident Reporting System (NHTSA)

**FAS** = Federation of American Scientists
= firsts and seconds

**FAST-TRAC** = faster and safer travel through traffic routing and advanced controls; computerized traffic lights

**FAT** = Fresno, California, airport

**FAT MAN** = code name for implosion-type plutonium bomb dropped on Nagasaki, Japan in WW II (see LITTLE BOY)

**FAX** = facsimile transmittal by telephone line

**FB** = fullback (football)

**FBA** = Federal Bar Association

**FBI** = Federal Bureau of Investigation

**FC** = fielder's choice (baseball)

**FCA** = Farm Credit Administration

**FCC** = Federal Communications Commission

**FCI** = Foreign Counterintelligence Division of the FBI, now NSD

**FCIS** = Fellow of the Chartered Institute of Secretaries

**FCRC** = Federal Contract Research Center

**FCS** = Fellow of the Chemical Society

**FCU** = Federal Credit Union

**FD** = fire department

**FDA** = Food and Drug Administration

**FDAA** = Federal Disaster Assistance Administration

**FDB** = Fahrenheit dry bulb

**FDIC** = Federal Deposit Insurance Corporation

**FDR** = Franklin Delano Roosevelt, 32nd president of the US

**Fe** = iron ( Latin: *ferrum*); a chemical element

**FEA** = Federal Energy Administration

**FEB** = February

**FEC** = Federal Election Commission

**FECU** = Federal Employees Credit Union

**FED** = federal; US government
    = Federal Reserve Board; "the Fed"
    = federation

**FED's** = US government employees or representatives

**FED EX** = Federal Express

**FEDP** = Federal Executive Development Program

**FEI** = Federal Executive Institute

**FEM** = female
    = feminine

**FEMA** = Federal Emergency Management Agency

**FEPC** = Fair Employment Practices Commission

**FERC** = Federal Energy Regulatory Commission

**FF** = fast forward (video tape recording)
    = following
    = fortissimo (music: very loud)
    = folios

**FFA** = Future Farmers of America (see NFFF)

**FFR** = Fellow of the Faculty of Radiologists

**FFRDC** = Federally Funded Research and Development Center

**FFV** = First Families of Virginia

**FG** = field goal (sports)

**FGAA** = Federal Government Accountants Association

**FGIS** = Federal Grain Inspection Service

**FHA** = Federal Housing Administration
    = Federal Highway Administration

**FHC** = fixed-head coupe; British hardtop

**F-HEAD** = engine with an F-shaped cylinder head
**FHLB** = Federal Home Loan Banks
**FHLBB** = Federal Home Loan Bank Board
**FHLMC** = Federal Housing Loan Mortgage Corporation; "FREDDY MAC"
**FHWA** = Federal Highway Administration
**FI** = fuel injection
　　= foreign intelligence
**FIA** = *Fédération Internationale de l'Automobile* (French)
**FIAT** = *Fabbrica Italiana Automobili Torino* (Italian)
**FIC** = Fellow of the Institute of Chemistry
**FICA** = Federal Insurance Contributions Act
**FICB** = Federal Insurance Corporation Banks
**FICT** = fiction
**FIDE** = International Chess Federation
**FIDO** = fog investigation dispersal operations (FAA)
**FIFO** = first in, first out
**FIG** = figure
　　= figurative
**FIM** = *Fédération Internationale Motocycliste* (French)
**FIN** = financial
　　= finish
　　= end (Latin)
**FINN** = Finnish
**FIR** = field information report
**FIREBASE** = Wildland Fire—Bibliographic Database
**FISA** = Foreign Intelligence Surveillance Act, for wiretapping
**FL** = Florida (postal code)
**FLA** = Florida
**FLAK** = antiaircraft shrapnel, from the German *Flieger Abwehr Kanone* for aircraft defense gun
**FLB** = Federal Land Banks

FLC = Federal Laboratory Consortium
FLETC = Federal Law Enforcement Training Center
FLEX = Federation Licensing Examination, by the Federation of State Medical Boards of the US, Inc.
FLIR = forward-looking infrared
FLL = Ft. Lauderdale, Florida, airport
FLN = *Front de Libération Nationale*; National Liberation Front of Algeria
FLOR = Florida
FL OZ = fluid ounce
FLRA = Federal Labor Relations Authority
FLRC = Federal Labor Relations Council
FLSA = Fair Labor Standards Act
FM  = frequency modulation band (radio; see AM)
    = Federated States of Micronesia (postal code)
    = field manual (US Army)
    = fathom
Fm = fermium; a chemical element
FMC = Ford Motor Company
      = Federal Maritime Commission
FMCS = Federal Mediation and Conciliation Service
FMFLANT = Fleet Marine Force Atlantic
FMFPAC = Fleet Marine Force Pacific
FMI = Food Marketing Institute
FMIS = Farm Market Infodata Service (USDA)
FN  = *Fabrique Nationale*; Belgian arms manufacturer
    = function
    = footnote
FNA = Federation of National Associations
FNIC = Food and Nutrition Information Center (USDA)
FNMA = Federal National Mortgage Association; "FANNY MAY"
FNT = Flint, Michigan, airport

**FO** = forward observer, usually for artillery targeting (military)
    = fly out (baseball)
    = first officer
    = flight officer
**FOB** = free on board
**FOC** = full operational capability
**FOE** = Fraternal Order of Eagles
    = Friends of the Earth
**FOI** = Freedom of Information Services
**FOIA** = Freedom of Information Act
**FOMOCO** = Ford Motor Company
**FOP** = Fraternal Order of Police
**FOPW** = Federation of Organizations for Professional Women
**FOR** = Fellowship of Reconciliation
**FORCECOM** = standing combat army (US Army)
**FOSIC** = Fleet Ocean Surveillance Information Center
**4-H** = Head, Heart, Hands, Health; educational organization
**FOURTH** = 4th of July; Independence Day
**FOW** = first open water
**FP** = freezing point
    = focal plane, of a camera
    = focal plane shutter, of a camera
**FPA** = Foreign Policy Association
**FPC** = Federal Power Commission
**FPDC** = Federal Procurement Data Center
**FPM** = feet per minute
**FPO** = fleet post office (USN)
**FPS** = Federal Protection Services
    = feet per second
**FR** = from
    = front
    = *franc* (French currency)
    = French

**Fr** = francium; a chemical element

**FRA** = Federal Railroad Administration

    = Fleet Reserve Association

**FRAG** = to kill with a fragmentation grenade (Vietnam war)

**FRB** = Federal Reserve Board

**FRCP** = Fellow of the Royal College of Physicians

**FRCS** = Fellow of the Royal College of Surgeons

**FREDDY MAC** = Federal Housing Loan Mortgage Corporation; FHLMC

**FREQ** = frequency

**FRERP** = Federal Radiological Emergency Response Plan

**FRG** = Federal Republic of Germany; (German: *Bundesrepublik Deutschland*)

**FRGS** = Fellow of the Royal Geographical Society

**FRI** = Friday

    = Food Research Institute

**FRIG** = Frigidaire

    = refrigerator

**FRISCO** = San Francisco

**FROG** = free rocket over ground; Soviet short-range missile

**FRS** = Federal Reserve System

**FRT** = front

**FSA** = flexible spending account

**FSH** = follicle-stimulating hormone

**FSLIC** = Federal Savings and Loan Insurance Corporation

**FSS** = fast sea-lift ship; large, fast cargo ships (USN)

**F-STOP** = camera lens aperture setting

**FT** = foot or feet

    = fort

    = full time

    = free throw (basketball)

**FTA** = fornicate the army (from the Vietnam war)

**FTC** = Federal Trade Commission

**FTD** = Florists Telegraph Delivery
**FTS** = Federal Telecommunications System
**FTSI** = Financial Times Stock Index, in London; "footsie"
**FT LB** = foot-pound
**FUBAR** = fouled up beyond all recognition
**FUR** = furlong
**FUSAG** = First US Army Group; phony decoy unit for D-Day
**FV** = on the back of the page (Latin: *folio verso*)
**FWB** = Fahrenheit wet bulb
**FWD** = front-wheel drive
　　　 = forward
**FWP** = Federal Women's Program
**FWPCA** = Federal Water Pollution Control Act
**FWY** = freeway
**FX** = effects (movies)
　　　 = function of X (mathematics)
**FY** = fiscal year
**FYI** = for your information
**FYP** = five-year plan

**G** = gravity
　　 = gram
　　 = goalie
　　 = good
　　 = goal (sports)
　　 = games (sports)
　　 = guard (sports)
　　 = grand, for thousand
　　 = general audiences: all ages admitted (movie rating)
　　 = guanine; one of four DNA building blocks (see C, A, T)
　　 = Great Britain (aircraft registration code)
**G-1** = personnel and administration (military)
**G-2** = intelligence (military)

**G-3** = operations (military)
**G-4** = logistics (military)
**G-5** = accurate, long-range artillery gun made in South Africa
**G7** = Group of Seven: US, Canada, UK, France, Germany, Japan, Italy
**GA** = Gamblers Anonymous
    = Georgia (postal code)
    = games away
    = goals against
    = general assistance
    = gas analysis
**Ga** = gallium; a chemical element
**GAAP** = generally accepted accounting principles
**GACIAC** = Tactical Weapons Guidance and Control Information and Analysis Center (DOD)
**GAEA** = Graphic Arts Employers of America
**GAL** = gallon
**GALV** = galvanized
**GAMA** = Gas Appliance Manufacturers Association
    = General Aviation Manufacturers Association
**GAO** = General Accounting Office; congressional spending watchdog
**GAR** = garage
    = Grand Army of the Republic (Civil War)
**GAS** = gasoline
    = Get Away Special; NASA Shuttle program
**GASP** = Group Against Smokers' Pollution
**GATT** = General Agreement on Tariffs and Trade
**GAW** = guaranteed annual wage
**GAY** = homosexual
**GAY 90's** = the happy 1890's
**GB** = Great Britain
    = games behind (sports)

**GBBL** = Girls Baseball League (started during WW II)
**GBF** = gay black female
**GBM** = gay black male
**GBU** = glide-bomb unit; laser-guided bombs
**GBZ** = Gibraltar (international car index mark)
**GC** = golf club
**GCA** = ground-controlled approach
    = Girl's Clubs of America
**GCB** = Knight Grand Cross of the Bath (British)
**GCCS** = Global Command and Control System (USAF)
**GCHQ** = Government Communications Headquarters (British version of NSA)
**GCI** = ground control intercept
**GCIU** = Graphic Communications International Union
**GCM** = General Court Martial (military)
**GCM** = Grand Cayman, West Indies, airport
**GCT** = Greenwich civil time
**GCW** = gross carrying weight
**Gd** = gadolinium; a chemical element
**GDI** = gross domestic income
**GDP** = gross domestic product
**GDR** = German Democratic Republic; former East Germany (see DDR)
**GE** = General Electric
**Ge** = germanium; a chemical element
**GED** = General Equivalency Diploma
**GEG** = Spokane, Washington, airport
**GEN** = general
    = generator
    = generation
    = genus
**GEN X** = generation X; generation without definition, born in the seventies

**GEO** = geosynchronous earth orbit
**GEODSS** = ground-based electro-optical deep space surveillance
**GEOG** = geography or geographical
**GEOL** = geology or geological
**GEOM** = geometry or geometrical
**GEOR** = Georgia
**GEOSAT** = geodetic satellite
**GER** = German
**GESTAPO** = *Geheime Staatspolizei*; Security State police in Nazi Germany
**GF** = General Foods
   = goals for (sports)
**GFE** = government-furnished equipment
**GFE&M** = government-furnished equipment and material
**GFP** = government-furnished property
**GFWC** = General Federation of Women's Clubs
**GFY** = government fiscal year
**GHA** = Greenwich hour angle
**GHQ** = general headquarters
**GI** = gastrointestinal
   = government issue
   = an American soldier
   = galvanized iron
**GIA** = Gemological Institute of America
   = Goodwill Industries of America
**GIANT TALK** = SAC communications network
**GIB** = Gibraltar
**GIC** = guaranteed investment contract, such as a fixed interest option
**GIDEP** = Government-Industry Data Exchange Program (DOC)
**GIGA** = prefix for billion

**GIGABIT** = billion bits (computers)
**GIGAFLOPS** = billion floating point operations per second (computers)
**GIGO** = garbage in, garbage out
**GINNY MAE** = Government National Mortgage Association; GNMA
**GITMO** = US Naval Base in Guantanamo, Cuba
**GK** = Greek
**GLAD** = Gay and Lesbian Advocates and Defenders
**GLAM** = glamor
**GLCM** = ground-launched cruise missile
**GLOSS** = glossary
**GLONASS** = Global Navigation Satellite System (Soviet)
**GM** = general manager
    = General Motors
    = gram
**GMAC** = General Motors Acceptance Corporation
**G-MAN** = government man, usually FBI
**GMAT** = Graduate Management Admission Test
**GMC** = General Motors Corporation
    = GM truck
**GMHC** = Gay Men's Health Crisis
**GMT** = Greenwich mean time, calculated from Greenwich Observatory in England
**GMV** = gram molecular volume
**GNMA** = Government National Mortgage Association "GINNY MAE"
**GNP** = gross national product
**GO** = general order
    = ground out (baseball)
**GOCO** = government-owned, contractor-operated

**GOP** = Grand Old Party (the Republican party)
**GOPAC** = GOP PAC
**GOTH** = gothic
**GOV** = governor
**GOVT** = government
**GP** = general practitioner
= general purpose
= games played
**GPA** = grade point average
= Gas Processors Association
**GPALS** = Global Protection Against Limited Strikes (military)
**GP** = general practitioner; medical doctor
= general purpose; derivative of WW II "jeep"
= group
= Grand Prix (French for grand prize)
**GPD** = gallons per day
**GPI** = ground position indicator
**GPM** = gallons per minute
**GPO** = Government Printing Office; also USGPO
**GPS** = gallons per second
= global positioning system; government network of 24 orbiting satellites for ground and sea navigation
**GPS/MET** = global positioning system/meteorological; satellite weather system
**GQ** = general quarters
**GR** = Greece (international car index mark)
**G-R** = Gallup-Robinson, survey organization
**GRAD** = graduate
**GRE** = Graduate Record Examination
**GREAT** = Gang Resistance, Education And Training
**GRID** = gay-related immunodeficiency disease; now designated AIDS
**GRO** = Gamma Ray Observatory in space (NASA)

**GRU** = Soviet military intelligence (Russian: *Glavnoye Razvedyvatelnoye Upravlenye*)

**GR WT** = gross weight

**GS** = general staff

= games started (baseball)

**GS-18** = highest rank in US civil service

**GSA** = General Services Administration

= Girl Scouts of America

= Geological Society of America

= Genetics Society of America

**GSC** = general staff corps

**GSMD** = General Society of Mayflower Descendants

**GSO** = general staff officer

= Greensboro and Winston-Salem, North Carolina, airport

**GSP** = Generalized System of Preferences (international trade)

**GST** = general sales tax

**G-STRING** = the stripper's last and most modest piece of apparel

**GT** = grand touring (automotive)

**GTD** = guaranteed

**GTO** = model of a Pontiac muscle car

= *gran turismo omologato* (Italian: homologated grand touring car produced in quantity of at least 1,000)

**GTW** = Grand Trunk Western (railroad)

**GU** = genitourinary

= Guam (postal code)

**GUT** = grand unified theory, of the universe

**GVW** = gross vehicle weight

**GWEN** = ground wave emergency communications network (US)

**GWF** = gay white female

**GWM** = gay white male

**GWT** = gross weight
**GYM** = gymnasium
**GYN** = gynecological


**H** = hydrogen; a chemical element
   = husband
   = height
   = hour
   = handicapped
   = hit (baseball)
   = heroin
   = hell
   = husband
   = Hungary (international car index mark)
**HARM** = air-to-ground missile that homes in on radar beams
**HASC** = House Armed Services Committee
**HASH** = hashish; gummy extract from the marijuana plant
**HAV** = Havana, Cuba, airport
**HAW** = Hawaii
**HB** = halfback (football)
   = handbook
**Hb** = hemoglobin; also Hg
**HBCU** = Historically Black Colleges and Universities
**HBHC** = hospital-based home care (VA)
**HBM** = His (Her) Britannic Majesty
**HBO** = Home Box Office
**H-BOMB** = hydrogen bomb
**HBP** = hit by pitcher (baseball)
**HBS** = Harvard Business School
**H-HOUR** = the designated hour

HC = House of Commons
HCC = hemispherical combustion chamber (automotive)
HCCA = Horseless Carriage Club of America
HCV = hydraulic control valve
HD = heavy duty
    = hard drive
    = head
    = high density
HDF = Hereditary Disease Foundation
HDL = high-density lipoprotein; "good" cholesterol (see LDL)
HDPE = high density polyethylene; recyclable pastic
HDT = hardtop (automotive)
HDTV = high-definition television
HDWE = hardware
HE = high efficiency
    = high explosive
    = human error
    = His Eminence
    = His Excellency
He = helium; a chemical element
HEARTHFIRE = high-energy accelerator reactor for thermonuclear fusion with ion beam of relativistic energy
HEAT = Help Eliminate Auto Thefts
HEB = Hebrew
HED = human engineering deficiency
    = human engineering discrepancy
HEI = Health & Energy Institute
HEIAC = Hydraulic Engineering Information Analysis Center (USACE)
HELO = helicopter; also CHOPPER
HEP = hydroelectric power
    = human-error probability

**HER** = human-error rate
= heraldry
**HEREIU** = Hotel Employees and Restaurant Employees International Union
**HESS** = History of Earth Sciences Society
**HEU** = highly enriched uranium; "weapons-grade"
**HEV** = hybrid electric vehicle
**HEW** = US Department of Health, Education and Welfare
**HEX** = hexagon
**HF** = high frequency
**HF/SSB** = high frequency single side band
**Hf** = hafnium; a chemical element
**HG** = hectogram; 100 grams
**Hg** = hemoglobin (also Hb)
= mercury (Latin: *hydrargyrum*); a chemical element
**HGT** = height
**HH** = His (Her) Highness
= His Holiness
**HHFA** = US Housing and Home Finance Agency
**HHS** = US Department of Health and Human Services; also DHHS
**HI** = Hawaii (postal code)
**HIAA** = Hobby Industry Association of America
**HID** = high-intensity discharge, automobile lights
**HI-FI** = high fidelity
**HILAT** = high latitude research satellite
**HIM** = His (Her) Imperial Majesty
**HI-REZ** = high resolution
**HIST** = history or historical
**HIV** = human immunodeficiency virus; AIDS virus
**HIV+** = HIV positive; possessing the AIDS virus

**HK** = Hong Kong
**HL** = hectoliter; 100 liters
     = House of Lords
**HM** = His (Her) Majesty
     = heavy metal
**HMAS** = His (Her) Majesty's Australian Ship
**HMCS** = His (Her) Majesty's Canadian Ship
**HMMWV** = high-mobility multipurpose wheeled vehicle; 4WD 4-passenger super jeep; "HUMVEE" or "HUMMER" (US Army)
**HMO** = health management organization
**HMS** = His (Her) Majesty's Ship
**HMSA** = Historic Motor Sports Association
**HNIS** = Human Nutrition Information Service (USDA)
**HNL** = Honolulu, Hawaii, airport
**HO** = high output
**H$_2$O** = chemical designation for water
**Ho** = holmium; a chemical element
**HOAA** = Home Office Association of America
**HON** = honorable
**HOR** = horizontal
**HORT** = horticulture or horticultural
**HOSP** = hospital
       = hospice
**HP** = horsepower
     = Highway Patrol
     = high pressure
     = high purity
**HPMA** = Hardwood Plywood Manufacturers Association
**HPSCI** = House Permanent Select Committee on Intelligence; "hipsy"
**HQ** = headquarters

**HQDA** = Headquarters, Department of the Army
**HR** = human resources; personnel
    = home run
    = House of Representatives
    = hour
**HRH** = His (Her) Royal Highness
**HRSA** = Health Resources and Services Administration (DHHS)
**HRT** = hormone-replacement therapy
**HS** = high school
**HSA** = Hispanic Society of America
**HSR** = Historic Sportscar Racing
**HT** = height
    = high tension
**HTLV** = human T-cell leukemia virus
**HTS** = heights
**HUAC** = House Un-American Activities Commission; "hew-ak"
**HUD** = US Department of Housing and Urban Development; "hud"
    = heads-up display; instruments projected on windshield
**HUFSM** = Highway Users Federation for Safety and Mobility
**HUMINT** = human intelligence; spies
**HUMMER** = civilian version of HMMVW, built by AM General
**HUMVEE** = variation of HMMVW
**HUT** = Hopkins Ultraviolet Telescope
**HV** = high voltage
**HVAC** = heating, ventilation and air conditioning
    = high-voltage alternating current
**HVDC** = high-voltage direct current

HVY = heavy
HW = hardware
    = heavy water
HWM = high-water mark
HWY = highway
HX = heat exchanger
HYD = hydraulic
HYDRO = hydroelectric
HYPER = hyperactive; abnormally active
HYPO = hypodermic syringe; "needle"
Hz = hertz or cycle, after Heinrich R. Hertz, German physicist

I = interstate highway, as in I-75
  = island
  = 1 in Roman numerals
  = incomplete, scholastic grade
  = Italy (international car index mark and aircraft code)
  = iodine; a chemical element
IA = Iowa (postal code)
IAAI = International Association of Arson Investigators
IABSOIW = International Association of Bridge, Structural and Ornamental Iron Workers
IAC = Intelligence Advisory Committee
IAC's = Information Analysis Centers (DOD)
IACP = International Association of Chiefs of Police
IAD = Dulles airport, Washington DC
IADB = Inter-American Defense Board
IADC = Inter-American Defense College
IADL = International Association of Democratic Lawyers
IAEA = International Atomic Energy Agency
IAFC = International Association of Fire Chiefs
IAFF = International Association of Fire Fighters

**IAGS** = InterAmerican Geodetic Survey (DOD)
**IAH** = International Airport, Houston, Texas
**IAI** = Israel Aircraft Industries
**IAICM** = International Association of Ice Cream Manufacturers
**IAMAW** = International Association of Machinists and Aerospace Workers
**IANEC** = Inter-American Nuclear Energy Commission
**IAP** = international airport
**IAPMO** = International Association of Plumbing and Mechanical Officials
**IAS** = indicated air speed
**IATSE** = International Alliance of Theatrical Stage Employees
**IAWP** = International Association of Women Police
**IB** = incendiary bomb
      = Iberia Airlines, Spain
**ib** = in the same place; also ibid (Latin: *ibidem*)
**IBEW** = International Brotherhood of Electrical Workers
**IBF** = International Boxing Federation
      = International Business Forum
**ibid** = in the same place; also ib (Latin: *ibidem*)
**IBM** = International Business Machines
**IBPAT** = International Brotherhood of Painters and Allied Trades
**IBRD** = International Bank for Reconstruction and Development; part of the World Bank (UN)
**IBS** = irritable bowel syndrome
**IBT** = International Brotherhood of Teamsters
**IC** = Index Catalog of Nebulae (astronomy)
      = Indian Airlines, India
**IC4A** = Intercollegiate Association of Amateur Athletes of America; also ICAAAA
**ICA** = International Credit Association

**ICAAAA** = Intercollegiate Association of Amateur Athletes of America; also IC4A

**ICAD** = International Confederation of Art Dealers

**ICAF** = Industrial College of the Armed Forces

**ICAO** = International Civil Aviation Organization (UN)

**ICAP** = International Code Assessment Program

**ICBM** = intercontinental ballistic missile

**ICC** = Interstate Commerce Commission
= Indian Claims Commission
= International Chamber of Commerce

**ICE** = in-car entertainment system; radio, CD, tape

**ICF** = inertial confinement fusion

**ICFA** = International Cystic Fibrosis Association

**ICFTU** = International Confederation of Free Trade Unions

**ICHTH** = ichthyology

**ICJ** = International Court of Justice

**ICLS** = International Courtly Literature Society

**ICMA** = International City Management Association

**ICMEA** = International Coroners and Medical Examiners Association

**ICODS** = Interagency Committee On Dam Safety

**ICONS** = Information Center On Nuclear Standards

**ICP** = International Center of Photography

**ICRDB** = International Cancer Research Data Base (NCI)

**ICRP** = International Commission on Radiological Protection

**ICRU** = International Commission on Radiation Units and Measurements

**ICSH** = interstitial cell-stimulating hormone

**ICST** = Institute for Computer Science and Technology (NBS)

**ICT** = Wichita, Kansas, airport

**ICWS** = Indy Car World Series

**ICWU** = International Chemical Workers Union
**ID** = identification
= inside diameter
= intelligence department
= Idaho (postal code)
**IDA** = Idaho
= intrusion detection alarm
= International Development Association, of the World Bank (UN)
**IDCA** = US International Development Cooperation Agency
**IDMS** = isotope dilution mass spectrometry
**IDSA** = Industrial Designers Society of America
**ie** = that is (Latin: *id est*; that is to say)
**IED** = improvised explosive device
**IEEE** = Institute of Electrical and Electronics Engineers
**IES** = Illumination Engineering Society
= Institute of Environmental Sciences
**IEW** = Illegal Exportation of War Materials Statute
**IF** = intermediate frequency
**IFAD** = International Fund for Agricultural Development (UN)
**IFB** = invitation for bids
**IFBB** = International Federation of Body Builders
**IFC** = International Finance Corporation (UN)
**IFCTU** = International Federation of Christian Trade Unions
**IFF** = identification, friend or foe (military)
**IFR** = instrument flight rules
**IFV** = infantry fighting vehicle
**IG** = inspector general
**IGA** = Independent Grocers Association

**IGB** = Prohibition of Illegal Gambling Business (US)
**IGCA** = International Guild of Candle Artisans
**IGFA** = International Game Fish Association
**IGS** = International Graphoanalysis Society
**IGY** = International Geophysical Year; the 18 months from July '57 to December '58
**I-HEAD** = engine with an I-shaped cylinder head
**IHF** = International Hospital Federation
**IHL** = International Hockey League
**IHM** = Servants of the Immaculate Heart of Mary; Catholic order of nuns
**IHOP** = International House of Pancakes
**IHP** = indicated horsepower
**IHPVA** = International Human Powered Vehicle Association
**IHRA** = International Hot Rod Association
**IHS** = Jesus; Roman transliteration of the Greek
     = International Health Society
     = International Horn Society
**IIE** = Institute of Industrial Engineers
**IIHS** = Insurance Institute for Highway Safety
**IISH** = International Institute of Safety and Health
**IISS** = International Institute for Strategic Studies
**IIVI** = International Institute for Visually Impaired
**IJA** = International Jugglers Association
**IJN** = Imperial Japanese Navy
**IKA** = International Kitefliers Association
**IL** = Illinois (postal code)
     = Israel (international car index mark)
     = Ilyushin; Soviet aircraft designer
**IL-96** = Soviet Ilyushin long-range passenger jet
**ILA** = International Longshoremen's Association

**ILAE** = International League Against Epilepsy
**ILAR** = International League Against Rheumatism
**ILDC** = International Legal Defense Council
**ILGWU** = International Ladies' Garment Workers' Union
**ILHR** = International League for Human Rights
**ILI** = International Law Institute
**ILL** = Illinois
    = illustrated or illustration
**ILO** = International Labor Organization (UN)
**ILPBC** = International League of Professional Baseball Clubs, Inc.
**ILS** = instrument landing system
**ILWC** = International League of Women Composers
**IMAEI** = International Meteorology Aviation and Electronics Institute
**IMET** = International Military Education and Training Program (DOD)
**IMF** = International Monetary Fund (UN)
**IMHO** = in my humble opinion
**IMI** = International Marketing Institute
**IMIT** = imitative or imitation
**IMMS** = International Material Management Society
**IMNSHO** = in my not-so-humble opinion
**IMO** = International Maritime Organization (UN)
**IMP** = import
    = imperial
    = imprimatur; let it be printed
**IMS** = Institute of Museum Services
    = Indianapolis Motor Sports
**IMSA** = International Motor Sports Association
**IN** = Indiana (postal code)
    = inch

**In** = indium; a chemical element
**INC** = incorporated
    = income
    = includes or included
    = incomplete (football)
    = inconclusive
**INCOG** = incognito
**INCR** = increase
**IND** = Indiana
    = Indianapolis, Indiana, airport
    = India (international car index mark)
    = independent
    = industry or industrial
**INEOA** = International Narcotic Enforcement Officers Association
**INF** = intermediate-range nuclear forces
    = infantry
    = infinite
**INFO** = information
**INIS** = International Nuclear Information System
**INMM** = Institute of Nuclear Materials Management
**INP** = International News Photo
**INPO** = Institute of Nuclear Power Operations
**INR** = Bureau of Intelligence and Research (DOS)
**INRI** = Jesus of Nazareth, King of the Jews; (Latin: *Iesus Nazarenus, Rex Iudaeorum*)
**INRO** = International Naval Research Organization
**INS** = US Immigration & Naturalization Service
    = International News Service
    = inspector
    = International Numismatic Society
**INSAG** = International Nuclear Safety Advisory Group
**INSCOM** = Intelligence and Security Command (US Army)

**INSP** = inspector
**INST** = instant
    = instance
    = institute
**INSTR** = instrument or instrumental
     = instructor
**INSTRAW** = International Research and Training Institute for the Advancement of Women (UN)
**INT** = international
    = interest
    = interior
    = intern
    = internal
    = interception (football)
**INTERNET** = millions of computers in 43,000 networks in 81 countries linked by telephone lines using a shared computer language
**INTL** = international
**INTRO** = introduction
**INV** = invoice
    = inventor
**IO** = initials only
**I/O** = input/output
**IOA** = International Ozone Association
**IOC** = International Olympic Committee
**IOF** = International Oceanographic Foundation
**IOOF** = Independent Order of Odd Fellows
**IORM** = Improved Order of Red Men
**IOU** = I owe you; informal promissory note
**IP** = instrument panel
    = innings pitched (baseball)
    = initial point
    = intermediate pressure

**IPA** = International Phonetic Alphabet
     = International Polka Association
**IPAA** = International Prisoners Aid Association
**IPCEA** = Insulated Power Cable Engineers Association
**IPI** = International Petroleum Institute
**IPMI** = International Precious Metals Institute
**IPO** = Independent Post Office
     = initial public offering (of stock)
**IPPF** = International Planned Parenthood Federation
**IPRA** = International Professional Rodeo Association
**IPS** = inches per second
     = income per share
**IPSA PIPELINE** = Iraqi oil pipeline via Saudi Arabia
**IQ** = intelligence quotient; index of relative intelligence
based on test scores:

| | |
|---|---|
| 140+ | near genius or genius |
| 120-140 | very superior |
| 110-120 | superior |
| 90-110 | average |
| 80-90 | dull normal |
| 70-80 | borderline deficiency |
| 50-70 | educable mentally retarded |
| 30-50 | trainable |
| 20-30 | severely mentally retarded |
| 0-20 | profoundly mentally retarded |

**IR** = infrared
    = Irish
**Ir** = iridium; a chemical element
**IRA** = individual retirement account
     = Irish Republican Army
**IRBM** = intermediate range ballistic missile
**IRC** = Internal Revenue Code
**IRCA** = International Radio Club of America
      = Immigration Reform & Control Act

**IRE** = Ireland

= Investigative Reporters and Editors

**IRL** = Indy Racing League (auto racing)

**IRO** = International Refugee Organization (UN)

**IROC** = International Race of Champions (auto)

**IRREG** = irregular

**IRS** = Internal Revenue Service

= independent rear suspension (automotive)

**IS** = island

**ISA** = International Society of Appraisers, Ltd.

= International Silo Association

= Intelligence Support Activity; Pentagon's intelligence and counter-terrorism unit

**ISAR** = International Society for Animal Rights

**ISB** = International Society of Bassists

**ISBN** = International Standard Book Number

**ISC** = Intelligence and Security Command (US Army)

= International Speed Challenge (automotive)

**ISCDS** = International Stop Continental Drift Society

**ISCS** = International Society for Cardiovascular Surgery

= International Sand Collector's Society

**ISL** = island

**ISLCBS** = International Seal, Label, and Cigar Band Society

**ISO** = International Organization for Standardization (not IOS)

**ISOHP** = International Society for Organ History and Preservation

**ISPMB** = International Society for the Protection of Mustangs & Burros

**ISPN** = International Society for Pediatric Neurosurgery

**ISR** = Institute for Social Research

= Israel

**ISSN** = International Standard Serial Number (magazines)

**ISTEA** = Intermodal Surface Transportation Efficiency act; requiring highway paving mixture of CRM and asphalt

**ISV** = International Scientific Vocabulary
**ISWAP** = International Society of Women Airline Pilots
**IT** = Italy
**ITA**  = International Television Association
     = International Trade Administration (DOC)
**ITAL** = italics
     = Italian
**IT BAND** = iliotibial tract; connective muscle from hip to leg
**ITC** = US International Trade Commission
**ITF** = International Tennis Federation
**ITG**  = International Trumpet Guild
     = Hilo, Hawaii, airport
**ITS**  = International Thespian Society
     = inflatable tubular structure; elongated air bag used over the door to protect head and neck in side impact (automotive and aerospace)
**ITT** = International Telephone and Telegraph
**ITU** = International Telecommunication Union (UN)
**IU** = international unit; specific biological quantity that produces a particular biological effect
**IUBAC** = International Union of Bricklayers and Allied Craftsmen
**IUCD** = intrauterine contraceptive device
**IUD** = intrauterine device
**IUEESMFW** = International Union of Electronic, Electrical, Salaried, Machine and Furniture Workers
**IUIS** = International Union of Immunological Societies
**IUOE** = International Union of Operating Engineers
**IUPAC** = International Union of Pure and Applied Chemistry
**IUPAP** = International Union of Pure and Applied Physics
**IV** = intravenous
**IVF** = in vitro fertilization
**IWF** = International Weightlifting Federation

**IWW** = Industrial Workers of the World
**IYRU** = International Yacht Racing Union

**J** = judge
   = justice
   = Japan (international car index mark)
**JA** = Junior Achievement Inc.
    = judge advocate
    = joint account
    = Japan (aircraft registration code)
**JACK** = hijack
**JAG** = Jaguar; British automobile
     = judge advocate general
**JAM** = Jamaica
**JAMA** = Japanese Automobile Manufacturers Association
       = Journal of the American Medical Association
**JAN** = January
     = Jackson, Mississippi, airport
**JAP** = Japanese
**JATO** = jet-assisted takeoff
**JAX** = Jacksonville, Florida, airport
**JC** = Jesus Christ
**JCAE** = Joint Committee on Atomic Energy
**JCC** = Junior Chamber of Commerce
**JCD** = doctor of canon law
**JCO** = justification for continued operation
**JCS** = Joint Chiefs of Staff (military)
**JCT** = junction
**JD** = doctor of law
**JDF** = Juvenile Diabetes Foundation
**JDS** = Joint Deployment System (military)
**JEEP** = joint emergency evacuation program of essential government workers; see COG

JFK = John Fitzgerald Kennedy, 35th US president
    = New York, NY, airport
JG = junior grade
JHVH = variation of YHWH
JHWH = variation of YHWH
JIS = Job Information Service (DOL)
JL = Japan Airlines
JND = just noticeable difference
JO = junior officer
JOT = junior officer trainee
JOUR  = journalist
      = journey
      = journeyman
JP  = jet propulsion
   = jet propulsion fuel, as in JP-4
   = justice of the peace
JPL = Jet Propulsion Laboratory (NASA)
JR = junior
JSOC = Joint Special Operations Command; supervises all military counter-terrorist forces
JSTARS = Joint Surveillance Tactical Attack Radar System; airborne radar for monitoring vehicles
JT = joint
JU-87 = WW II German Junkers divebomber; "STUKA"
JUL = July
JUN = June
JUNC = junction
JUV = juvenile
JV = junior varsity
JVC = Japanese Victor Company
JWV = Jewish War Veterans

**K** = kilo; thousand (metric system)

= kilometer; thousand meters

= knot; one nautical mile per hour

= strikeout (baseball)

= kicker (football)

= king (chess)

= karat; variation of carat

= Kelvin; temperature unit or scale

= potassium (Latin: *kalium*); a chemical element

= Köchel; for Dr. Ludwig von Köchel who cataloged Mozart's works

**K-9** = canine

**K-12** = kindergarten through grade twelve

**KAN** = Kansas

**KANS** = Kansas

**KATUSA** = Korean Augmentation to US Army; Korean conscripts for US Army during Korean war

**KB** = kilobyte; thousand bytes

= king's bishop (chess)

= Knight Bachelor (British)

= Knight of the Bath (British)

= king's bench

**KBE** = Knight Commander of the (Order of the) British Empire

**KBPS** = kilobytes per second; thousand bytes per second

**KC** = kilocycle; thousand cycles (also KHZ)

= Knights of Columbus

= Kansas City

= king's counsel

**KC-135** = military midair refueling tanker plane; Boeing "Stratotanker"

**KCB** = Knight Commander of the Bath (British)

**KDI** = Kidney Disease Institute
**KEN** = Kentucky
**KENT** = Kentucky
**KFC** = Kentucky Fried Chicken
**KG** = kilogram; thousand grams
    = Knight of the (Order of the) Garter (British)
**KGB** = Soviet Committee of State Security (Russian: *Komitet Gosudarstvennoye Bezhopaznosti*); Soviet intelligence and security agency similar to the FBI, CIA and Border Patrol combined
**KGPS** = kilograms per second
**KH-11** = US spy satellite
**KHz** = kilohertz; thousand hertz or cycles (also KC)
**KIA** = killed in action
**KID** = child
**KID VID** = children's video
**KIN** = Kingston, Jamaica, airport
**KIWI** = resident of New Zealand
**KKK** = Ku Klux Klan
**KL** = kiloliter; thousand liters
    = Kuala Lumpur, city in Malaysia
    = Royal Dutch Airlines
**KLEPTO** = kleptomaniac; addicted to stealing
**KLM** = Royal Dutch Airlines
**KM** = kilometer; thousand meters
**KMA** = freebie, favor from "kiss my you-know-what"
**KMAG** = Korean Military Assistance Group
**KMPS** = kilometers per second
**KN** = king's knight (chess)
    = knot; one nautical mile per hour
**kN** = kilonewton (measure of force)
**KNEECAP** = see NEACP
**KOA** = Kona, Hawaii, airport

**K of C** = Knights of Columbus
**K of P** = Knights of Pythias
**KO** = knockout (boxing)
    = kickoff (football)
**KP** = kitchen police; kitchen duty (military)
**KPC** = kilo parsecs (astronomy)
**KPNO** = Kitt Peak National Observatory, Tucson, Arizona
**KR** = king's rook (chess)
**Kr** = krypton; a chemical element
**K RATIONS** = US Army field rations; one day's rations in three small cardboard boxes
**KS** = Kansas (postal code)
**KSA** = Kafka Society of America
**KT** = karat (see C = CARAT)
    = knight
**Kt** = knight; also N (chess)
**KTO** = Kuwait Theater of Operations (Gulf War)
**KV** = kilovolt; thousand volts
**KW** = kilowatt; thousand watts
**KWH** = kilowatt hour; one thousand watts per hour
**KY** = Kentucky (postal code)

**L** = left
    = large
    = liter
    = lost
    = lake
    = length
    = Latin
    = 50 in Roman numerals
    = *lira* (Italian currency)
    = Luxembourg (international car index mark)

**L88** = GM designation for 427-cubic-inch Corvette V-8
**LA** = Louisiana (postal code)
   = Los Angeles
**La** = lanthanum; a chemical element
**LAB** = League of American Bicyclists
   = laboratory
   = Labrador
   = labrador, breed of dog
**LAIRS** = Labor Agreement Information Retrieval System (OPM)
**LAM** = laminated
**LAMBO** = Lamborghini; Italian automobile
**LAN** = Lansing, Michigan, airport
**LAND** = League Against Nuclear Dangers
**LANG** = language
**LANL** = Los Alamos National Laboratories
**LANTCOM** = Atlantic Command; US Unified Command HQ
**LAPD** = Los Angeles Police Department
**LAS** = Las Vegas, Nevada, airport
**LA SED** = Latin Americans for Social and Economic Development
**LASER** = light amplification by stimulated emission of radiation
**LAT** = latitude
   = Latin
   = local apparent time
**LATA** = local access transport area, of local and long-distance phone coverage
**LATINO** = Latin American
**LAV** = lavatory
   = light armored vehicle

**LAX** = Los Angeles, California, airport
**LB** = pound
   = linebacker (football)
**LBJ** = Lyndon Baines Johnson, 36th US president
**LB ST** = pounds static thrust (jet engines)
**LBW** = long wheelbase (automotive)
**LC** = lower case
   = landing craft
   = Library of Congress
**LCCC** = Library of Congress Computerized Catalog
**LCD** = liquid-crystal display; a type of video screen
   = lowest common denominator
**LCM** = least common multiple
**LCOL** = lieutenant colonel; also LTCOL
**LCOM** = lieutenant commander; also LTCOM
**L/CPL** = lance corporal
**LCT** = local civil time
   = landing craft, tank; barge-like vessel with a bow
ramp (USN)
**LD** = lethal dose
   = long distance
   = load
   = lord
**LDC** = less-developed country
**LDG** = landing
   = loading
**LDL** = low-density lipoprotein; "bad" cholesterol (see HDL)
**LDR** = leader
**LDS** = Latter-Day Saints
**LE** = left end (football)
   = limit of error
**LEAA** = Law Enforcement Assistance Administration
**LED** = light-emitting diode
   = type of illuminated video screen

**LEG** = legislature
    = legal
    = legato (music: smooth and connected)
**LEGIT** = legitimate
     = good drama, not burlesque
**LEM** = Lunar Excursion Module (NASA)
**LEO** = low earth orbit
**LESA** = Lunar Exploration System for Apollo (NASA)
**LEU** = low-enriched uranium
**LEV** = Lunar Excursion Vehicle (NASA)
**LF** = low frequency
   = left field (baseball)
**LFA** = Lupus Foundation of America
    = lead federal agency
**LG** = left guard (sports)
   = large
**LGA** = LaGuardia Airport, New York, NY
**LGB** = Long Beach, California, airport
**LGEN** = lieutenant general; also LTGEN
**LGM** = little green men; visitors from outer space
**LH** = left hand
   = Lufthansa Airlines, Germany
**LHA** = Lincoln Highway Association
**LHD** = left hand drive
    = doctor of humanities
**LI** = Long Island
**Li** = lithium; a chemical element
**LIA** = Laser Institute of America
**LIB** = liberal
   = liberation
   = library or librarian
**LIC** = license
**LIEUT** = lieutenant, also LT
**LIFO** = last in first out

**LIHEAP** = Low-Income Housing Energy Assistance Program
**LIMA** = Licensing Industry Merchandisers' Association
**LIMO** = limousine
**LIN** = lineal or linear
**LING** = linguistics
**LIQ** = liquid
  = liquor
**LIT** = literature or literary
  = literally
  = literary college
  = Little Rock, Arkansas, airport
**LitB** = bachelor of literature
**LitD** = doctor of literature
**LITHO** = lithography
**LITTLE BOY** = code name for gun-type uranium bomb dropped on Hiroshima in WW II (see FATMAN)
**LIUNA** = Laborers' International Union of North America
**LLB** = bachelor of laws
  = Little League Baseball
**LLD** = doctor of laws
**LLNL** = Lawrence Livermore National Laboratory
**LLM** = Lunar Landing Module (NASA)
**LLRW** = low-level radioactive waste
**LM** = Lunar Module (NASA)
  = legion of merit
**LMG** = light machine gun
**LMP** = Literary Market Place (publication)
**LMT** = local mean time
**LN** = lane
**LNG** = liquid natural gas

**LO** = LOT Polish Airlines
**L/O** = layout
**LOA** = letter of agreement
**LOB** = left on base (baseball)
**LOD** = line-of-duty (military)
**LOG** = logarithm
**LOND** = London
**LONG** = longitude
**LOOM** = Loyal Order Of Moose
**LOR** = Lunar Orbit Rendezvous (NASA)
**LORAN** = long-range aids to navigation
**LOX** = liquid oxygen; rocket fuel
    = smoked salmon
**LP** = long play; medium VCR recording speed
    = low pressure
    = long-playing record: 33 1/3 rpm
    = limited partnership
    = listening post
**LPA** = Little People of America
**LPB** = Lunar and Planetary Bibliography (NASA)
**LPG** = liquid petroleum gas
    = low-pressure gas
**LPGA** = Ladies' Professional Golfers' Association
**LPI** = lines per inch
    = Lightning Protection Institute
    = Lunar and Planetary Institute
**LPLNG** = low-pressure liquid natural gas
**LPN** = Licensed Practical Nurse
**LPTV** = low-power television
**LPZ** = low-population zone
**LR** = living room
**LRL** = Lawrence Radiation Laboratory

**LS** = long shot (cinematography)
    = left side
**LSA** = Leukemia Society of America
    = Learn and Serve America
    = Linguistic Society of America
**LSD** = lysergic acid diethylamide; "acid;" synthetic hallucinogen
    = limited-slip differential (automotive)
**LS/MFT** = Lucky Strike means fine tobacco; ad slogan
**LST** = landing ship, tank; flat-bottom transport (USN)
    = lost
    = local solar time
**LT** = lieutenant
    = light
**LT1** = GM designation for 350-cubic-inch Corvette V-8
**LT5** = GM designation for Corvette ZR1 DOHC V-8
**LTA** = Lawn Tennis Association
**LTBT** = Limited Test Ban Treaty
**LT COL** = lieutenant colonel; also LCOL
**LT COM** = lieutenant commander; also LCOM
**LTD** = limited
**LT GEN** = lieutenant general; also LGEN
**LT GOV** = lieutenant governor
**LTjg** = lieutenant, junior grade (USN)
**LTM** = low-trajectory missile
**LTR** = letter
**Lu** = lutetium; a chemical element
**LUB** = lubrication
**LUBE JOB** = lubrication of an automobile
**LUGG** = luggage
**LV** = leaves or leaving
**LW** = left wing (sports)

Lw = lawrencium; a chemical element
LWCA = Long Wave Club of America
LWIR = long-wavelength infrared
LWM = low-water mark
LWOP = leave without pay
LWV = League of Women Voters
LY = El Al Israel Airlines
LZ = landing zone (military)

M = male
= married
= medium
= mile
= minute
= month
= meter
= mega or million
= mass
= Mach; the speed of sound, after the Austrian physicist
= Messier Catalog of Nebulae, after French astronomer
= 1,000 in Roman numerals
= fictional code name for head of James Bond's secret service
= Malta (international car index mark)
M-31 = Andromeda Nebula; actually a galaxy
MA = Massachusetts (postal code)
= master of arts
= mental age
= Mistresses Anonymous
M/A = manual or automatic
MAA = Mathematical Association of America
= Moped Association of America
MAAG = Military Assistance Advisory Group

**MAC** = Macintosh computer
= MacDonald's hamburger
= Mothers Against Carjackers
= Military Airlift Command
= Military Assistance Command
= Multipurpose Arthritis Center

**MACE** = methylchloroform chloroacetophenone; toxic chemical compound once used for riot control

**MACH** = machine
= machinist
= ratio of speed to speed of sound; "mock," after the Austrian physicist

**MACIPS** = Military Airlift Command Information Processing System

**MACV** = Military Assistance Command in Vietnam; "mac-vee"

**MAD** = mutual assured destruction (military)
= magnetic anomaly detector (for finding sunken treasure or hidden submarines)

**MADD** = Mothers Against Drunk Driving

**MAF** = Marine Amphibious Force

**MAG** = magazine (publication)
= magazine (for ammunition)
= magnitude
= magnetic
= magnesium; also Mg
= Marine Aviation Group

**MAGIC** = WW II code for intelligence culled from enemy codes; US version of British ULTRA

**MAG-LEV** = magnetic levitation; train that runs on a magnetic field

**MAJ** = major

**MAJ GEN** = major general

**MALDEF** = Mexican American Legal Defense and Educational Fund
**MAN** = manual
    = Manitoba
**M&M** = sugarcoated chocolate candy pellet
    = Mars and Mars, for John and Forrest Mars, candy tycoons
**MANHATTAN PROJECT** = variation of Manhattan Engineer District; code name for WW II atomic-bomb project
**MAP** = municipal airport
**MAP-EX** = map exercise; review of battle plans (US Army)
**MAPI** = Machinery and Allied Products Institute
**MAPP** = Modern Age Planning Program; simulates battle scenarios (military)
**MAR** = March
**MARC** = machine-readable cataloging (LC)
**MARK 17** = first deliverable H-bomb of 21 tons
**MARS** = Military Affiliate Radio System
**MARU** = Middle American Research Unit
**MASC** = masculine
**MASER** = microwave amplification by stimulated emission of radiation
**MASH** = Mobile Army Surgical Hospital
**MASS** = Massachusetts
**MASS SPEC** = mass spectrometry
**MATH** = mathematics
**MATS** = Military Air Transport Service
**MAUFS** = Municipal Arborists Urban Foresters Society
**MAX** = maximum
**MAYO** = mayonnaise
**MB** = Manitoba (postal symbol)
    = motor boat
    = Mercedes Benz; German automobile

**MBA** = master of business administration
    = Military Brats of America
**MBAA** = Mortgage Bankers Association of America
**MBC** = meteor burst communication; reflecting VHF radio signals off meteor trails
**MBDA** = Minority Business Development Agency (DOC)
**MBDC** = Minority Business Development Centers (DOC)
**MBFR** = Mutual and Balanced Force Reductions
**MBMA** = Metal Building Manufacturers Association
**MBO** = management by objective
**MBS** = Mutual Broadcasting System
**MBT** = main battle tank
**MC** = master of ceremonies
    = message center
    = Marine Corps
    = Master Card credit card
    = megacycle; million cycles; also MHz
    = Monaco (international car index mark)
**MCA** = Music Corporation of America
    = Missing Children of America
**MCAA** = Mason Contractors Association of America
**MCC** = master control center (mobile communications)
**MCI** = Museum Consultants International
    = Kansas City, Missouri, International Airport
**MCIC** = Metals and Ceramics Technologies Center (DOD)
**MCL** = Marine Corps League
**MCO** = Orlando, Florida, International Airport
**MCU** = medium close up (movies)
**MD** = medical doctor
    = medical department
    = Maryland (postal code)
    = McDonnell Douglas

**Md** = mendelevium; a chemical element

**MDA** = Muscular Dystrophy Association

**MDR** = minimum daily requirement, usually vitamins

**MDS** = master of dental surgery

**MDSE** = merchandise

**MDT** = mountain daylight time
= mobile data terminal (mobile communications)

**MDU** = motion detection unit

**MDW** = Midway Airport, Chicago, Illinois

**ME** = medical examiner
= mechanical engineer
= Maine (postal code)
= Middle English
= Middle East

**Me** = Messerschmitt; German aircraft designer

**Me 109** = WW II German Messerschmitt pursuit plane; also Bf 109, after *Bayerische Flugzeugwerke*, predecessor company where it was designed

**Me 262** = first WW II jet fighter; German Messerschmitt

**MEB** = US Marine Expeditionary Brigade (Gulf War)

**MECH** = mechanical
= mechanic
= mechanized

**MECO** = main engine cutoff (NASA)

**MED** = medical
= medium
= medieval
= minimal effective dose
= minimal erythemal dose; time it takes sunlight to turn skin pink
= Manhattan Engineer District; code name for WW II atomic-bomb project; also MANHATTAN PROJECT

**MEd** = master of education
**MEDEVAC** = medical evacuation, usually by helicopter
**MEDICAID** = medical aid for poor and impoverished elderly
**MEDICARE** = medical care for the elderly
**MEECN** = minimum essential emergency communications network
**MEF** = median energy of fission
**MEGA** = million
**MEI** = Middle East Institute
**MEM** = member
    = memorial
    = Memphis, Tennessee, airport
**MEMO** = memorandum
**MENS** = Mission Element Need Statements (DOD)
**MEP** = mean effective pressure
    = Marine Environmental Protection
**MER** = meridian
**MERC** = Mercury
    = Mercedes Benz
**MESBIC** = Minority Enterprise Small Business Investment Companies
**MESSRS** = plural of Mr. (French: *Messieurs*)
**MESUR** = Mars Environmental Survey Project (NASA)
**MET** = metropolitan
    = Metropolitan Opera Theatre of New York; also MOT
    = meteorology
**METO** = Middle East Treaty Organization
**METRO** = metropolitan
    = Paris subway
**METS** = New York Metropolitans baseball team
**METT-T** = mission, enemy, terrain, troops and time (US Army)

**MEV** = million electron volts
**MEX** = Mexico (international car index mark)
     = Mexican
     = Mexico City airport
**MF** = medium frequency
   = mezzo forte (music: medium loud)
**MFA** = master of fine arts
**MFCC** = Marriage, Family, Child Counselor
**MFG** = manufacturing
**MFGA** = Master Furriers Guild of America
**MFH** = master of fox hounds
**MFI** = multi-port fuel injection
**MFN** = most-favored nation
**MFR** = manufacturer
**MFT** = Marriage and Family Therapist
**MG** = milligram; one-thousandth of a gram
   = machine gun
   = military government
   = British car, after Morris Garages
**Mg** = magnesium; a chemical element
**MGA** = British sports car (also MGB, MG TC, MG TD and MG TF)
**MGB** = Soviet Ministry of State Security (Russian: *Ministerstvo Gosudarstvennoi Bezopasnosti*); predecessor to Soviet KGB
**MGCA** = Men's Garden Clubs of America
**MGF** = Myasthenia Gravis Foundation
**MGM** = Metro-Goldwyn-Mayer
      = Montgomery, Alabama, airport
**MGMT** = management
**MGM/UA** = Metro-Goldwyn-Mayer/United Artists
**MGR** = manager
**MGT** = management
**MH** = medal of honor
   = Marshall Islands (postal code)

MHI = Mental Health Institute

MHW = mean high water

MHz = megahertz; million hertz or cycles

MI = Michigan (postal code)

    = mile

    = military intelligence

MI5 = British Military Intelligence, section 5; equivalent to the FBI; "Security Service"

MI6 = British Military Intelligence, section 6; equivalent to the CIA; "Secret Service" or "Secret Intelligence Service"

MIA = missing in action

     = Marble Institute of America

     = Miami, Florida, airport

MICE = money, ideology, compromise, ego; ways to compromise a spy

MICH = Michigan

MICKEY D's = MacDonald's

MICOM = Army Missile Command HQ

MICR = magnetic ink character recognition

MID = middle

MIDN = midshipman

MiG = various Soviet fighter planes; after designers Mokoyan and Gurevich

MIL = military

MILSTAR = nuclear weapons communications satellite

MIN = minute (of time)

     = minimum

     = minority

     = minister

     = minor

MINN = Minnesota

MIO = minimum identifiable odor

MIRV = multiple individually-targeted reentry vehicle; missile with multiple warheads

MISC = miscellaneous
MISS = Mississippi
MIT = Massachusetts Institute of Technology
MITI = Ministry of International Trade & Industry (Japan)
MIXT = mixture
MJ = Mary Jane, alias for marijuana
    = marijuana
MK = mark
MKE = Milwaukee, Wisconsin, airport
MKT = market
ML = milliliter; one-thousandth of a liter
MLA = Modern Language Association
MLB = middle linebacker (football)
MLBPA = Major League Baseball Players Association
MLC = Money Laundering Control Act (US)
MLD = minimum lethal dose
    = median lethal dose
MLR = minimum lending rate
MLRS = multiple-launch rocket system (US Army)
MLS = microwave landing system, for major airports
MLW = mean low water
MM = millimeter; one-thousandth of a meter
    = million in Roman numerals
MMA = Monorail Manufacturers Association
MME = madame (French for Mrs.)
MMFPA = Man-Made Fiber Producers Association
MMM = Minnesota Mining and Manufacturing; also 3M
MN = Minnesota (postal code)
    = magnetic north
Mn = manganese; a chemical element
MNC = multinational corporation
MNE = Maine

**MO** = Missouri (postal code)
    = month
    = modus operandi (method of operation)
    = medical officer
    = money order
    = mail order
**Mo** = molybdenum; a chemical element
**MOB** = main operating base
**MOD** = modern
    = modified or modification
    = model
**MOL** = manned orbital laboratory
**MOMA** = Museum of Modern Art, NY
**MON** = Monday
    = Montana
    = monetary
**MONO** = mononucleosis
    = monaural, in contrast to stereo
    = monophonic, in contrast to stereophonic
**MONT** = Montana
**MOPAR** = Chrysler Corporation's Motor Parts
    = Chrysler Corporation car: Plymouth, Dodge, DeSoto, Chrysler
**MORC** = Market Opinion Research Center
**MOS** = military occupational specialty
    = months
    = without sound, from "mit out sound" (movies)
**MOSSAD** = Israeli secret service
**MOT** = Metropolitan Opera Theater
**MOTOWN** = Motor Town (Detroit)
    = recording company
**MOUSE** = Minimum Orbital Unmanned Satellite of Earth
**MOX** = mixed-oxide fuel

**MP** = military police
= Mounted Police
= melting point
= missing person
= member of parliament
= Northern Mariana Islands (postal code)
**MPA** = Magazine Publishers Association
**MPAA** = Motion Picture Association of America (ratings board)
**MPC** = multimedia personal computer
= mega parsecs (astronomy)
**MPD** = maximum permissible dose
**MPE** = maximum permissible exposure
**MPG** = miles per gallon
**MPH** = miles per hour
**MPI** = Medicine in the Public Interest
= multi-port injection, as in an automobile engine
**MPS** = meters per second
**MR** = mister
**MRA** = Moral ReArmament
**MRAA** = Mental Retardation Association of America
**MRCP** = Member of the Royal College of Physicians
**MRD** = motorized rifle division
**MRI** = magnetic resonance imaging
**MRIA** = Model Railroad Industry Association
**MRS** = mistress (married)
**MS** = multiple sclerosis
= Miss or Mrs.
= Mississippi (postal code)
= medium shot (movies)
= manuscript
= master of science
= Microsoft
= motor ship

**MSA** = Mineralogical Society of America
**MSC** = Military Sealift Command
     = Materials Science Center
**MSc** = master of science
**MSEC** = millisecond; one-thousandth of a second
**MSF** = Motorcycle Safety Foundation
**MSFC** = Marshall Space Flight Center (NASA)
**MSG** = monosodium glutamate; flavor enhancer
     = message
**MSGR** = monseigneur
**MSGT** = master sergeant
**MSI** = Marine Sciences Institute
**MSL** = mean sea level
**MSN** = Madison, Wisconsin, airport
**MSP** = Minneapolis-St. Paul, airport
**MSRP** = manufacturer's suggested retail price
**MSS** = manuscripts
**MST** = mountain standard time
**MSTS** = Military Sea Transport Service
**MSY** = New Orleans, Louisiana, airport
**MT** = Montana (postal code)
     = mount
     = mountain time
**MTBE** = methyl tertiary-butyl ether; oxygenated gasoline additive
**MTG** = meeting
**MTGE** = mortgage
**MTN** = mountain
**MTO** = Mediterranean Theater of Operations (WW II)
**MTOUSA** = Mediterranean Theater of Operations, US Army (WW II)
**MTPS** = Modern Talking Picture Service
**MTV** = Music Television

**MUMS** = Multiple Use MARC System (LC)
**MUN** = municipal
**MUNI** = municipal
    = municipal bond
**MUS** = museum
    = music
    = musician
**MUSE** = Musicians United for Safe Energy
**MV** = millivolt; one-thousandth of a volt
**MVA** = motor-vehicle accident
**MVD** = Soviet Ministry for Internal Affairs (Russian: *Ministerstvo Vnutrennykh Del*); predecessor to KGB
**MVICSA** = Motor Vehicle Information and Cost Savings Act (US)
**MVMA** = Motor Vehicle Manufacturers Association
**MVP** = most valuable player
**MVPA** = Military Vehicle Preservation Association
**MVT** = motor vehicle theft
    = Motor Vehicle Theft Law Enforcement Act (US)
**MW** = milliwatt; one-thousandth of a watt
**MWA** = Modern Women of America
**MY** = model year (automotive)
**MYTD** = model year to date (automotive)
**MW** = microwave
**MWWU** = Marine Wing Weapons Unit
**MX** = motocross; cross-country motorcycle racing
    = ICBM, renamed "Peacekeeper"
**MYOB** = mind your own business
**MYSTIC STAR** = President's radio communications network
**MYTH** = mythical
    = mythology

**N** = north
= name
= noun
= neuter
= number
= noon
= no
= navy
= normal
= knight; also кt (chess)
= nitrogen; a chemical element
= Norway (international car index mark)
= United States (aircraft registration code)
**NA** = Native American
= not applicable
= not available
= Narcotics Anonymous
= Nicotine Anonymous
= no account
**Na** = sodium (Latin: *natrium*); a chemical element
**NAA** = National Archery Association
= National Aeronautic Association
= Newspaper Association of America
= National Association of Accountants
= National Archery Association
= neutron activation analysis
**NAAAA** = National Association of Area Agencies on Aging
**NAAB** = National Association of Animal Breeders
**NAACP** = National Association for the Advancement of Colored People
**NAADAA** = National Antique and Art Dealers Association of America
**NAADC** = North American Aerospace Defense

Command

**NAAFA** = National Association to Advance Fat Acceptance

**NAAMM** = North American Academy of Manipulative Medicine

**NAANAD** = National Association of Anorexia Nervosa and Associated Disorders

**NAAQS** = National Ambient Air Quality Standards

**NAARPR** = National Alliance Against Racist and Political Repression

**NAAV** = National Association of Atomic Veterans

**NAB** = National Alliance of Businessmen

= National Association of Broadcasters

**NABA** = National Association of Black Accountants

**NABET** = National Association of Broadcast Employees and Technicians

**NABJ** = National Association of Black Journalists

**NABM** = National Association of Bedding Manufacturers

**NABOB** = National Association of Black-Owned Broadcasters

**NABS** = National Association of Barber Schools

= North American Bluebird Society

**NACA** = National Advisory Committee for Aeronautics; now NASA

= National Association for Children of Alcoholics

= North American College of Acupuncture

= National Air Carrier Association

**NACDL** = National Association of Criminal Defense Lawyers

**NACO** = National Association of Counties

**NACW** = National Association of Career Women

**NAD** = National Association of the Deaf

= National Academy of Design

**NADA** = National Automobile Dealers Association

**NADAA** = National Association of Dance and Affiliated Artists

**NADAP** = National Association on Drug Abuse Problems

**NADC** = National Animal Disease Center
**NADS** = National Association of Diaper Services
**NAE** = National Academy of Engineering
    = National Academy of Education
    = National Adoption Exchange
**NAEMT** = National Association of Emergency Medical Technicians
**NAEP** = National Assessment of Educational Programs (ED)
**NAF** = National Abortion Federation
**NAFA** = North American Falconers' Association
**NAFCU** = National Association of Federal Credit Unions
**NAFE** = National Association for Female Executives
**NAFI** = National Association of Fire Investigators
**NAFLFD** = National Association of Federally Licensed Firearms Dealers
**NAFO** = Northwest Atlantic Fisheries Organization
**NAFT** = no accounting for taste
**NAFTA** = North American Free Trade Agreement
**NAGA** = North American Gamebird Association
**NAGCR** = North American Guild of Change Ringers
**NAIA** = National Association of Intercollegiate Athletics
**NAIAS** = North American International Automobile Show, in Detroit
**NAIC** = National Astronomy and Ionosphere Center
**NAJCA** = National Association of Juvenile Correctional Agencies
**NAKBA** = National Association to Keep and Bear Arms
**NALC** = National Association of Letter Carriers
**NALU** = National Association of Life Underwriters
**NAM** = National Association of Manufacturers
    = Vietnam
**NAMA** = North American Mycological Association
**NAMC** = National Association of Minority Contractors

**NAME** = National Association of Medical Examiners
**NAMM** = National Association of Margarine Manufacturers
**NAN** = National Association of Neighborhoods
    = Nuclear Awareness Network
**NAPA** = National Automotive Parts Association
**NAPBIRT** = National Association of Professional Band Instrument Repair Technicians
**NAPCA** = National Air Pollution Control Administration
**NAPCC** = National Animal Poison Control Center
**NAPE** = National Association of Power Engineers
    = National Association of Professional Educators
    = napalm; jellied gasoline
**NAPH** = National Association of the Physically Handicapped
**NAPM** = National Association of Purchasing Management
**NAPWPT** = National Association of Professional Word Processing Technicians
**NAR** = National Association of Rocketry
**NARA** = National Archives and Records Administration
**NARAL** = National Abortion Rights Action League
**NAR-ANON** = narcotics anonymous, support group for families of narcotics users (not part of NA)
**NARAS** = National Academy of Recording Arts and Sciences, Inc.
**NARC** = narcotics officer
    = DEA officer
**NARD** = National Association of Retail Druggists
**NAREIT** = National Association of Real Estate Investment Trusts
**NARFE** = National Association of Retired Federal Employees
**NARI** = National Association of Recycling Industries
**NARP** = National Association of Railroad Passengers
**NARS** = National Archives and Records Service (DOD)

**NAS** = National Academy of Sciences
   = National Astrological Society
   = National Avionics Society
   = naval air station
   = Nassau, Bahamas, airport
**NASA** = National Aeronautics and Space Administration
**NASACU** = National Association of State Approved Colleges & Universities
**NAS&FP** = National Asset Seizure and Forfeiture Program
**NASC** = National Alliance of Senior Citizens
**NASCAR** = National Association of Stock Car Racing
**NASCD** = National Association for Sickle Cell Disease
**NASD** = National Association of Securities Dealers
**NASDAQ** = National Association of Securities Dealers Automated Quotation System
**NASE** = National Association of the Self-Employed
**NASIS** = National Association for State Information Systems
**NASMV** = National Association on Standard Medical Vocabulary
**NASP** = National Aerospace Plane project; X-30 project
**NASS** = National Alliance for Safe Schools
   = National Accident Sampling System (NHTSA)
**NASW** = National Association of Social Workers
   = National Association of Science Writers, Inc.
**NASWA** = North American Shortwave Association
**NAT** = national
   = native
   = natural
**NATA** = National Air Transportation Association
**NATAS** = National Appropriate Technology Assistance Service (DOE)
**NATCC** = North American Touring Car Championship
**NATL** = national

**NATO** = North Atlantic Treaty Organization
     = North African Theater of Operations (WW II)
**NATOUSA** = North African Theater of Operations, US Army (WW II)
**NATS** = National Association of Teachers of Singing
**NAUI** = National Association of Underwater Instructors
**NAUS** = National Association of Uniformed Services
**NAUT** = nautical
**NAV** = net asset value
     = naval
     = navigation
**NAVAIR** = US Naval Air
**NAVS** = National Anti-Vivisection Society
     = North American Vegetarian Society
**NAVSPASUR** = Naval Space Surveillance System
**NAVSTAR** = US navigation system using time and ranging
**NAWAS** = national warning system
**NAWBO** = National Association of Women Business Owners
**NAWL** = National Association of Women Lawyers
**NAZI** = Hitler's *National Sozialist* party organization (see NSDAP)
**NB** = New Brunswick
     = northbound
**Nb** = niobium; a chemical element
**nb** = note carefully (Latin: *nota bene*)
**NBA** = National Basketball Association
     = National Boxing Association
**NBC** = National Broadcasting Company
     = National Baseball Congress
     = National Bowling Council
**NBME** = National Board of Medical Examiners
**N-BOMB** = neutron bomb; H-bomb that emits neutrons instead of heat

**NBRA** = National Bench Rest Association (shooting)
**NBRMP** = National Board of Review of Motion Pictures
**NBS** = National Bureau of Standards; now NIST
    = National Biological Service
**NBTA** = National Business Travel Association
**NC** = North Carolina (postal code)
    = no charge
    = no comment
    = National Conservation
**NC-17** = no children under 17 admitted (movies)
**NCA** = National Command Authority
    = National Constructors Association
    = National Council on Alcoholism
    = National Council on the Aging
    = National Carousel Association
    = National Caves Association
    = National Coal Association
    = National Confectioners Association
**NCAA** = National Collegiate Athletic Association
**NCAC** = National Clean Air Coalition
    = National Coalition Against Censorship
    = National Council of Acoustical Consultants
**NCADD** = National Council on Alcoholism and Drug Dependence
**NCADI** = National Clearinghouse for Alcohol and Drug Information
**NCADP** = National Coalition Against the Death Penalty
**NCAI** = National Clearinghouse for Alcohol Information
    = National Congress of American Indians
**NCAP** = New Car Assessment Program, by NHTSA
**NCAR** = National Center for Atmospheric Research (NSF)
    = North Carolina
**NCBH** = National Coalition to Ban Handguns
**NCBI** = National Cotton Batting Institute

**NCCA** = National Cotton Council of America
**NCCBA** = National Caucus & Center on Black Aged
**NCCCD** = National Center for Computer Crime Data
**NCCD** = National Council on Crime and Delinquency
**NCCG** = National Council on Compulsive Gambling
**NCCJ** = National Conference of Christians and Jews
**NCCM** = National Council of Christian Men
**NCCPB** = National Council of Commercial Plant Breeders
**NCCW** = National Council of Catholic Women
**NCDB** = National Consumer Data Base
**NCDE** = National Center for Death Education
**NCE** = New Catholic Edition, of the Bible
**NCEA** = National Catholic Educational Association
      = National Center for Economic Alternatives
**NCEC** = National Committee for an Effective Congress
**NCEE** = National Council on Economic Education
**NCFA** = National Committee For Adoption
      = Narcolepsy and Cataplexy Foundation of America
**NCFR** = National Council on Family Relations
**NCFT** = National Center for Families and Television
**NCGA** = National Computer Graphics Association
**NCGIC** = National Cartographic and Geographic Information Center (DOI)
**NCGSTDS** = National Coalition of Gay Sexually Transmitted Disease Services
**NCH** = National Cocaine Hotline
**NCHE** = National Center for Health Education
**NCHS** = National Center for Health Statistics
**NCI** = National Cancer Institute
    = Nuclear Control Institute
**NCIC** = National Crime Information Center (DOJ)
    = National Cartographic Information Center (DOI)
**NCJA** = National Criminal Justice Association
**NCJJ** = National Center for Juvenile Justice

125

**NCJRS** = National Criminal Justice Reference Service
**NCJW** = National Council of Jewish Women
**NCL** = National Consumers League
**NCLC** = National Child Labor Committee
**NCLEX** = National Council Licensure Examination
**NCLEX-PN** = NCLEX for Practical Nurses
**NCLEX-RN** = NCLEX for Registered Nurses
**NCMA** = National Concrete Masonry Association
**NCMC** = NORAD Cheyenne Mountain Center
**NCMEC** = National Center For Missing and Exploited Children
**NCMR** = National Clearinghouse on Marital Rape
**NCO** = non-commissioned officer
**NCOA** = National Change of Address System
        = National Corvette Owners Association
**NCPA** = National Cleft Palate Association
**NCPCA** – National Committee for Prevention of Child Abuse
**NCPCR** = National Center for the Prevention and Control of Rape
**NCR** = National Cash Register
**NCRFP** = National Council for a Responsible Firearms Policy
**NCRP** = National Committee for Responsive Philanthropy
**NCS** = national communications system
        = National Cartoonists Society
        = National Council on Stuttering
        = nuclear criticality safety
**NCSA** = National Center for Supercomputing Applications
        = National Computer Security Association
**NCSC** = National Child Safety Council
        = National Council of Senior Citizens
**NCSCI** = National Center for Standards and Certification Information (NBS)

**NCSCPAS** = National Center for the Study of Corporal Punishment and Alternatives in the Schools
**NCSL** = National Conference of State Legislatures
**NCSO** = National Council of Salesmen's Organizations
**NCSP** = National Center for Surrogate Parenting
**NCSS** = National Crash Severity Study (NHTSA)
**NCTA** = National Cable Television Association
    = Navajo Code Talkers Association
    = National Christmas Tree Association
**NCTE** = National Council of Teachers of English
**NCTIP** = National Committee on the Treatment of Intractable Pain
**NCTV** = National Coalition on Television Violence
**NCUA** = National Credit Union Administration
**NCUED** = National Council for Urban Economic Development
**NCUTLO** = National Committee on Uniform Traffic Laws and Ordinances
**NCV** = no commercial value
**NCWUS** = National Council of Women of the United States
**ND** = North Dakota (postal code)
    = no date
**Nd** = neodymium; a chemical element
**NDA** = no detectable activity
**NDAA** = National District Attorneys Association
**NDAK** = North Dakota
**NDC** = National Dairy Council
**NDDS** = Nuclear Detonation Detection System
**NDE** = near-death experience
**NDI** = National Dance Institute
**NDRC** = National Defense Research Committee
**NDRI** = National Diabetes Research Interchange
**NDSS** = National Down Syndrome Society

NDU = National Defense University
NE = Nebraska (postal code)
     = New England
     = northeast
Ne = neon; a chemical element
NEA = National Endowment for the Arts
     = Nuclear Energy Agency
     = Nuclear Engineering Associates
     = National Education Association of the United States
NEACP = national emergency airborne command post; "kneecap"
NEB = nebula
     = New English Bible
NEBR = Nebraska
NEC = National Electric Code
NECO = National Ethnic Coalition of Organizations
NED = New English Dictionary
NEDC = National Entrepreneurial Development Center
NEDRES = National Environmental Data Referral System (NOAA)
NEFA = National Education Foundation of America
NEG = negative
NEH = National Endowment for the Humanities
NEHA = National Environmental Health Association
     = National Executive Housekeepers Association
NEI = National Eye Institute
     = not elsewhere included
NEIC = National Earthquake Information Center
     = National Energy Information Center
NEISS = National Electronic Injury Surveillance System (NHTSA)
NEJM = New England Journal of Medicine
NELIA = Nuclear Energy Liability Insurance Association

**NEMA** = National Electrical Manufacturers Association
**NEPA** = National Environmental Policy Act
**NERSC** = National Energy Research Supercomputer Center
**NES** = not elsewhere specified
**NESAC** = National Education Standards And Counsel
**NESHAP** = National Emission Standards for Hazardous Air Pollutants
**NEST** = Nuclear Energy Search Team
**NET** = National Educational Television
    = Internet; international network of computer users
**NETH** = Netherlands
**NEURO** = neurology or neurological
**NEUT** = neutral
    = neuter
**NEV** = Nevada
**NEW** = Nuclear Energy Women
**NEW ENG** = New England
**NEWSTAR** = nuclear energy waste space transportation and removal
**NEXT** = Nationwide Examination of X-Ray Trends (DHHS)
**NF** = Newfoundland (postal symbol)
    = no funds
**NFA** = National Foundation for Asthma
    = National Flute Association
**NFB** = National Federation of the Blind
**NFC** = National Football Conference
    = National Forensic Center
    = no further consequences
**NFDA** = National Funeral Directors Association
**NFDC** = National Flight Data Center
    = National Fertilizer Development Center
**NFEC** = National Food and Energy Council
**NFFA** = National Future Farmers of America
    = National Frozen Foods Association

**NFFAR** = National Foundation for AIDS Relief, Inc.
**NFFE** = National Federation of Federal Employees
**NFFPC** = National Foundation to Fight Political Corruption
**NFIB** = National Federation of Independent Business
**NFIC** = National Foundation for Ileitis and Colitis
= Natural Fibers Information Center
**NFIS** = National Film Information Service
**NFJGD** = National Foundation for Jewish Genetic Diseases
**NFL** = National Football League
**NFLD** = Newfoundland
**NFLPA** = National Football League Players Association
**NFLPN** = National Federation of Licensed Practical Nurses
**NFMC** = National Federation of Music Clubs
**NFO** = National Farmers Organization
**NFPA** = National Fire Protection Association
= National Food Processors Association
**NFPAC** = Nuclear Freeze Political Action Committee
**NFPCA** = National Fire Prevention and Control Administration
**NFPW** = National Federation of Press Women
**NG** = National Guard
= no good
= nitroglycerin
= noble gas
**NGA** = National Glass Association
= National Gardening Association
**NGC** = New General Catalog of Nebulae and Clusters of Stars
**NGD** = National Guild of Decoupeurs
**NGF** = National Genetics Foundation
= National Golf Foundation
**NGHEF** = National Gay Health Education Foundation
**NGIC** = National Geodetic Information Center
**NGLTF** = National Gay and Lesbian Task Force

**NGS** = National Genealogical Society
= National Geriatrics Society
**NGTF** = National Gay Task Force
**NGV** = natural gas vehicle
**NH** = New Hampshire (postal code)
**NHA** = National Hearing Association
= National Handbag Association
**NHAMP** = New Hampshire
**NHC** = National Health Council
= National Hurricane Center
**NHCA** = National Hairdressers and Cosmetologists Association
**NHC** = National Health Federation
**NHDA** = National Huntington's Disease Association
**NHF** = National Hemophilia Foundation
**NHI** = National Highway Institute
**NHL** = National Hockey League
**NHLA** = National Hardwood Lumber Association
**NHLBI** = National Heart, Lung, and Blood Institute
**NHMA** = National Housewares Manufacturers Association
**NHO** = National Hospice Organization
**NHPIC** = National Health Planning Information Center
**NHRA** = National Hot Rod Association
= National Housing Rehabilitation Association
**NHSF** = National Highway Safety Foundation
**NHTSA** = National Highway Traffic Safety Administration; "Nitsa"
**Ni** = nickel; a chemical element
**NIA** = National Institute on Aging
**NIAA** = National Institute on Alcohol Abuse and Alcoholism (DHHS)
**NIADA** = National Independent Automobile Dealers Association

**NIADDKD** = National Institute of Arthritis, Diabetes, Digestive and Kidney Diseases

**NIAID** = National Institute of Allergy and Infectious Diseases

**NIASE** = National Institute for Automotive Service Excellence

**NIB** = National Information Bureau
= National Industries for the Blind

**NIBM** = National Institute for Burn Medicine

**NIC** = National Institute of Corrections
= newly-industrializing country

**NICAD** = nickel-cadmium battery; also NICD

**NICB** = National Insurance Crime Bureau

**NICD** = nickel-cadmium battery; also NICAD

**NICHHD** = National Institute of Child Health and Human Development

**NICJ** = National Institute of Criminal Justice

**NICRAD** = Navy/Industry Cooperative Research and Development Program

**NID** = National Intelligence Daily, produced by CIA for top officials

**NIDA** = National Institute on Drug Abuse

**NIDR** = National Institute of Dental Research

**NIE** = National Institute of Education

**NIEHS** = National Institute of Environmental Health Sciences

**NIGMS** = National Institute of General Medical Sciences

**NIH** = National Institutes of Health
= not invented here

**NIICU** = National Institute of Independent Colleges & Universities

**NIJ** = National Institute of Justice

**NIJD** = National Institute of Judicial Dynamics

**NIKE** = US Army's first ground-to-air missile, after the Greek winged goddess of victory

**NILECJ** = National Institute of Law Enforcement and Criminal Justice
**NIMH** = National Institute of Mental Health
= nickel metal-hydride battery
**NINCDS** = National Institute for Neurological Communicative Disorders and Stroke
**NIOSH** = National Institute for Occupational Safety and Health
**NIPP** = National Institute for Public Policy
**NIRL** = negligible individual risk level
**NIS** = US Naval Investigative Service
= National Intelligence Survey
**NIST** = National Institute of Standards and Technology
**NIV** = National Institute of Victimology
**NJ** = New Jersey (postal code)
**NKF** = National Kidney Foundation
**NKO** = need to know only
**NKVD** = Soviet People's Commissariat of Internal Affairs (Russian: *Narodnyi Komissariat Vnutrennikh Del*); a predecessor to Soviet KGB
**NL** = National League (baseball)
= Netherlands (international car index mark)
**nl** = it is not permitted (Latin: *non licet*)
**NLADA** = National Legal Aid & Defender Association
**NLC** = National Leadership Council
= National League of Cities
**NLEF** = National Lupus Erythematosus Foundation
**NLF** = National Leukemia Foundation
**NLI** = National Lead Industries
**NLM** = National Library of Medicine
**NLN** = National League for Nursing
**NLRB** = National Labor Relations Board
**NLSMB** = National Live Stock and Meat Board

**NLUS** = Navy League of the United States
**NM** = New Mexico (postal code)
= nautical mile
**NMA** = National Meat Association
= National Medical Association
= National Motorists Association
**NMB** = National Mediation Board
**NMC** = National Meteorological Center
= National Music Council
**NMD** = National Missile Defense
**NMEX** = New Mexico
**NMF** = National Migraine Foundation
**NMFS** = National Marine Fisheries Service (DOC)
**NMHA** = National Mental Health Association
**NMHC** = National Multi Housing Council
**NMI** = no middle initial
**NMIC** = Naval Military Intelligence Center
**NMMA** = National Marine Manufacturing Association
**NMPA** = National Music Publishers Association, Inc.
**NMPF** = National Milk Producers Federation
**NMR** = nuclear magnetic resonance
**NMRL** = National Materials Research Laboratory Program (DOC)
**NMSS** = National Multiple Sclerosis Society
**NMVRSF** = National Motor Vehicle Research Safety Foundation
**NNA** = National Newspaper Association
**NNLDA** = National Network of Learning Disabled Adults
**NNN** = net, net, net; net of (not including) taxes, maintenance and insurance; "triple net" (real estate)
**NNPA** = National Newspaper Publishers Association
= Nuclear Non-Proliferation Act

**NNRLIS** = National Natural Resources Library and Information System

**NNS** = National News Service

**NO** = number

= north

**No** = nobelium; a chemical element

**NO 1** = number one; first mate, British navy

**NOA** = National Opera Association

**NOAA** = National Oceanic and Atmospheric Administration (DOC)

**NOF** = National Osteopathic Foundation

**NOFODIS** = no foreign dissemination (US)

**NOL** = Naval Ordnance Laboratory

**NOM** = nomenclature

= nominal

**NON-U** = not upper-class; low-class

= not university

**NOP** = not otherwise provided for

**NORAD** = North American Aerospace Defense Command

**NORBA** = National Off-Road Bicycle Association

**NORC** = National Opinion Research Center

**NORD** = National Organization for Rare Disorders

**NORF** = National Obesity Research Foundation

**NORM** = normal

= naturally occurring radioactive material

**NORML** = National Organization for the Reform of Marijuana Laws

**NOS** = numbers

= not otherwise specified

**NOSC** = Naval Ocean Systems Center (USN)

**NOTA** = none of the above

**NOT SAFE** = National Organization Taunting Safety and Fairness Everywhere

**NOUE** = notification of unusual event

**NOV** = November

**NOVA** = National Organization for Victim Assistance

**NOW** = National Organization of Women

**NOX** = nitrous oxide; auto-exhaust emission and smog constituent

**NP** = neuropsychiatry

    = notary public

    = newspaper

    = nuclear power

**Np** = neptunium; a chemical element

**NPA** = Newspaper Association of America

    = National Pasta Association

**NPAP** = National Psychological Association for Psychoanalysis

**NPC** = National Press Club

    = National Peach Council

**NPCA** = National Parks & Conservation Association

    = National Pest Control Association

    = National Paint and Color Association

**NPCSIB** = National Police Chiefs and Sheriffs Information Bureau

**NPDES** = National Pollutant Discharge Elimination System

**NPF** = National Parkinson Foundation

    = National Psoriasis Foundation

    = not provided for

**NPG** = negative population growth

**NPI** = National Preservation Institute

**NPIC** = National Photographic Interpretation Center

**NPIS** = New Product Information Service (DOC)

**NPO** = National Program Office; representatives from CIA, State, Defense and FEMA

**NPPA** = National Press Photographers Association

**NPR** = National Public Radio
**NPRA** = National Petroleum Refiners Association
**NPS** = National Park Service
**NPT** = Non-Proliferation Treaty (Nuclear)
    = national pipe thread
**NQAA** = Nuclear Quality Assurance Agency
**NQOS** = not quite our sort
**NR** = near
    = number
**NRA** = National Rifle Association of America
    = Nuclear Regulatory Agency
    = National Recovery Administration
    = National Restaurant Association
    = National Rehabilitation Association
**NRAO** = National Radio Astronomy Observatory in Charlottesville, VA
**NRB** = National Research Bureau
**NRBA** = National Radio Broadcasters Association
**NRC** = National Research Council
    = Nuclear Regulatory Commission
    = National Radio Club
    = National Recycling Coalition
    = National Referral Center (LC)
**NRCM** = National Referral Center Master List (LC)
**NRCPC** = National Rural Crime Prevention Center
**NREN** = National Research and Education Network (computers)
**NRG** = Nautical Research Guild
**NRIC** = National Ridesharing Information Center (NIE)
    = National Rehabilitation Information Center
**NRL** = Naval Research Laboratory
**NRLC** = National Right to Life Committee, Inc.
**NRMS** = Natural Resource Management Systems

**NRO** = National Reconnaissance Office
**NROTC** = Naval Reserve Officer Training Corps
**NRPB** = National Radiological Protection Board
**NRPC** = National Railroad Passenger Corporation; Amtrak
**NRRC** = nuclear risk reduction centers; Soviet arms control agreement
**NRSA** = National Research Service Awards
**NRSF** = National Reye's Syndrome Foundation
**NS** = Nova Scotia (postal symbol)
**NSA** = National Security Agency; cryptanalysts
     = National Standards Association
     = National Sheriffs' Association
     = Nuclear Safety Agency
     = National Speakers Association
     = National Stroke Association
     = National Shipping Authority
     = National Shuffleboard Association
**NSC** = National Security Council
     = National Safety Council
     = Nuclear Science Center
**NSCAA** = National Society for Children & Adults with Autism
**NSCIA** = National Spinal Cord Injury Association
**NSCID** = National Security Council Intelligence Directive
**NSD** = National Security Directive
**NSDA** = National Soft Drink Association
**NSDAP** = Hitler's *National Sozialist Deutsche Arbeite Partei* (National Socialist German Workers Party); forerunner of NS or "NAZI"
**NSDD** = National Security Decision Directive
**NSF** = National Sports Foundation
     = National Science Foundation
     = Nuclear Science Foundation
     = National Scoliosis Foundation
     = not sufficient funds

**NSGA** = National Sporting Goods Association
**NSI** = National Space Institute
    = national security information
**NSIC** = Nuclear Safety Information Center
**NSIDSF** = National Sudden Infant Death Syndrome Foundation
**NSIS** = National Shut-In Society
**NSMR** = National Society for Medical Research
**NSPA** = National Society of Public Accountants
**NSPB** = National Society to Prevent Blindness
**NSPCB** = National Society for the Preservation of Covered Bridges
**NSPE** = National Society of Professional Engineers
**NSPIC** = Nuclear Standards Program Information Center (DOE)
**NSPS** = New Source Performance Standards (US)
**NSRDS** = National Standards Reference Data System (NBS)
**NSS** = National Sculpture Society
**NSSA** = National Skeet Shooting Association
**NSSAR** = National Society of the Sons of the American Revolution
**NSSDC** = National Space Science Data Center (NASA)
**NSSL** = National Severe Storms Laboratory
**NSTAF** = National Solar Technical Audience File (DOE)
**NSTF** = National Science Teachers Association
**NSTL** = National Space Technology Laboratories (NASA)
**NSWMA** = National Solid Wastes Management Association
**NT** = Northwest Territories, Canada
    = New Testament
**NTA** = National Technical Association
**NTE** = not to exceed
**NTF** = National Turkey Foundation
**NTFP** = National Task Force on Prostitution

**NTIA** = National Telecommunications and Information Administration (DOC)
**NTIS** = National Technical Information Service (DOC)
**NTP** = National Toxicology Program (NIEHS)
     = normal temperature and pressure
**NTPA** = National Truck Pullers Association
**NTSADA** = National Tay-Sachs and Allied Diseases Association
**NTSB** = National Transportation Safety Board
**NTSC** = National Television Standards Committee; TV broadcasting and receiving standards in North America (see PAL)
**NTU** = National Taxpayers Union
**NT WT** = net weight
**NU** = name unknown
**NUC** = National Urban Coalition
**NUL** = National Urban League
**NUM** = numeral
**NUMBER ONE** = first mate, British navy
**NUSC** = Naval Underwater Systems Center (USN)
**NV** = Nevada (postal code)
     = nonvoting
**NVA** = North Vietnamese Army; US designation of Viet Nam People's Army
**NVC** = nonverbal communication
**NVH** = noise, vibration and harshness (automotive)
**NW** = northwest
     = Northwest Airlines
**NWA** = Northwest Airlines
     = National Weather Association
**NWC** = National War College
     = Naval Weapons Center
     = National Writers Club
**NWCSC** = Nuclear Weapons Council Standing Committee

**NWCTU** = National Women's Christian Temperance Union; also WCTU
**NWF** = National Wildlife Federation
**NWFL** = National Women's Football League
**NWS** = National Weather Service
**NWT** = Northwest Territories
**NWU** = National Writers Union
**NY** = New York (postal code)
**NYA** = National Youth Administration
**NYC** = New York City
      = New York Central Railroad
**NYME** = New York Mercantile Exchange
**NYMPHO** = nymphomaniac; female obsessed with sex
**NYPD** = New York Police Department
**NYSE** = New York Stock Exchange
**NZ** = New Zealand
    = Air New Zealand

**O** = oxygen; a chemical element
  = ovation
  = blood type (also A, B and AB)
  = hitless or scoreless (sports)
  = ohm
  = Ohio
**O's** = Baltimore Orioles baseball team
**OA** = Overeaters Anonymous
    = Olympic Airways
**OAA** = Opticians Association of America
**OAAU** = Organization of Afro-American Unity
**OADEMQA** = Office of Acid Deposition, Environmental Monitoring & Quality Assurance
**OAG** = Official Airline Guides; flight schedules
**OAK** = Oakland, California, airport

**OAM** = Office of Aviation Medicine
**OAPP** = Office of Aviation Policy & Plans
**OAR** = Organization of American Rivers
    = Office of Air & Radiation
**OAS** = Organization of American States
    = Office of American Studies
    = *Organisation de l'Armée Secréte*; French anti-independence group in Algeria
**OB** = on base (baseball)
    = out of bounds (sports)
    = obstetrics
**OBCA** = Outboard Boating Club of America
**OBD** = on-board diagnostics (automotive)
**OBE** = Office of Business Economics
    = Order of the British Empire
**OBEMLA** = Office of Bilingual Education & Minority Language Affairs
**OB-GYN** = obstetrics-gynecology (babies and females)
**OBI** = Office of Basic Intelligence (CIA)
**OBIT** = obituary
**OBJ** = object
    = objection
**OBS** = obscure
    = observatory
    = obsolete
**OBV** = obverse
**OCARM** = Order of Carmelites
**OCART** = Order of Carthusians
**OCAWIU** = Oil, Chemical and Atomic Workers International Union
**OCC** = occupied
    = Order of Calced Carmelites
**OCCA** = Office of Compliance and Consumer Assistance

**OCD** = Office of Civil Defense
**OCDM** = Office of Civil and Defense Mobilization
**OCI** = Office of Current Intelligence (CIA)
**O CLUB** = officers club (military)
**OCONUS** = outside the continental United States (military)
**OCR** = optical character recognition
    = optical character reader (computers)
    = Office for Civil Rights (DHHS)
    = Office of Civil Rights (ED)
**OCRWM** = Office of Civilian Radioactive Waste Management
**OCS** = officer candidate school
**OCSO** = Order of Cistercians of the Strict Observance
**OCT** = October
    = octagon
    = octave
    = octet
**OD** = overdose
    = doctor of optometry
    = officer of the day (military)
    = officer of the deck (naval)
    = olive drab (US Army)
    = outside diameter
    = overdraft
**O/D** = overdrive
**ODC** = Overseas Development Council
    = Order of Discalced Carmelites
**ODO** = odometer
**OE** = original equipment (automotive)
    = operating engineer
    = old English
**OECD** = Organization for Economic Cooperation and Development

**OEEC** = Organization for European Economic Cooperation

**OED** = Oxford English Dictionary

**OEM** = original equipment manufacturer (automotive)
= Office of Emergency Management

**OES** = Office of Emergency Services
= Order of the Eastern Star
= Office of Endangered Species

**OEVE** = Office of Earthquakes, Volcanoes, and Engineering

**OFA** = Office of Family Assistance

**OFC** = officer

**OFCCP** = Office of Federal Contract Compliance Programs

**OFE** = Office of Fusion Energy

**OFF** = office
= officer
= official

**OFFY** = Offenhauser; 4-cylinder Mayer & Drake engine powering Indy-500 cars in the fifties

**OFM** = Order of Friars Minor

**OFPP** = Office of Federal Procurement Policy

**OFS** = Orange Free State

**OGE** = Office of Government Ethics

**OGPS** = Office of Grants and Program Systems

**OH** = Ohio (postal code)

**O/H** = overhead

**OHA** = overseas housing allowance

**OHC** = overhead cam, in an engine

**OHDS** = Office of Human Development Services (DHHS)

**OHER** = Office of Health and Environmental Research (DOE)

**OHM** = British civil servant, from OHMS

**OHMO** = Office of Health Maintenance Organizations

**OHMS** = On His (Her) Majesty's Service; franking of official British government mail

**OHV** = overhead valves, in an engine
**OIA** = Office of International Aviation
**OIC** = officer in charge
**OICA** = Office of Information & Consumer Affairs
**OICD** = Office of International Cooperation and Development
**OICW** = objective individual combat weapon; laser-sighted rifle also firing air-bursting ammunition
**OIT** = Office of International Trade
**OJ** = orange juice
**OJARS** = Office of Justice Assistance, Research and Statistics
**OJT** = on-the-job training
**OK** = Oklahoma (postal code)
      = okay; all right
**OKC** = Oklahoma City
**OKLA** = Oklahoma
**OLB** = outside linebacker (football)
**OLDS** = Oldsmobile
**OM** = Odyssey of the Mind; academic games, kindergarten through college
      = order of merit
**OMA** = Omaha, Nebraska, airport
**OMB** = Office of Management and Budget
**OMI** = Oblates of Mary Immaculate
**ON** = Ontario (postal symbol)
**ONAE** = Office of Naval Architecture and Engineering
**ONAP** = Office of Native American Programs
**ONDCP** = Office of National Drug Control Policy
**ONE** = Office of National Estimates (CIA)
**ONI** = Office of Naval Intelligence
**ONLINE** = connected to the Internet (computers)
**ONR** = Office of Naval Research
**ONS** = Oncology Nursing Society

**ONT** = Ontario
**OOBE** = out-of-body experience
**OOS** = out of service
    = out of sequence
**OP** = observation post
    = opus; work
    = out of print
    = Order of Preachers
**OPA** = overall paid attendance (sports)
    = office of public affairs
    = Office of Price Administration
**OPC** = old people's center
**op cit** = in the work cited (Latin: *opere citato*)
**OPEC** = Organization of Petroleum Exporting Countries
**OP ED** = opposing editorial
**OPEI** = Outdoor Power Equipment Institute
**OPEIU** = Office and Professional Employees International Union
**OPIC** = Office of Public Insurance Counsel
    = Overseas Private Investment Corporation
**OPM** = other people's money
    = Office of Personnel Management (US)
**OPP** = opposite
    = opposing
**OPR** = Office of Public Records
**OPS** = operations
    = Office of Price Stabilization
**OPT** = optional
**OPTI** = Office of Productivity, Technology and Innovation (DOC)
**OR** = Oregon (postal code)
    = operating room
    = owner's risk

**ORC** = Opinion Research Center
= Organized Reserve Corps
**ORCH** = orchestra
**ORD** = O'Hare Airport, Chicago, Illinois
= ordinary
= order
= ordnance
**ORE** = Oregon
**OREG** = Oregon
**ORG** = organization
= organic
**ORIG** = original
**ORNL** = Oak Ridge National Laboratory
**OS** = operating system (computers)
**O/S** = out of stock
**Os** = osmium; a chemical element
**OSA** = Optical Society of America
**OSB** = Order of Saint Benedict
**OSDBU** = Office of Small and Disadvantaged Business Utilization (SBA)
**OSF** = Order of Saint Francis
= Open Software Foundation
**OSFA** = Office of Student Financial Assistance
**OSH** = Office on Smoking & Health
**OSHA** = Occupational Safety and Health Administration
**OSHRC** = Occupational Safety and Health Review Commission
**OSI** = Office of Special Investigations (military)
**OSM** = Order of the Servants of Mary
**OSO** = Orbiting Solar Observatory (NASA)
**OSRD** = Office of Standard Reference Data
**OSS** = Office of Strategic Services; predecessor of CIA
**OST** = Office of Science & Technology (DEA, FCC)

**OSU** = Order of St. Ursula
**OT** = out of town
    = overtime
    = Old Testament
**OTA** = Office of Technology Assessment
**OTAF** = Office of Technology Assessment and Forecast
**OTC** = Over-The-Counter stock exchange
    = over-the-counter (pharmaceuticals)
    = Ozone Transport Commission; 12 eastern states
and DC
**OTEC** = Ocean Thermal Energy Conversion (NOAA)
**OTH** = over the horizon, radar
**OTH-B** = over-the-horizon backscatter
**OTMA** = Office Technology Management Association
**OTP** = Office of Telecommunications Policy
**OTR** = one-time recording, of video tape
**OTRA** = other than regular army
**OTS** = officers' training school
    = open two-seater; British roadster
**O/U** = over and under; shotgun with one barrel over another
**OUI** = operating under the influence; driving a car after excess use of alcohol or narcotics
**OUO** = official use only
**OWADP** = Organization of Women Architects and Design Professionals
**OWLA** = Organization of Women for Legal Awareness
**OWM** = Office of Weights & Measures
**OWVL** = one-way voice link (radio communications)
**OZ** = ounce
**OZ TR** = ounce troy; 1/12 pound troy, equivalent to 1.097 oz AVDP

**P** = page
  = pint
  = parking, usually with the international "no" symbol
  = passing w/o grade, scholastic grade
  = piano (music: soft)
  = port, or left side of a ship
  = pawn (chess)
  = pitcher (baseball)
  = point (basketball)
  = punter (football)
  = pursuit (US Air Force)
  = *pistole* (German military)
  = parabellum
  = phosphorus; a chemical element
  = *peso* (currency)
  = Portugal (international car index mark)

**P-08** = *Pistole* 08 (German for 1908 pistol); WW II Luger

**P-38** = WW II US twin-boom pursuit plane; Lockheed "Lightning"
  = *Pistole* 1938; German Walther semiautomatic pistol (WW II)

**P-40** = WW II US pursuit plane, Curtiss "Warhawk;" used by Flying Tigers

**P-47** = WW II US pursuit plane; Republic "Thunderbolt"

**P-51** = WW II US long-range escort pursuit plane; North American "Mustang;" re-designated F-51

**P-61** = WW II US twin-prop night pursuit plane; Northrup "Black Widow"

**P-80** = first US jet pursuit plane, flew in january, 1944; Lockheed "Shooting Star;" changed to F-80

**PA** = Pennsylvania (postal code)
    = public address (system)
    = press agent
    = purchasing agent
    = power amplifier
    = Parents Anonymous
    = Potsmokers Anonymous
    = Pills Anonymous
    = Privacy Act
    = Panama (international car index mark)
**Pa** = protactinium; a chemical element
**PAA** = Population Association of America
**PAAO** = Pan American Association of Ophthalmology
**PABA** = para-aminobenzoic acid; no longer used in sunburn lotion
**PABX** = private automatic branch exchange
**PAC** = Political Action Committee
    = Pacific
    = public affairs coordinator
**PACCS** = Post-Attack Command and Control System; SAC airborne command posts
**PACFLT** = Pacific Fleet
**PACOM** = Pacific Command; US Unified Command HQ
**PAHO** = Pan American Health Organization
**PAK** = Pakistan (international car index mark)
**PAL** = Police Athletic League
    = European video standard of higher resolution than NTSC
**PAN** = Panama
**PAN AM** = Pan American
       = Pan American Airways
**P&G** = Procter and Gamble
**P&L** = profit and loss
**P&O** = Pacific and Orient Steamship Lines

**P&W** = Poets & Writers
**PANE** = People Against Nuclear Energy
**PAO** = public affairs officer
**PAP** = as in Pap test; for the detection of uterine cancer; after Dr. Papanicolaou who originated it
**PAR** = paragraph
    = parallel
    = phased-array radar
**PARA** = parabellum; for war or combat
    = paratrooper
**PARENS** = parentheses
**PARNTS** = People of America Responding to Needs in Today's Society
**PARSEC** = distance at which a star shows a parallax of one second of arc, equal to 32.6 light years
**PAS** = Physicians for Automotive Safety
**PASCOS** = particles, strings and cosmology (astronomy)
**PASS** = passenger
    = passive
    = Procurement Automated Source System (SBA)
**PAT** = Political Action Team; CIA's 40-man commando groups in Vietnam
    = patent
    = point after touchdown (football)
**PATH** = pathology or pathological
**PAU** = Pan American Union
**PAVE PAWS** = precision acquisition of vehicle entry—phased array warning system; SLBM early-warning radar
**PAWA** = Pan American World Airways
**PAX** = private automatic exchange
**PAYE** = pay as you earn
    = pay as you enter
**PAYT** = payment

**PB** = passed ball (baseball)
**Pb** = lead (Latin: *plumbum*); a chemical element
**PBA** = Professional Bowlers Association
**PB&J** = peanut butter and jelly sandwich
**PBGC** = Pension Benefit Guaranty Corporation (US)
**PBI** = West Palm Beach, Florida, airport
**PBS** = Public Broadcasting System
**PBX** = private branch exchange
**PBY** = WW II US flying boat; Consolidated "Catalina"
**PC** = personal computer
    = politically correct
    = Professional Corporation
    = piece
    = percent
    = parsec
    = police constable
    = privy council
**PCB's** = polychlorinated biphenyls; bio-accumulating toxin
**PCC** = Panama Canal Commission
**PCCW** = Public Citizen Congress Watch
**PCDS** = Parents of Children with Down's Syndrome
**PCH** = Pacific Coast Highway
**PCIE** = President's Council on Integrity and Efficiency
**PCN** = payroll change notice
    = procedure change notice
**PCP** = phencyclidine; hallucinogenic street drug aka "angel dust," "crystal," "rocket fuel"
**PCS** = pieces
    = permanent change of station
**PCT** = percent
    = precinct
**PCV** = positive crankcase ventilation (automotive)
    = pressure control valve

**PD** = police department
    = paid
    = *per diem* (Latin: by the day)
    = population density
**Pd** = palladium; a chemical element
**PDCA** = Painting and Decorating Contractors of America
    = Purebred Dairy Cattle Association
**PDF** = Parkinson's Disease Foundation
**PDQ** = pretty damned quick
    = cancer therapy database (NCI)
**PDR** = Physicians' Desk Reference
**PDT** = Pacific daylight time
**P/E** = price to earnings ratio (stock market)
**PE** = professional engineer
    = probable error
    = Prince Edward Island (postal symbol)
**PEA** = Public Education Association
**PEHA** = Pony Express Historical Association
**PEI** = Prince Edward Island
**PEM** = proton exchange membrane, in fuel cells or batteries
**PEN** = peninsula
    = International Association of Poets, Playwrights, Editors, Essayists and Novelists
    = penalty minute; also PM (hockey)
**PENN** = Pennsylvania
    = Pennsylvania Railroad
**PENNA** = Pennsylvania
**PERF** = perfect
    = perforated
**PERK** = percolate
    = perquisite
**PERM** = permanent (woman's hair treatment)
    = permanent

153

**PERS** = personal
= person
**PERT** = pertaining
= program evaluation and review technique
**PET** = petroleum
= positron emission tomography
**PETA** = People for the Ethical Treatment of Animals
**PF** = personal foul (basketball)
**PFC** = private first class
**PFD** = preferred
**PFFLG** = Parents, Families, and Friends of Lesbians and Gays
**PFIAB** = President's Foreign Intelligence Advisory Board; "piffiab"
**PG** = parental guidance suggested (movie rating)
= page
= pregnant
= postgraduate
**PG-13** = parents strongly cautioned to give guidance to children 13 and under; some material may be inappropriate (movie rating)
**PGA** = Professional Golfers' Association
**PGI** = Pyrotechnics Guild International
**PGRI** = Public Gaming Research Institute
**PHARM** = pharmacy or pharmacist
**PH** = philosophy
= purple heart
**pH** = potential of hydrogen; degree of acidity or alkalinity, as in pH factor
**PhD** = doctor of philosophy
**PHENOM** = phenomenon
**PHILA** = Philadelphia
**PHILLY** = Philadelphia
**PHON** = phonetics

**PHOTO** = photograph
**PHOTOG** = photographer
**PHS** = Public Health Service; also USPHS
**PHX** = Phoenix, Arizona, airport
**PHYS** = physics
          = physical
          = physician
**PHYS-ED** = physical education
**PI** = private investigator
**PIA** = Plastics Institute of America
         = Peoria, Illinois, airport
**PIC** = picture
         = public information center
**PICO** = one trillionth, as in picosecond
**PIN** = personal identification number
**PIO** = public information officer
**PIRG** = Public Interest Research Group
**PIT** = Pittsburgh, Pennsylvania, airport
**PIX** = pictures
**PJ's** = pajamas
**PK** = park
        = peak
        = psychokinesis
        = place kicker (football)
        = Pakistan International Airlines
**PKG** = package
**PKS** = Parkes Catalog (astronomy)
**PKT** = packet
**PL** = place
        = plural
        = Poland (international car index mark)
**PLA** = Palestine Liberation Army
         = People's Liberation Army of China
**PL&R** = postal laws and regulations

**PLASTEC** = Plastics Technical Evaluation Center (US Army)
**PLAT** = platoon
**PLATO** = Program Logic for Automatic Teaching Operations (SBA)
**PLC** = public limited company
**PLF** = plaintiff
**PLI** = Public Lands Institute
**PLO** = Palestine Liberation Organization
**PLU** = plural
**PM** = *post meridiem* (Latin for after noon)
    = *post mortem* (Latin for after death); autopsy
    = premium
    = postmaster
    = provost marshall
    = prime minister
    = preventative maintenance
    = penalty minute; also PEN (hockey)
**Pm** = promethium; a chemical element
**PMA** = Publishers Marketing Association
    = Pharmaceutical Manufacturers Association
    = Polyurethane Manufacturers Association
**PMMI** = Packaging Machinery Manufacturers Institute
**PMP** = preventative maintenance procedure
    = probable maximum precipitation
**PMS** = pre-menstrual stress
**PMT** = payment
**PMTC** = Pacific Missile Test Center
**PMW** = probable maximum wind
**PMWP** = probable maximum winter precipitation
**PMY** = professional man-year
**PN** = promissory note
**PNAF** = primary nuclear airlift force
**PNE** = peaceful nuclear explosion

**PNET** = Peaceful Nuclear Explosion Treaty
**PNG** = persona non grata; undesirable person
**PNLM** = Palestine National Liberation Movement
**PNP** = plug and play (electronics)
**PNS** = Pensacola, Florida, airport
**PO** = purchase order
  = post office
  = petty officer
  = put out (baseball)
**Po** = polonium; a chemical element
**POA** = Police Officers Association
  = Pacific Ocean Areas
**POAC** = Pentagon Officers' Athletic Club
**POC** = port of call
**POD** = pay on delivery
  = probability of detection
**PO'D** = pissed off
**POE** = port of entry
  = port of embarkation
**POGS** = milk bottle caps
**POL** = politician
  = political
  = Poland or Polish
  = possession-only license
  = provisional operating license
**POLARIS** = first US nuclear-powered missile submarine
  = first US submarine-launched ballistic missile
**POLIT** = political
**POM** = Australian term for Brits; from Prisoner of His Majesty
**POP** = popular
  = population
  = point of purchase
  = proof of principle

**POR** = point of no return; when proceeding is shorter than going back

= Press-On-Regardless car road rally

**PORT** = Portugal or Portuguese

**POS** = positive

= position

= point of sale

**POSH** = elegant or luxurious; from port out, starboard home: British steamship reservations to India that avoided the hot sun

**POSS** = possessive

**POSSLQ** = person of opposite sex sharing living quarters

**POT** = potential

**POTS** = plain old telephone system

**POV** = point of view

= privately owned vehicle

**POW** = prisoner of war

**PP** = pianissimo (music; very soft)

= pages

= parcel post

= past participle

= polypropylene; a form of plastic

**PPA** = Professional Photographers of America

**PPD** = prepaid

**PPFA** = Planned Parenthood Federation of America

**PPG** = Pittsburgh Plate and Glass

**PPHRII** = Parents of Premature and High Risk Infants International

**PPM** = parts per million

**PPO** = Preferred Provider Organization

**PPP&B** = paper, plates, print and bind (book publishing)

**PPQ** = National Plant Pest Quarantine Office (USDA)

**PPS** = post post script

= pulses per second

**PPT** = precipitate
**PPTN** = precipitation
**PPV** = pay per view; pay for a television program upon viewing
**PQ** = Province of Quebec (postal symbol)
**P's and Q's** = to be careful, as in minding one's P's and Q's
**PR** = public relations
= Puerto Rican
= pair
= price
= pronoun
= Puerto Rico (postal code)
= Philippine Airlines
**Pr** = praseodymium; a chemical element
**PRB** = Private Radio Bureau
**PRC** = People's Republic of China
= Postal Rate Commission
**PRCA** = Professional Rodeo Cowboys Association
**PREC** = precedent
= preceding
**PRECIP** = precipitation; rain or snow
**PREEMIE** = premature baby
**PREF** = preferred
**PRELIM** = preliminary
**PREM** = premium
**PRE MED** = premedical
**PREP** = prepare
= preparatory, as in prep school
= preparation
= preposition
**PREPPIE** = a callow person; one in prep school
**PRES** = president
= present
**PREV** = previous

159

**PREZ** = president
**PRF** = proof
**PRI** = Public Radio Institute
**PRIMUS** = Primary Medical Care for the Uniformed Services
**PRIV** = private
**PRM** = presidential review memorandum
**PRNDL** = automatic transmission quadrant: park, reverse, neutral drive, low; "prindle"
**PRO** = public relations officer
  = professional
  = advocate, as in pro-choice
**PROB** = probable
  = problem
**PROD** = producer
  = production
**PROF** = professor
**PROG** = program
  = progressive
**PROM** = programmable read-only memory
  = promontory
**PROMO** = promotional advertising
**PRON** = pronoun
**PROP** = propeller
  = proprietor
  = proposition
  = property
**PROS** = Professional Reactor Operator Society
**PRO TEM** = temporary; for the time being (Latin: *pro tempore*)
**PROV** = provincial
  = provisional
  = provost
**PRS** = pairs
**PRSA** = Public Relations Society of America

**PRU** = Provincial Reconnaissance Unit; CIA assassination squads in Vietnam

**PRV** = pressure relief valve

**PS** = post script

= public school

**PSA** = public service announcement, TV spot

= Photographic Society of America

= Poetry Society of America

= Professional Salespersons of America

= prostate specific antigen; blood test for presence of antigens that could indicate prostate cancer

**PSAT** = Pre-SAT; Pre Scholastic Aptitude Test

**PSCA** = Profit Sharing Council of America

**PSF** = pounds per square foot

**PSGA** = Parkinsonian Support Groups of America

**PSI** = pounds per square inch

= Professional Secretaries International

**PSP** = Palm Springs, California, airport

**PSR** = PULSAR

= Physicians for Social Responsibility

**PSRS** = Public Safety Radio Services

**PSS** = Port Safety and Security (USCG)

**PST** = Pacific standard time

**PSTIAC** = Pavements and Soil Trafficability Information Analysis Center (USACE)

**PSYCH** = psychology

**PT** = patrol torpedo, as in PT boat

= physical training

= Pacific time

= physical therapy

= pint

= point

= part time

= port

Pt = platinum; a chemical element
PT-109 = President Kennedy's WW II PT boat
PTA = Parent-Teachers Association
PTG = printing
PTO = Patent and Trademark Office
= please turn over
PTSA = Parents, Teachers and Students Association
PTSD = post-traumatic stress syndrome
PTY = proprietary
PU = it stinks; "pee-you!"
= pickup
Pu = plutonium; chemical element used in A-bombs
PUB = publication
= tavern, from British public house
= public
= publish
= publisher
PUD = pickup and delivery
PULSAR = pulsating star
PURPLE = Japanese WW II diplomatic code
PUSH = People United to Save Humanity
PVA = Paralyzed Veterans of America
PVC = polyvinyl chloride; a form of plastic
= plastic pipe
PVD = Providence, Rhode Island, airport
PVP = pre-volume production (automotive)
PVT = private
PW = prisoner of war (also POW)
= Palau (postal code)
PWA = Public Works Administration
PWP = Parents Without Partners
PWR = power
PX = post exchange

Q  = question
   = quart
   = queen (chess)
   = quotient
QA = quality assurance
Q&A = questions and answers
    = questionnaire
QANTAS = Queensland and Northern Territory Air Service
QB = quarterback
   = queen's bishop (chess)
   = queen's bench
QC = quality control
   = queen's council
QDA = quantity discount agreement
QED = which was to be demonstrated (Latin: *quod erat demonstrandum*)
QEF = which was to be done (Latin: *quod erat faciendum*)
QEI = which was to be found out (Latin: *quod erat inveniendum*)
QF = Qantas Airways, Australia
QID = four times a day (Latin: *quater in die*)
QM = quartermaster
QMC = quartermaster corps
QMG = quartermaster general
QN = queen's knight (chess)
QR = quarter or quarterly
   = queen's rook (chess)
QRA = quick-reaction alert
QRI = Qualitative Requirements Information (US Army)
QRT = quart
    = Quick Reaction Team; US Army counterintelligence unit

**QSR** = QUASAR
**QT** = quart
= quiet
**QTY** = quantity
**QUAD** = quadrangle
= quadrant
**QUASAR** = quasi-stellar radio source; distant starlike object that emits powerful radio waves
**QUE** = Quebec
**qv** = which see (Latin: *quod vide*)
**QY** = query

**R** = restricted: under 18 requires accompanying parent or guardian (movie rating)
= right
= river
= Republican
= runs (baseball)
= reserve
= rook (chess)
= railway
= rabbi
= royal
= radius
= restricted
= resistance
= roentgen
= *rex* (Latin for king)
= *regina* (Latin for queen)
**RA** = regular army
= rear admiral
= royal academy
= Russia (aircraft registration code)

**Ra** = radium; a chemical element

**RAAF** = Royal Australian Air Force

**RAB** = Radio Advertising Bureau

**RAC** = Royal Automobile Club

    = Reliability Analysis Center (USAF)

**RACES** = Radio Amateur Civil Emergency Service

**RAD** = radical

    = radiator (automotive)

    = radius

    = radiation absorbed dose

    = rapid access data

**RADAR** = radio detection and ranging

        = Radio Association Defending Airwave Rights; car-radar lobby

**RADIUS** = Research And Development Institute of the United States

**RADM** = rear admiral

**RAF** = Royal Air Force

**RAM** = random access memory (computers)

    = radioactive material

**RAND** = research and development

        =RAND Corporation; the first think tank

**R&A** = Royal and Ancient Golf Club of St. Andrews, Scotland

**R&B** = rhythm and blues

**R&D** = research and development

**R&R** = rest and recuperation

**RANN** = Research Applied to National Needs Program

**RAPID** = Recovery Assistance Program Information and Delivery (FEMA)

**RATO** = rocket-assisted takeoff

**RB** = running back

    = review board

**Rb** = rubidium; a chemical element

**RBC** = red blood cells
**RBE** = relative biological effectiveness
**RBI** = runs batted in
**RBS** = Recreational Boating Safety (USCG)
    = radar bomb scoring
**RC** = Red Cross
    = Roman Catholic
    = Royal Crown Cola
**RCA** = Radio Corporation of America
    = Radiation Control Agency
**RCAF** = Royal Canadian Air Force
**RCCA** = Relocation Counseling Center of America
**RCH** = residential care program (VA)
**RCMA** = Radio Communications Monitoring Association
**RCMP** = Royal Canadian Mounted Police
**RCP** = Royal College of Physicians
**RCS** = Royal College of Surgeons
**RCT** = regimental combat team
    = recruit
**RCWP** = Rural Clean Water Program (USDA)
**RD** = Registered Dietician
    = rural delivery
    = road
    = rod
    = round
    = restricted data
**RDA** = recommended dietary allowance
    = recommended daily allowance
**RD&T** = research, development and testing
**RDF** = radio direction finder
**RDH** = Registered Dental Hygienist
**RDLP** = Research and Development Limited Partnership (DOC)
**RDT&E** = research, development, testing and evaluation

RDU = Raleigh/Durham, North Carolina, airport
RE = regarding
    = rare earth
    = right end (sports)
Re = rhenium; a chemical element
REA = Rural Electrification Administration (USDA)
REAC = Radiological Emergency Assistance Center
REACT = Radio Emergency Associated Communications Teams
REB = rebound
REBAR = reinforcement bar; steel bar used to strengthen concrete
REC = record
    = recreation
RECAP = recapitulation
RECD = received
RECIP = reciprocal
RECON = reconnaissance
RECPT = receipt
REC SEC = recording secretary
RECT = rectangle
REDCOM = Readiness Command; US Unified Command HQ
REF = referee
    = reference
    = refund
    = refinery
    = referral
REFRIG = refrigerator
REG = regulation
    = regular
    = regiment
    = regulator
    = region

**REGD** = registered
**REGT** = regiment
**REHAB** = rehabilitate, people or property
**REIC** = Radiation Effects Information Center
**REINF** = reinforced
**REIT** = Real Estate Investment Trust
**REL** = relative
    = religion or religious
**REM** = rapid eye movement (during sleep, associated with dreaming)
    = remote
    = unit of radiation dose
**REP** = reputation
    = representative
    = republic
    = Republican
    = report
    = reporter
**REPT** = report
**REQ** = requisition
    = require
    = request
**REQD** = required
**RERF** = Radiation Effects Research Foundation
**RES** = reserve
    = residence
    = resolution
**RESP** = respectively
**R-E-S-P-E-C-T** = what Aretha Franklin demands
**RET** = retired
    = retard
**RETD** = retained
    = returned

RETRO = retrograde
        = the way it used to be
REV = revolution, as in an engine
      = reverse
      = revision or revised
      = revenue
      = reverend
      = review
REV UP = increase revolutions of an engine
REW = rewind
REZ = resolution
RF = radio frequency
    = right field (baseball)
RFD = rural free delivery
RFE = Radio Free Europe
RFG = reformulated gasoline, for lower emissions
RFP = request for proposal
     = request for procurement
RFQ = request for quotation
RG = right guard (sports)
    = Varig Brazilian Airlines
RGB = red, green and blue, color television tube
RGS = Royal Geographical Society
RH = relative humidity
    = right hand
Rh = rhodium; a chemical element
RHD = right hand drive
RHET = rhetoric
RHIP = rank has its privileges
RI = Rhode Island (postal code)
    = Rock Island Line (railroad)
RIA = Robotic Industries Association
RIAA = Recording Industry Association of America

**RICO** = Racketeering Influenced and Corrupt Organizations Act (US)
**RID-USA** = Remove Intoxicated Drivers—USA
**RIF** = reduction in force
**RIM** = resin injected molding; a form of plastic
= Recreation Information Management (USDA)
= Revolutionary Internationalist Movement; the *Sindero Luminoso* of Peru (Spanish for Shining Path)
**RIP** = rest in peace (Latin: *requiescat in pace*)
**RIS** = Russian Intelligence Services (CIA term)
**RIT** = ritardando (music: retard)
**RIV** = river
= Buick Riviera
**RLHS** = Railway and Locomotive Historical Society
**RM** = room
= Royal Marines
**RMA** = Rubber Manufacturers Association
= Royal Military Academy at Sandhurst, England
**RMS** = Royal Mail Service
= Royal Mail Steamship, as in RMS Titanic
**RN** = Registered Nurse
= Royal Navy
**Rn** = radon; a chemical element
**RNA** = ribonucleic acid
**RNC** = Republican National Committee
**RND** = round
**RNO** = Reno, Nevada, airport
**RNZAF** = Royal New Zealand Air Force
**RO** = Romania (international car index mark)
**ROAUS** = Reserve Officers Association of the US
**ROC** = Republic of China, on Taiwan
= Rochester, New York, airport
**ROK** = Republic of Korea

**ROLLER** = Rolls-Royce
**ROLLS** = Rolls-Royce
**ROM** = Roman
**ROP** = run of paper
**ROTC** = Reserve Officers' Training Corps
**ROW** = right of way
**RP** = received pronunciation; correct pronunciation
**RPI** = Retinitis Pigmentosa International
**RPM** = revolutions per minute
**RPS** = revolutions per second
**RPT**  = report
    = repeat
**RR** = rural route
   = railroad
   = rear
   = right rear
   = Rolls-Royce
**RRB** = Railroad Retirement Board
**RRCA** = Road Runners Club of America
**RS** = Royal Society
**RSA**  = Russian Space Agency
    = Rhetoric Society of America
**RSC** = Royal Shakespeare Company
**RSCJ** = Religious of the Sacred Heart of Jesus
**RSFSR** = Russian Soviet Federated Socialist Republic; Russia as part of the Soviet Union
**RSM** = regimental sergeant major
**RSNA** = Radiological Society of North America
**RSO** = reconnaissance systems officer (military)
**RST** = Rochester, Minnesota, airport
**RSTN** = regional seismic test network
**RSV** = Revised Standard Version, of the Bible
**RSVP** = please reply (French: *répondez s'il vous plaît*)

**RSWC** = right side up with care
**RT** = right
= right tackle (football)
**RTA** = Railway Tie Association
**RTE** = route
**RTECS** = Registry of Toxic Effects of Chemical Substances (NIOSH)
**RTG** = radioisotope thermal-electric generator (NASA)
**RTM** = resin transfer molding; a form of plastic
**RU** = rat unit; amount sufficient to produce a response in lab rats
**Ru** = ruthenium; a chemical element
**RU-486** = French abortion pill
**RUSS** = Russian
= Russia
**RV** = recreational vehicle
= reentry vehicle (aerospace)
**RVIA** = Recreation Vehicle Industry Association
**RW** = right wing (sports)
= railway
**RWDSU** = Retail, Wholesale, and Department Store Union
**RWV** = rear-wheel drive
**RWY** = railway

**S** = south
= small
= singular
= satisfactory, scholastic grade
= second
= starts (baseball)
= safety; defensive back (football)
= safety; 2-point score for the defense (football)
= Sweden (international car index mark)
= sulfur; a chemical element

**SA** = Salvation Army

= sex appeal

= South America

= South Africa

= Sexaholics Anonymous

= *société anonyme* (French for anonymous society or corporation)

= *Sturm Abteilung*; Nazi storm troopers

**Sa** = save (hockey)

**SAA** = single action army, Colt .45 revolver

= Society of Automotive Analysts

= Society of American Archivists

= Stepfamily Association of America

**SAAI** = Specialty Advertising Association International

**SAAMI** = Sporting Arms and Ammunition Manufacturers' Institute

**SAC** = Strategic Air Command

**SACCS** = SAC Airborne Command and Control System

**SACEUR** = Supreme Allied Commander Europe (NATO)

**SACLANT** = Supreme Allied Commander Atlantic (NATO)

**SACMED** = Supreme Allied Commander, Mediterranean (WW II)

**SAD** = seasonal affected disorder

**SADD** = Students Against Driving Drunk

**SAE** = Society of Automotive Engineers

**SAF** = Society of American Florists

= Society of American Foresters

**SAFE** = Society for the Advancement of Fission Energy

**SAG** = Screen Actors Guild

**SALT** = Strategic Arms Limitation Talks

**SAM** = surface-to-air missile

**SAMA** = Specialty Automotive Manufacturers Association

= Scientific Apparatus Makers Association

**SAMI** = Society of American Magicians, International
**SAMOS** = satellite and missile observatory system; first US spy satellite
**SAMS** = School for Advanced Military Studies
**SAMSO** = Space and Missile Systems Organization
**SAN** = sanitarium
= San Diego, California, airport
**SANA** = Soyfoods Association of North America
**S&L** = savings and loan
**S&M** = sadism and masochism
**S&P** = Standard & Poor's, Publishers
**S&P 500** = Standard & Poor's index of 500 common stocks
**S&W** = Smith & Wesson
**SANE** = Committee for a Sane Nuclear Policy
**SAPS** = signal algorithmic processing system
**SAR** = Society of Authors' Representatives
= search and rescue
= synthetic-aperture radar; near-photographic-quality radar
**SASE** = self-addressed stamped envelope
**SASK** = Saskatchewan
**SAT** = Saturday
= San Antonio, Texas, airport
**SATCOM** = satellite communication
**SATD** = saturated
**SAU** = standard advertising unit, in newspapers
**SAX** = saxophone
**SB** = stolen base (baseball)
= southbound
= bachelor of science
**Sb** = antimony (Latin: *stibium*); a chemical element
**SBA** = Small Business Administration

**SBAA** = Spina Bifida Association of America
**SBDC** = Small Business Development Centers (SBA)
**SBF** = single black female
**SBI** = Small Business Institute
**SBIR** = Small Business Innovation Research Program
**SBM** = single black male
**SBW** = Small Business Tax Workshop (IRS)
**SC** = South Carolina (postal code)
    = scene
    = Supreme Court
    = Security Council (UN)
    = small capitals
    = Sisters of Charity
**Sc** = scandium; a chemical element
**SCA** = Shipbuilders Council of America
**SCAP** = Supreme Commander, Allied Powers (in occupied Japan)
**SCAR** = South Carolina
**SCATANA** = Security Control of Air Traffic and Air Navigation Aids; FAA plan to ground all aircraft in US and Canada in an emergency
**SCC** = Slidell Computer Complex (NASA)
**SCCA** = Sports Car Club of America
**SCCM** = Society of Critical Care Medicine
**ScD** = doctor of science
**SCFMA** = Summer and Casual Furniture Manufacturers Association
**SCH** = school
**SCI** = science
**SCI FI** = science fiction
**SCORE** = Service Corps of Retired Executives (SBA)
**SCOT** = Scottish
    = Scotland

**SCR** = screen

= screenplay

**SCRAMJET** = supersonic combustion ramjet

**SCS** = Soil Conservation Service (USDA)

**SCSA** = Soil Conservation Society of America

**SCTA** = Southern California Timing Association (automotive)

**SCUBA** = self-contained underwater breathing apparatus, invented by Jacques Cousteau

**SCUD** = Soviet mid-range battlefield missile

**SCUS** = Supreme Court of the United States

**SD** = South Dakota (postal code)

= special delivery

= standard deviation

= *sine die*; adjourned indefinitely (Latin for without a day)

= *Sicherheitsdienst*; German WW II security service

**SDAK** = South Dakota

**SDECE** = *Service de Documentation Extérieure et de Contre-Espionnage*, now DGSE; French CIA; "ess-deck"

**SDF** = Louisville, Kentucky, airport

**SDI** = Strategic Defense Initiative; "Star Wars"

**SDS** = Students for a Democratic Society

**SE** = southeast

= split end (football)

= Sweden (aircraft registration code)

**Se** = selenium; a chemical element

**SEA** = Seattle/Tacoma, Washington, airport

**SEABEES** = Construction Battalions; CB's (USN)

**SEAL's** = US Navy elite combat unit; after Sea, Air, Land

**SEASPRAY** = CIA-Army aviation unit

**SEA-TAC** = Seattle-Tacoma International Airport

**SEATO** = Southeast Asia Treaty Organization

**SEC** = Securities and Exchange Commission (stock-market watchdog)

    = second

    = secretary

    = security

    = Sexual Exploitation of Children statute (US)

**SEC DEF** = Secretary of Defense

**SEC NAV** = Secretary of the Navy

**SECT** = section

**SECY** = secretary

**SEE** = Society of Explosive Engineers

**SEG** = Screen Extras Guild

**SEIA** = Solar Energy Industries Association

**SEIU** = Service Employees International Union

**SEM** = scanning electron microscope

    = seminary

**SEMA** = Special Equipment Market Association (automotive)

**SEN** = senate

    = senator

**SEP** = separate

    = September

    = simplified employee pension

**SEPT** = September

    = septuagenarian; person in one's seventies

**SER** = serial

    = series

**SERB** = Serbian

**SERE TRAINING** = survival, evasion, resistance and evacuation training (military)

**SERI** = Solar Energy Research Institute (DOE)

**SERV** = service

**SES** = Society of Eye Surgeons

SETI = search for extraterrestrial intelligence (aerospace)
SETP = The Society of Experimental Test Pilots
SF = San Francisco
   = single female
   = science fiction
   = sinking fund
   = sacrifice fly (baseball)
   = Finland (international car index mark)
SFA = Saks Fifth Avenue
SFC = sergeant first class
    = Sport Fishing Institute
SFI = sequential fuel injection (automotive)
SFO = San Francisco, California, airport
SFSA = Steel Founders' Society of America
SFTE = Society of Flight Test Engineers
SFX = sound effects (movies and radio)
SGA = The Songwriters Guild of America
SGAA = Stained Glass Association of America
SGBF = single gay black female
SGBM = single gay black male
SGD = signed
SGF = Springfield, Missouri, airport
SGMA = Sporting Goods Manufacturers Association
SGP = Singapore (international car index mark)
SGT = sergeant
SGWF = single gay white female
SGWM = single gay white male
SH = share
   = sacrifice hit (baseball)
Sh = shot (hockey)
SHAEF = Supreme Headquarters of the Allied Expeditionary Force (WW II)

**SHAPE** = Supreme Headquarters of the Allied Powers in Europe (NATO)
**SHF** = super-high frequency
**SHO** = shutout (baseball)
**SHOT** = Society for the History of Technology
**SHOT SHOW** = Shooting, Hunting, Outdoor Trade Show
**SHP** = shaft horsepower
**SHSA** = Steamship Historical Society of America
**SHV** = Shreveport, Louisiana, airport
**SI** = Smithsonian Institution
    = Society of Illustrators
**Si** = silicon; a chemical element
**SIA** = Securities Industry Association
      = Semiconductor Industry Association
      = Survivors of Incest Anonymous
**SIAM** = Society for Industrial & Applied Mathematics
**sic** = as originally spelled (Latin for thus)
**SIDS** = sudden infant death syndrome; crib death
**SIETAR INTERNATIONAL** = Society for Intercultural Education, Training and Research—International
**SIF** = Scleroderma International Foundation
**SIG** = stellar inertial guidance
     = signal
     = signature
**SIGINT** = signals intelligence
**SIIC** = self-incriminating infringement of copyright
**SINET** = shared information network
**SING** = singular
**SIOC** = Strategic Information Operations Center
**SIOP** = single integrated operational plan; master plan for nuclear war
**SIPI** = Scientists Institute for Public Information

**SIRS** = Soils Information Retrieval System (USDA)
**SIRTF** = Space Infrared Telescope Facility (curtailed)
**SIS** = Secret Intelligence Service; British MI6
    = Soviet Intelligence Services
    = Signal Intelligence Satellites (military)
    = Special Intelligence Service; FBI unit for counter-intelligence in Latin America during WW II
**SITE R** = underground Pentagon in Raven Rock Mountain, PA
**SIT REP** = situation report
**SIU** = Society for the Investigation of the Unexplained
**SJ** = Society of Jesus; Jesuits
**SJC** = Senate Judiciary Committee
**SJD** = doctor of juridical science
**SJU** = San Juan, Puerto Rico, airport
**SK** = Saskatchewan (postal symbol)
    = SAS (Scandinavian Air)
**SKT** = Sanskrit
**SKU** = stock keeping unit
**SL** = sea level
**SLA** = Symbionese Liberation Army; erstwhile US mini revolutionary group
**SLAN** = *sine loco, anno, vel nomine* (Latin for without place, year or name)
**SLBM** = submarine-launched ballistic missile
**SLCM** = sea-launched cruise missile
**SLC** = Salt Lake City, Utah, airport
**SLCM** = sea-launched cruise missile
**SLFCS** = survivable low-frequency communications system
**SLG** = slugging percentage (baseball)
**SLP** = super long play; slowest video recording speed
**SLR** = single-lens reflex, as in a camera

**SM** = small
    = single male
    = Society of Mary
**Sm** = samarium; a chemical element
**SMACCNA** = Sheet Metal and Air Conditioning Contractors' National Association
**SMC** = sheet molding compound; a form of plastic
**SMERSH** = Russian acronym for *smyert shpionem*: death to spies
    = WW II Soviet Army secret police unit
    = reputed secret assassination section of KGB
**SMF** = Sacramento, California, airport
**SMIAC** = Soil Mechanics Information Analysis Center (USACE)
**SMLE** = short magazine Lee-Enfield; British WW II rifle
**SMPTE** = Society of Motion Picture & Television Engineers
**SMR** = specialized mobile radio
**SMSA** = standard metropolitan statistical area
**SMWIA** = Sheet Metal Workers' International Association
**SMYAL** = Sexual Minority Youth Assistance League
**SN** = Sabena Airlines, Belgium
**Sn** = tin (Latin: *stannum*); a chemical element
**SNA** = Orange County, California, airport
**SNAFU** = situation normal, all fouled up
**SNAG** = Society of North American Goldsmiths
**SNAME** = The Society of Naval Architects and Marine Engineers
**SNAP** = systems for nuclear auxiliary power; atomic batteries
**SNCC** = Student Non-Violent Coordinating Committee; "snick"
**SNG** = synthetic natural gas
**SNL** = Sandia National Laboratories

**SNM** = Society of Nuclear Medicine
**SO** = sold out
    = south
    = Standard Oil
    = sellers option
    = strikeout (K in baseball)
**$SO_2$** = sulfur dioxide; contributor to acid rain
**SOB** = son of a bitch
**SOC** = social
    = social studies; "soash"
**SOCONY** = Standard Oil Company of New York
**SOD** = Save Our Doves
    = Special Operations Division; coordinates US Army special operations and counter-terrorist units
**SOE** = Special Operations Executive; WW II British sabotage organization
**SOF** = sound on film; sound synchronized to motion picture
**SOHC** = single overhead camshaft, in an engine
**SOHIO** = Standard oil of Ohio
**SOI** = Special Olympics International, Inc.
**SOL** = "somewhat" out of luck
    = soluble
**SOLN** = solution
**SONAR** = sound navigation and ranging; locating by reflected sound
**SOON** = Solar Observing Optical Network (USAF)
**SOP** = standard operating procedure
**SOPA** = senior officer present afloat
**SOPAC** = South Pacific
**SOPH** = sophomore
**SOS** = distress signal in Morse code; "save our souls"
    = Save Our Sons
    = "something" on a shingle; chipped beef on toast (military)

**SOSUS** = sound (or sonar) surveillance system
**SOVREN** = Society of Vintage Racing Enthusiasts
**SP** = standard play; fastest video recording speed
    = special
    = species
    = state police
    = spelling
    = Spain
    = Spanish
    = Shore Police (USN MP's)
    = Southern Pacific (railroad)
    = self-propelled
    = single pole
**SPA** = Society of Professional Archaeologists
**SPAAMFAA** = Society for the Preservation and Appreciation of Antique Motor Fire Apparatus in America
**SPACECOM** = Space Command HQ
**SPADATS** = space detection and tracking system
**SPAM** = spiced ham in a can, by Hormel
**SPAR** = member of women's USCG Reserve; from the USCG motto: *Semper Paratus* (Latin for always ready)
**SPC** = Soy Protein Council
**SPCA** = Society for the Prevention of Cruelty to Animals
**SPCC** = Society for the Prevention of Cruelty to Children
**SPD** = speed
**SPE** = Society of Plastics Engineers
**SPEBSQSA** = Society for the Preservation and Encouragement of Barber Shop Quartet Singing in America, Inc.
**SPEC** = specification
    = specialist; as SPEC 1 in the army
**SPECS** = eyeglasses
**SPEEDO** = speedometer
    = competitive swim wear

**SPERDVC** = Society to Preserve and Encourage Radio Drama, Variety, and Comedy
**SPF** = sun protection factor
**SP GR** = specific gravity
**SPI** = Society of Professional Investigators
    = Society of the Plastics Industry
    = Sports Philatelists International
    = Springfield, Illinois, airport
**SPINOFF** = NASA's annual report
**SPJ** = Society of Professional Journalists
**SPORT UTE** = sport-utility vehicle; also SUV
**SPQR** = *senatus populusque Romanus* (Latin for the senate and people of Rome)
    = small profits, quick returns
**SPR** = Society for Psychical Research
**SPUTNIK** = first man-made satellite in orbit, by the Soviets
**SQ** = square
    = Singapore Airlines
**SQN** = squadron
**SR** = senior
    = Swissair
**Sr** = strontium; a chemical element
**S-R** = stimulus-response
**SR-71** = two-seat high-altitude reconnaissance plane; Lockheed "Blackbird"
**SRA** = Science Research Associates
**SRAM** = short-range attack missile
**SRBM** = short-range ballistic missile
**SRC** = Survey Research Center
**SRD** = Society for the Right to Die
**SRO** = standing room only
**SRQ** = Sarasota/Bradenton, Florida, airport
**SRS** = supplemental restraint system; air bag

**SRSS** = square root of the sum of the squares
**SS** = super stock (automotive)
    = super sport (automotive)
    = shortstop (baseball)
    = same size
    = steamship
    = stainless steel
    = USN designation for submarines
    = Security Service; British MI5
    = *Schutzstaffel*; Hitler's protection department or bodyguard
**SSA** = Social Security Administration
    = Soaring Society of America
**SSB** = strategic nonnuclear-powered ballistic missile submarine
**SSBN** = strategic nuclear-powered ballistic missile submarine
**SSCI** = Senate Select Committee on Intelligence; "sissy"
**SSDC** = Society of Stage Directors and Choreographers
**SSGA** = Sterling Silversmiths Guild of America
**SSGN** = nuclear-powered guided (cruise) missile submarine
**SSGT** = staff sergeant
**SSI** = Supplemental Security Income
**SSM** = surface-to-surface missile
**SSN** = Social Security number
    = nuclear-powered attack submarine
**SSR** = Soviet Socialist Republic
**SSRC** = Social Science Research Council
**SSRT** = single-stage rocket technology; see DC-X
**SSS** = Selective Service System; the draft
    = submarine version of SOS distress signal
**SST** = supersonic transport, like the Concorde or Tu-144
**ST** = street
    = saint

**STA** = station

= Science and Technology Agency

= Special Temporary Authority; temporary broadcasting license

**STAR** = Scientific and Technical Aerospace Reports (NASA)

**START** = Strategic Arms Reduction Talks

**STAT** = immediately (Latin: *statim*)

= statute

**STBD** = starboard

**STD** = sexually transmitted disease

= standard

**STEALTH** = advanced technology bomber designed to evade radar; B-2

**STEP** = Standard for Exchange of Product Model Data (automotive)

**STEREO** = stereophonic; recording and transmitting on two channels

**stet** = let it stand (Latin); proofreader's term

**STK** = streak

= stock

**STL** = St. Louis, Missouri, airport

**STOL** = short takeoff and landing aircraft

**STOP** = single title order plan (book publishing)

**STP** = standard temperature and pressure

**STR** = stereo

= submarine thermal reactor

= Special Representative for Trade Negotiations

**STRANGELOVE** = code name for Continuation of Government plan, or COG

**STT** = St. Thomas, Virgin Islands, airport

**STU** = secure telephone unit; "scrambled" phone

**STUD** = student

**STUKA** = WW II German divebomber; Junkers JU-87; from German *Sturzkampfflugzeug* for divebomber

**STY** = story
**SU**  = state university
     = Skinners Union; British manufacturer of automotive carburetors
     = former USSR (international car index mark)
     = Aeroflot, Russian airline
**SUB** = substitute (sports)
     = submarine
**SUBJ** = subject
**SUBROC** = submarine rocket
**SUM** = shallow underwater missile
**SUN** = Sunday
**SUP** = superior
**SUPP** = supplement
**SUPT** = superintendent
**SUPVR** = supervisor
**SURVIAC** = Survivability/Vulnerability Information Analysis Center (DOD)
**SUV** = sports utility vehicle
**SV**  = safety valve
     = solenoid valve
     = saves, by a relief pitcher (baseball)
     = saves, by a goalie (hockey)
**S-VHS** = super VHS; S-video video format
**S-VIDEO** = super video; high-definition video
**SVRA** = Sportscar Vintage Racing Association
**SW** = southwest
     = shortwave
**SWAK** = sealed with a kiss
**SWAPO** = South-West African People's Organization
**SWAT** = special weapons and tactics
**SWB** = short wheelbase (automotive)
**SWBD** = switchboard

**SWE** = Society of Women Engineers
**SWF** = single white female
**SWG** = standard wire gauge
**SWM** = single white male
**SWO** = stop-work order
**SWPA** = Southwest Pacific Area
**SX** = Greece (aircraft registration code)
**SYM** = symbol
= symphony
**SYN** = synonym
= synthetic
**SYS** = system

**T** = true
= total
= tied
= tablespoon
= ton
= tackle (football)
= standard shot-size designation (.20 inch)
= tritium; radioactive isotope of hydrogen
= thymine; one of four DNA building blocks (see C, G, A)
**t** = teaspoon
**T-34** = Soviet WW II tank
**T-72** = the ultimate Soviet tank
**T/A** = Trans Am, from Trans America (auto racing)
**Ta** = tantalum; a chemical element
**TAC** = Tactical Air Command (USAF)
= tactical
**TACAMO** = take charge and move out; relay aircraft for submarines (USN)
**TACC** = Tactical Air Control Center (military)
**TACOM** = US Tank-Automotive and Armaments Command

**TAF** = tactical air force
**TALCM** = Tomahawk air-launched cruise missile
**T&E** = test and evaluation
**TARP** = tarpaulin
**TARSA** = Thromboctyopenia Absent Radius Syndrome Association
**TAS** = true air speed
**TASH** = The Association for Persons with Severe Handicaps
**TASS** = Telegraph Agency of the Soviet Union (Russian: *Telegranoe Agentsvo Sovetskovo Soyuza*); official Soviet news agency
**TB** = tuberculosis
   = total bases (baseball)
   = tiny bladder
**Tb** = terbium; a chemical element
**TBA** = to be announced
**TBD** = to be determined
**TBF** = WW II USN torpedo-bomber; Grumman "Avenger"
**T-BILL** = US Government treasury bill; savings bond of 1 year or less
**T-BONE** = beefsteak with a t-shaped bone
**TBS** = talk between ships
**TBSP** = tablespoon
**TC** = Twin Cities; Minneapolis and St. Paul, MN
   = Transportation Command (US Army)
   = traction control (automotive)
**Tc** = technetium; a chemical element
**T/C** = thermocouple
**TCA** = Tanners' Council of America
    = Train Collectors Association
**TCBY** = The Country's Best Yogurt
**TCE** = Tax Counseling for the Elderly (IRS)

**TCH** = delta-9-tetrahydro-cannabinol; potent ingredient of marijuana

**TCIU** = Transportation Communications International Union

**TD** = touchdown (football)

**T-DAM** = time series database of agricultural commodities and macro-economic data (USDA)

**TDD** = telecommunication device for the deaf (see TTY)

**TDI** = turbo direct injection, in diesel engines

**TDP** = US Trade and Development Program

**TDWR** = terminal doppler weather radar

**TDY** = temporary duty

**TE** = tight end (football)

**Te** = tellurium; a chemical element

**TECH** = technical
= technician
= technology

**TECLAB** = Federal Laboratory Technological Innovation Cases Data Base at the University of California

**TECTRA** = Federal Laboratory Technological Innovation Transfer Cases Data Base at the University of California

**TEL** = telephone
= telegraph
= tetraethyl lead

**TELLY** = television (British)

**TEMP** = temporary
= temperature

**TENN** = Tennessee

**TERA** = trillion

**TERAFLOPS** = trillion floating point operations per second (computers)

**TERR** = territory

**TESL** = Teaching of English as a Second Language

**TESOL** = Teachers of English to Speakers of Other Languages
**TEX** = Texas
**TEXACO** = Texas Corporation
**TEX-MEX** = Texan-Mexican, food or music
**TF** = task force
    = technical foul (basketball)
    = till forbidden
**TGD** = Transportation of Gambling Devices Statute (US)
**TGIF** = thank goodness it's Friday
**TGT** = target
**TGV** = high-speed train: *Trés Grand Vitesse* (French for very high speed)
**TH** = Thursday
    = true heading
**Th** = thorium; a chemical element
**ThD** = doctor of theology
**THEOL** = theology or theological
**THERM** = thermometer
**THERP** = technique for human error rate prediction
**THOU** = thousand
**THP** = thrust horsepower
**THURS** = Thursday
**Ti** = titanium; a chemical element
**TIAA** = Teachers Insurance and Annuity Association
    = Travel Industry Association of America
**TIB** = Temporary Importation Under Bond
**TIC** = Technical Information Center (DOE)
**TID** = three times a day (Latin for *ter in die*)
**TIG** = time in grade
**TIMA** = Thermal Insulation Manufacturers Association
**TIP** = to insure promptness
**TIP-FIDDLE** = time-phased deployment list; order and time of deployment of military units (military)

**TIPS** = threats, interrogation, promises, spying; federally prohibited employer conduct in union organizing campaigns
**TIROS** = Television and Infra Red Observatory Satellite; NASA weather satellite
**TIS** = time in service
**TKO** = technical knockout; beaten but unbowed (boxing)
**TKT** = ticket
**Tl** = thallium; a chemical element
**TLAM** = Tomahawk Land Attack Missile
**TLC** = tender loving care
**TLO** = total loss only
**TM** = trademark
　　= technical manual
　　= training manual
**Tm** = thulium; a chemical element
**TMA** = Turnaround Management Association
**T-MAN** = US Treasury agent
**TMAUS** = Tobacco Merchants Association of the US
**TMD** = Theater Missile Defense
**TMI** = taxes, maintenance and insurance (real estate)
**TN** = Tennessee (postal code)
　　= true north
　　= town
　　= train
　　= ton
**TNG** = training
**T-NOTE** = US Government treasury note; savings bond of 1 to 7 years
**TNPK** = turnpike
**TNT** = trinitrotoluene; a high explosive
　　= Turner Network Television

**TO** = table of organization
   = turn over
   = time out (sports)
**T-O** = take-off
**TOC** = tactical operations center
**TOE** = tables of organization and equipment (military)
**TOP** = Trade Opportunities Program (DOC)
**TOPS** = Take Off Pounds Sensibly
**TOT** = total
   = time on target
**TOW** = tube-launched optically-tracked wire-guided missile
**TP** = township
**TPA** = Tampa/St. Petersburg, Florida, airport
**TPK** = turnpike
**TR** = transpose, as letters in a word
   = troop
   = treble
   = Teddy Roosevelt, 26th US president
   = transmit/receive
**TR-1** = modernized U-2 spy plane
**TRAA** = Towing and Recovery Association of America
**TRAC** = Telecommunications Research and Action Center
**TRACON** = terminal radar approach control
**TRADOC** = Army Training and Doctrine Command
**TRANA** = Thoroughbred Racing Associations of North America
**TRANS** = transmission
   = transportation
   = translation
   = transaction
**TRANSCOM** = Transportation Command (US Army)
**TREAS** = treasurer
   = treasury

**T-REX** = Tyrannosaurus rex; prehistoric carnivore, largest in history
**TRF** = tuned radio frequency
**TRI** = Toxic Release Inventory; US law requiring industry reports
**TRIB** = tributary
**TRIG** = trigonometry
**TRI-POWER** = Pontiac engine with three 2-barrel carburetors
**TRU** = transuranium
**TS** = tough you-know-what; too bad
　　 = tropical storm
　　 = tensile strength
**TSA** = Tourette Syndrome Association
**TSCA** = Toxic Substances Control Act
**TSGT** = technical sergeant
**TSLS** = toxic shock-like syndrome
**TSP** = teaspoon
**TSS** = Trumpeter Swan Society
**T-STORM** = thunder storm
**TSVP** = please turn over; (French: *tournez s'il vous plaît*)
**TTBT** = Threshold Test Ban Treaty
**TTFN** = ta ta for now
**TTMA** = Truck Trailer Manufacturers Association
**TTY** = teletypewriter
　　 = typewriter used by the hearing impaired to communicate via phone
**TU** = trade union
　　 = Trout Unlimited
**Tu** = Tupolev, Soviet aircraft designer
**Tu-95** = Soviet Tupolev strategic bomber; "Bear"
**Tu-144** = Soviet Tupolev supersonic transport
**TUE** = Tuesday
**TUL** = Tulsa, Oklahoma, airport

**TURBO** = turbo-charge
       = turbine
**TURK** = Turkish
      = Turkey
**TUS** = Tucson, Arizona, airport
**TUT** = Tutankhamen; ancient Egyptian boy pharaoh
**TUX** = tuxedo
**TV** = television
   = terminal velocity
**TVA** = Tennessee Valley Authority
**TVM** = TV movie; made-for-television movie
**TVP** = textured vegetable protein
**TV-Q** = television quotient; popularity rating of television performers
**TW** = Trans World Airlines
**TWA** = Trans World Airlines
**TWOFER** = two for the price of one
**TWOS** = Total Warrant Officer System (military)
**TWP** = township
**TX** = Texas (postal code)
**TYPO** = typographical
      = typographical error
**TYS** = Knoxville, Tennessee, airport

**U** = university
  = unsatisfactory, scholastic grade
  = uranium; a chemical element
  = you
  = upper-class; snooty
**U-2** = high altitude spy plane, by Lockheed
**U-235** = rare isotope of uranium used in A-bombs
**U-238** = natural uranium, from its atomic weight
**UA** = United Airlines
  = United Artists

**UAA** = Unicyclists Association of America

**UAAAIW** = United Automobile, Aerospace, and Agricultural Implement Workers

**UACC** = Universal Autograph Collectors Club

**UAE** = United Arab Emirates

**UAJAPPFIUSC** = United Association of Journeymen and Apprentices of the Plumbing and Pipe Fitting Industry of the United States and Canada

**UAR** = United Arab Republic

**UAW** = United Auto Workers

**UBC** = Uniform Building Code

**UBCJA** = United Brotherhood of Carpenters and Joiners of America

**U-BOAT** = German WW II submarine; German: *Unterseeboot*

**UC** = upper case

**UCMJ** = Uniform Code of Military Justice

**UCPA** = United Cerebral Palsy Associations

**UCPNW** = United Campuses to Prevent Nuclear War

**UCPS** = Universal Coterie of Pipe Smokers

**UCS** = Union of Concerned Scientists

**UDA** = United Dairy Association

**UDC** = universal decimal classification

**UDT** = Underwater Demolition Team; WW II "frogmen"

**UEL** = United Empire Loyalist; Americans who moved to Canada during the Revolutionary War

**UFCWIU** = United Food and Commercial Workers International Union

**UFFVA** = United Fresh Fruit and Vegetable Association

**UFL** = upper flammability limit

**UFO** = unidentified flying object

**UFOIRC** = UFO Information Retrieval Center

**UFVA** = University Film and Video Association

**UHCA** = ultra-high capacity aircraft, proposed by Airbus

UHF = ultra-high frequency (on TV, channels 14-83)
UHS = ultimate heat sink
= ultra-high speed
UHV = ultra-high voltage
U/I = unidentified
UIATF = United Indians of All Tribes Foundation
UJA = United Jewish Appeal
U-JOINT = universal joint (automotive)
UK = United Kingdom (Great Britain)
UL = Underwriters Laboratories, Inc.; testing laboratories for electric appliances
ULEV = ultra-low-emissions vehicle
ULPA = United Lightning Protection Association
ULT = ultimate
ULTRA = WW II British code name for intelligence culled from the breaking of enemy codes
UMP = umpire
UMT = Universal Military Training
UMTA = Urban Mass Transportation Administration (DOT)
UMWA = United Mine Workers of America
UN = United Nations
UNABOM = universities and airlines bomber (FBI); also "unabomer" and "unabomber"
UNCA = United Neighborhood Centers of America
UNCF = United Negro College Fund Inc.
UNCHS = UN Center for Human Settlements
UNCTAD = UN Conference on Trade and Development
UNDOF = UN Disengagement Observer Force
UNDP = UN Development Program
UNDRO = Office of the UN Disaster-Relief Coordinator
Une = unnilennium; a chemical element

**UNEP** = UN Environment Program
**UNESCO** = UN Educational, Scientific and Cultural Organization
**UNFPA** = UN Population Fund
**Unh** = unnilhexium; a chemical element
**UNHCR** = Office of the UN High Commissioner for Refugees
**UNIA** = Universal Negro Improvement Association
**UNICEF** = UN International Children's Emergency Fund
**UNIPDEE** = International Union of Producers and Distributors of Electrical Energy
**UNITAR** = UN Institute for Training and Research
**UNIV** = university
**UNIVAC** = Universal Analog Computer; first large commercial computer produced by Remington Rand
**UNO** = United Nations Organization
**Unp** = unnilpexium; a chemical element
**UNPROFOR** = UN Protection Force, in Bosnia; "un-pro-for"
**Unq** = unnilquadium; a chemical element
**UNRWA** = UN Relief and Works Agency
**Uns** = unnilseptum; a chemical element
**UNSCEAR** = UN Scientific Committee on the Effects of Atomic Radiation
**UNTAG** = UN Transition Assistance Group
**UNTSO** = UN Truce Supervision Organization
**UNU** = UN University, in Tokyo
**UOA** = United Ostomy Association
**UP** = Upper Peninsula in Michigan
**UPAO** = University Professors for Academic Order
**UPC** = universal product code; bar code
**UPF** = United Parkinson Foundation
**UPG** = upgrade
**UPHA** = United Professional Horsemen's Association
**UPI** = United Press International
**UPN** = United Paramount Network

**UPS** = United Parcel Service; "ups"

= Universal Press Syndicate

= uninterruptible power supply

**UPU** = Universal Postal Union (UN agency in Switzerland)

**URA** = Universities Research Association

**URCLPWA** = United Rubber, Cork, Linoleum, and Plastic Workers of America

**UROL** = urology or urological

**URW** = United Rubber Workers

**US** = United States

**USA** = United States of America

= US Army

= Unicycling Society of America

**USAAC** = US Army Air Corps, until June, 1941; then USAAF

**USAAF** = US Army Air Force, until July, 1947; then USAF

**USAB** = US Amateur Boxing, Inc.

**USABA** = US Association for Blind Athletes

**USAC** = US Automobile Club

**USACE** = US Army Corps of Engineers

**USAF** = US Air Force

**USAFA** = US Air Force Academy (Colorado Springs)

**USAFI** = US Armed Forces Institute

**USAFR** = US Air Force Reserve

**USAHA** = US Animal Health Association

**USAID** = US Agency for International Development

**USAMRIID** = US Army Medical Research Institute of Infectious Diseases

**USAR** = US Army Reserve

**USAREC** = US Army Recruiting Command

**USAREUR** = US Army in Europe

**USARJ** = US Army in Japan

**USARV** = US Army in Vietnam

**USAS** = United States of America Standards

**USASI** = United States of America Standards Institute
**USASOC** = US Army Special Operations Command
**USAT** = US Army transport (ship)
**USBR** = US Bureau of Reclamation
**USBSA** = US Beet Sugar Association
**USC** = United States Code
**USCA** = US Court of Appeals
**USC&GS** = US Coast and Geodetic Survey
**USCCR** = US Commission on Civil Rights
**USCEA** = US Committee for Energy Awareness
**USCF** = US Chess Federation
**USCG** = US Coast Guard
**USCGA** = US Coast Guard Academy
**USCMA** = US Catholic Mission Association
**USCS** = US Customs Service
**USCT** = US Colored Trooper; on tombstones at Arlington National Cemetery
**USDA** = US Department of Agriculture
**USES** = US Employment Service
**USFRA** = Utah Salt Flats Racing Association (automotive)
**USFSA** = US Figure Skating Association
**USGA** = US Golf Association
**USGF** = US Gymnastics Federation
**USGPO** = US Government Printing Office
**USGS** = US Geological Survey
**USHA** = US Homeopathic Association
**USHSLA** = US Hide, Skin & Leather Association
**USIA** = US Information Agency
**USICA** = US International Communication Agency (USIA)
**USIDCA** = US International Development Cooperation Agency
**USIHR** = US Institute of Human Rights
**USITC** = US International Trade Commission

USLTA = US Lawn Tennis Association
USM = US Mail
USMA = US Military Academy at West Point, NY
        = US Metric Association
USMC = US Marine Corps
USMCR = US Marine Corps Reserve
USMLE = US Medical Licensing Examination
USMM = US Merchant Marine
USMMA = US Merchant Marine Academy
USMS = US Marshals Service
USN = US Navy
USNA = US Naval Academy at Annapolis, MD
USNI = US Naval Institute
USNO = US Naval Observatory
USNR = US Naval Reserve
USNS = US Navy Ship
USO = United Services Organization
USOC = US Olympic Committee
USP = US Pharmacopoeia
     = Unique Selling Proposition (advertising)
USPA = US Parachute Association
      = US Polo Association
      = US Potters Association
USPCA = US Police Canine Association
USPGA = US Professional Golfers' Association
USPHS = US Public Health Service; also PHS
USPS = US Postal Service
USR = user
USRA = US Railway Association
USS = United States Ship
USSA = US Sailing Association
      = US Student Association
USSOCOM = US Special Operations Command

**USSR** = Union of Soviet Socialist Republics
**USTA** = US Tennis Association
       = US Trademark Association
       = US Trotting Association
**USTFA** = US Trout Farmers Association
**USU** = usually
**USWA** = United Steel Workers of America
**USWB** = US Weather Bureau
**USYRU** = US Yacht Racing Union
**UT** = Utah (postal code)
     = Universal Time; see CUT
**UTU** = United Transportation Union
**UU** = ultimate user
**UV** = utility vehicle
     = ultraviolet
**UV's** = ultraviolet rays
**UVA** = ultraviolet rays that can pass through glass and penetrate deeply into the skin, aging it
**UVB** = ultraviolet rays that cause sunburn and skin cancer; they cannot pass through glass
**UW** = United Way
**UXB** = unexploded bomb
**UZI** = 9mm submachine gun


**V** = verb
   = valve
   = verb
   = volts
   = 5 in Roman numerals
   = victory
   = against (Latin: *versus*); also vs
   = velocity
   = volume
   = vanadium; a chemical element

**V1** = *Vergeltungswaffe eins*; (German for retaliation weapon one) Hitler's first vengeance weapon; a cruise-type missile; the "buzz bomb"

**V2** = *Vergeltungswaffe zwei*; (German for retaliation weapon two) Hitler's second vengeance weapon; a somewhat-guided missile

**V6** = engine with six cylinders arranged in a V

**V8** = engine with eight cylinders arranged in a V

**V10** = engine with ten cylinders arranged in a V

**V12** = engine with twelve cylinders arranged in a V

**V16** = engine with sixteen cylinders arranged in a V

**VA** = Virginia (postal code)
   = Veterans' Administration
   = Veterans' Affairs
   = Volunteers of America

**VAC** = vacuum

**VADM** = vice admiral

**VAGA** = Visual Artists and Galleries Association

**VAL** = value

**VALNET** = Veterans Administration Library Network

**VAMA** = Voluntary Affirmative Marketing Agreement (HUD)

**VAR** = variation
   = variable
   = various

**VARA** = Vintage Auto Racing Association

**VAT** = value-added tax

**VB** = verb

**VC** = Viet Cong
   = Victor Charlie; military for Viet Cong
   = veterinary corps
   = vice-consul
   = Victoria Cross (British)

**V-CHIP** = device in TV to block violent programs

**VCR** = video cassette recorder
**VD** = venereal disease
**VDT** = video data terminal (mobile communications)
    = video display terminal
**VDU** = visual display unit; screen
**VEBA** = voluntary employee beneficiary association
**V-E DAY** = Victory-in-Europe Day (ww ii)
**VEG** = vegetable
**VEGGIES** = vegetables
**VEL** = velocity
**VEN** = venerable
**VENT** = ventilate
**VER** = Vermont
**VERS** = version
**VERT** = vertical
    = vertebrate
**VET** = veteran
    = veterinarian
**VETTE** = Corvette sports car
**VEVRA** = Vietnam Era Veterans' Readjustment Assistance Act
**VF** = very fine
    = video frequency
**VFD** = volunteer fire department
**VFR** = visual flying rules
**VFW** = Veterans of Foreign Wars
**VG** = very good
**VH** = Australia (aircraft registration code)
**VHAD** = vehicle headlamp aim device
**VHF** = very high frequency (on TV, channels 2-13)
**VHS** = video home system
**VI** = Virgin Islands (postal code)
    = volume indicator
    = viscosity index

**VIA** = by way of
**VIC** = vicinity
**VICA** = Vocational Industrial Clubs of America
**VID** = visual identification
**VIL** = village
**VIN** = vehicle identification number
**VIP** = very important person
**VIS** = visibility
    = visual
**VISTA** = Volunteers in Service to America
**VITA** = Volunteer Income Tax Assistance (IRS)
    = Volunteers in Technical Assistance
**viz** = namely (Latin: *videlicet,* for one may see)
**V-J DAY** = Victory-over-Japan Day (WW II)
**VLA** = Very Large Array; 27 mobile antennas near Socorro, NM combined to make the world's most powerful radio telescope (see VLBA)
**VLBA** = Very Long Baseline Array; 10 radio dishes from Hawaii to the Virgin Islands (see VLA)
**VLBI** = very long baseline interferometry
**VLF** = very low frequency (navigation and submarine communication)
**VLR** = very long range
**VMI** = Virginia Military Institute
**VNA** = Visiting Nurse Association
**VO** = voice over picture (TV commercials)
    = very old
    = verbal order
**VOA** = Voice of America (USIA)
**VOC** = vocal
**VOCA** = Volunteers in Overseas Cooperative Assistance
**VOCG** = verbal order of the commanding general

**VOL** = volume
= volunteer
**VOQ** = visiting officer quarters
**VOR** = very-high-frequency omni range
**VOX** = voice activated (mobile communications)
**VP** = vice-president
= variable pitch
**VPA** = Videotape Production Association
**VQ** = visitors' quarters
**VR** = virtual reality
**VRRV** = virtual reality roving vehicle
**VS** = against (Latin: *versus*)
= veterinary surgeon
**VSA** = Violin Society of America
= Victorian Society in America
**VSCCA** = Vintage Sports Car Club of America
**VSI** = voluntary separation incentive
**VSTOL** = vertical/short takeoff and landing aircraft
**VT** = Vermont (postal code)
= vacuum tube
= variable time
**VTEC** = variable valve timing and lift electronic control; Honda engine
**VTOL** = vertical takeoff and landing aircraft
**VTR** = video tape recorder
**VU** = view
**VV** = vice versa
**VVAOV** = Vietnam Veterans Agent Orange Victims
**VW** = Volkswagen
**VWO** = valve wide open

**W** = wife
   = west
   = width
   = won
   = watt
   = with
   = week
   = weight
   = walkover; won by forfeit or concession (tennis)
   = tungsten (wolfram); a chemical element
**W-2** = income and tax statement
**W-33** = old US atomic artillery shell
**W-79** = newer model US atomic artillery shell
**WA** = Washington (postal code)
**WAAC** = Women's Auxiliary Army Corps; predecessor to WAC
**WAC** = Women's Army Corps (WW II)
**WAE** = when actually employed
**WAF** = Women in the United States Air Force
   = Women in the Arts Foundation
**WAFFEN SS** = armed SS; military units formed from Hitler's bodyguard
**WAFS** = Women's Auxiliary Ferrying Squadron (WW II)
**WAND** = Women's Action for New Directions
**WANO** = World Association of Nuclear Operators
**WAOB** = World Agricultural Outlook Board
**WAPOR** = World Association for Public Opinion Research
**WAR** = Women Against Rape
**WARN** = Worker Adjustment and Retraining Notification Act
**WAS** = World Archaeological Society
**WASH** = Washington State
   = Washington, D.C.

**WASP** = white anglo-saxon Protestant
     = Women's Airforce Service Pilots (WW II)
**WB** = Warner Brothers
     = westbound
     = weather bureau
     = wingback (football)
**WBA** = World Boxing Association
**WBC** = white blood cells
     = white blood count
     = World Boxing Council
**WBDNA** = Women Band Directors National Association
**WBF** = World Boxing Association
**WBN** = Warner Brothers Network
**WBS** = World Biological Society
**WC** = water closet (toilet)
     = without charge
**WCC** = World Council of Churches
**WCCA** = Whooping Crane Conservation Association
**WCCU** = World Council of Credit Unions
**WCF** = World Crafts Foundation
**WCTU** = Women's Christian Temperance Union; see NWCTU
**WD** = wood
     = word
     = War Department
**WDA** = Wildlife Disease Association
**WDC** = World Data Center
**WDL** = Workers Defense League
**WDTR** = World Traders Data Report (DOC)
**WEAL** = Women's Equity Action League
**WEC** = World Environment Center
**WED** = Wednesday
**WEIU** = Women's Educational and Industrial Union
**WEPR** = Women Executives in Public Relations

**WESTCOM** = Western Command (US Army)
**WESTLANT** = Western Atlantic Command HQ (NATO)
**WESTPAC** = Western Pacific Command (USN)
**WF** = white female
   = wrong font
**WFA** = white female American
   = World Federalists Association
**WFC** = World Food Council (UN)
**WFH** = World Federation of Hemophilia
**WFMH** = World Federation for Mental Health
**WFP** = World Food Program (UN)
**WFPHA** = World Federation of Public Health Associations
**WFTU** = World Federation of Trade Unions
**WG** = wing
   = wire gauge
**WGA** = Writers Guild of America
   = Western Golf Association
   = Wild Goose Association
**WGN** = wagon
**WH** = watt-hour
   = white
**WHES** = World Hunger Education Service
**WHL** = World Hockey League
**WHO** = World Health Organization (UN)
**WHOI** = Woods Hole Oceanographic Institution
**WHP** = water horsepower
**WHSE** = warehouse
**WI** = Wisconsin (postal code)
   = West Indies
   = wrought iron
   = Wine Institute
**WIA** = wounded in action
**WIBC** = World Institute of Black Communications
   = Women's International Bowling Congress

**WIC** = Women, Infants and Children, government food program
**WID** = widow
       = widower
**WILPF** = Women's International League for Peace and Freedom
**WIMA** = Writing Instrument Manufacturers Association
**WIN** = Windows; computer operating system
       = Work Incentive Program (DOL)
       = Women's International Network
**WINBA** = World International Nail and Beauty Association
**WIPO** = World Intellectual Property Organization (UN)
**WIR** = Wire Interception and Interception of Oral Communications Statute (US)
**WIS** = Wisconsin
**WISC** = Wisconsin
**WISH** = Workers' Institute for Safety and Health
**WISH LIST** = Women in the Senate and House list; PAC for pro-choice Republican women
**WK** = week
      = work
**WL** = white-lettered tires
      = wavelength
      = water line
**WLA** = White Lung Association
**WMA** = white male American
       = World Medical Association
       = World Modeling Association
       = Wheelchair Motorcycle Association
**WMK** = watermark
**WMO** = World Meteorological Organization (UN)
**WMS** = waste management system
**WN** = Southwest Airlines

**WO** = warrant officer
**W/O** = without
**WOC** = without compensation
**WOG** = disparaging British term for Orientals; from stencil on native workers' shirts: WOGS, for working on government services
**WOW** = Wider Opportunities for Women
**WP** = white phosphorous; a type of bomb (military)
    = weather permitting
    = wild pitch (baseball)
**WPA** = Works Progress Administration
    = War Pricing Administration
**WPB** = wastepaper basket
**WPC** = watts per candle
**WPCF** = Water Pollution Control Federation
**WPF** = World Peace Foundation
**WPI** = World Policy Institute
**WPM** = words per minute
**WPN** = weapon
**WPS** = World Population Society
**WPSA** = World's Poultry Science Association
**WR** = wide receiver (football)
**WRAP** = Woodland Resource Analysis Program (TVA)
**WRC** = World Rally Championship (automotive)
    = Water Resources Center
**WREE** = Women for Racial and Economic Equality
**WREI** = Women's Research & Education Institute
**WRL** = War Resisters League
**WRRC** = Water Resources Research Center
**WRRI** = Water Resources Research Institute
**WRSIC** = Water Resources Scientific Information Center (DOI)
**WS** = Women for Sobriety
**WSA** = World Sign Association

**WSMR** = White Sands Missile Range (US Army)
**WT** = weight
    = warrant
    = wireless telegraph
**WTO** = World Trade Organization
**WV** = West Virginia (postal code)
**WVA** = West Virginia
**WW** = whitewall tires
    = world war
**WWF** = World Wildlife Fund
      = World Wrestling Federation
**WWI** = Working Women's Institute
**WW I** = World War I
**WW II** = World War II
**WWMCCS** = World Wide Military Command and Control System; "wimmex"
**WWRF** = Who's Who Resource File (DOC)
**WWWC** = World Without War Council
**WY** = Wyoming (postal code)
**WYO** = Wyoming

**X** = no one under 18 admitted (movie rating)
    = unknown
    = experimental
    = 10 in Roman numerals
    = takes or captures (chess)
    = a certain destination
**X-1** = first plane to exceed speed of sound on October 14, 1947, by Bell Aircraft
**X-15** = rocket engine high-speed high-altitude research plane, by North American Aviation
**X-30** = National Aerospace Plane Project (NASP)
**XA, XB, XC** = Mexico (aircraft registration codes)

212

XCU = extreme close up (movies)
XD = without dividend (stock market)
X DIV = without dividend (stock market)
Xe = xenon; a chemical element
XEROX = copy
       = Xerox Corporation
XL = extra large
XLS = extreme long shot (movies)
XMAS = Christmas
XN = Christian
XNTY = Christianity
XO = executive officer (military)
XP = experimental
XR = without rights
XRF = x-ray florescence
XW = without warrants
XYZPDQ = examine your zipper pretty darn quick

Y   = yes
     = YMCA
     = YWCA
     = yard
     = year
     = yttrium; a chemical element
YAF = Young Americans for Freedom
YAK = various Soviet fighter and transport planes; after designer Yakovlev
YB = yearbook
Yb = ytterbium; a chemical element
YC = yacht club
YCA = Young Concert Artists
YD = yard
YEG = Edmonton, Alberta International Airport

**YG** = year group
**YHA** = Youth Hostels Association
**YHWH** = Yahweh; Hebrew "incommunicable name" for God; also JHVH, JHWH, YHVH
**YHZ** = Halifax, Nova Scotia, airport
**YID** = Yiddish
**YITB** = yours in the bond
**YMCA** = Young Men's Christian Association
**YMHA** = Young Men's Hebrew Association
**YMQ** = Montreal, Quebec, airport
**YOW** = Ottawa, Ontario, airport
**YQB** = Quebec City, Quebec, airport
**YQR** = Regina, Saskatchewan, airport
**YQX** = Gander, Newfoundland, airport
**YR** = year
    = your
    = Young Republicans
**YRS** = years
    = yours
**YT** = Yukon Territory, Canada
**YTO** = Toronto, Ontario, airport
**YVR** = Vancouver, British Columbia, airport
**YWCA** = Young Women's Christian Association
**YWG** = Winnipeg, Manitoba, airport
**YWHA** = Young Women's Hebrew Association
**YXD** = Edmonton, Alberta, airport
**YXE** = Saskatoon, Saskatchewan, airport
**YXU** = London, Ontario, airport
**YYC** = Calgary, Alberta, airport

**Z** = zero
   = zone
   = zulu time; military for Greenwich Mean Time
   = Japanese code for the attack on Pearl Harbor
**Z's** = sleep, as in "catch some Z's"
**Z-28** = model of Chevrolet Camaro sports car
**Z-COVERAGE** = FBI mail intercept program
**ZD** = zero defects
**ZEKE** = Allied code name for Mitsubishi Zero-Sen, WW II Japanese pursuit plane
**ZERO** = WW II Japanese pursuit plane; Mitsubishi Zero-Sen A6M
**ZEV** = zero emissions vehicle; electric automobile
**ZI** = zone of interior
   = Zinc Institute
**ZIP** = Zone Improvement Program; postal code
**ZK** = New Zealand (aircraft registration code)
**ZN** = zone
   = azimuth
**Zn** = zinc; a chemical element
**ZOA** = Zionist Organization of America
**ZOO** = zoological park
**ZOOl** = zoology or zoological
**ZPG** = zero population growth
   = Zero Population Growth
**Zr** = zirconium; a chemical element
**ZR1** = model of Chevrolet Corvette with LT5 DOHC engine
**ZS** = South Africa (aircraft registration code)

# Specialized
# Supplements

# *LEGAL LINGO*
(In Latin and English except where noted)

**ABSENTE REO** = defendant being absent
**AD ABSURDUM** = to the point of absurdity
**AD HOC** = for the purpose
**AD HOMINEM** = personal
**AD IDEM** = to the same point
**AD INFINITUM** = to infinity; without end
**AD INTERIM** = in the meantime
**ADIRATUM** = strayed or lost
**AD LITEM** = for the suit or action
**AD QUOD DAMNUM** = to what damage; how much damage would something do
**AD NAUSEUM** = to the point of nausea
**ADS** = *ad sectum*; at the suit of
**ADVOCATUS DIABOLI** = devil's advocate
**AEQUITAS SEQUITUR LEGEM** = equity follows the law, except where fraud would ensue
**AFFIDAVIT** = sworn statement
**ALGOR MORTIS** = the chill of death
**ALR** = American Law Reports
**AMICUS CURIAE** = friend of the court
**ANIMUS CAPIENDI** = the intention of taking
**ANIMUS FURANDI** = the intention of stealing
**A POSTERIORI** = after the facts
**APPELLATE COURT** = court of appeals; court that reviews a case
**A PRIORI** = before the facts

**BONA FIDE** = in good faith
**BONUM PUBLICUM** = the public good

217

**BRIEF** = legal document analyzing a case or position

**CASUS BELLI** = a cause for war
**CAUSE CÉLÈBRE** = celebrated cause or case (French)
**CAVEAT** = let him beware
**CAVEAT EMPTOR** = let the buyer beware
**CAVE CANEM** = beware of the dog
**CERTIORARI** = to be certified
**CIRCUIT COURT** = jurisdiction extends over counties and districts
**CODICIL** = supplement to a will
**CORPUS DELICTI** = body of the crime
**COMPOS MENTIS** = of sound mind
**CULPA** = fault or negligence
**CULPA LATA** = gross negligence
**CULPA LEVIS** = excusable neglect
**CURIA ADVISARI VULT** = the court wishes to consider
**CURSUS CURIAE EST LEX CURIAE** = the practice of the court is the law of the court
**CUSTODIA LEGIS** = in the custody of the law

**DAMNUM ABSQUE INJURIA** = loss without injury
**DEBITUM** = a debt
**DE BONIS ASPORTATIS** = of goods carried off
**DE BONIS NON ADMINISTRATIS** = of goods not yet administered
**DE FACTO** = in reality
**DE FIDE ET OFFICIO JUDICIS NON RECIPITUR QUAESTIO** = of the good faith and duty of the judge, no question can be permitted
**DE JURE** = by law
**DELICTUM** = wrongful act
**DE LUNATICO INQUIRENDO** = writ inquiring into a person's sanity

218

**DEPOSITION** = written statement under oath, presented as evidence
**DIES DATUS** = day appointed for a hearing
**DIES JURIDICUS** = a court day
**DIES NON (JURIDICUS)** = not a court day
**DISTRAIN** = seize goods for compensation
**DOCKET** = brief formal record of court proceedings
**DROIT** = legal right (French)

**ENTAIL** = settling an estate beyond one generation
**ESCROW** = safekeeping by a third party
**ESTOVERS** = things that can be removed legally by a renter
**ET AL** = *et alii*; and others
**EX BONA FIDE** = on one's honor
**EX CURIA** = out of court
**EX DELICTO** = by reason of an objectionable wrong
**EX DESUETUDINE AMITTUNTER**
  **PRIVILEGIA** = rights are forfeited by disuse
**EX FACIE** = on its face; evidently
**EX GRATIA** = by favor; in the absence of legal right
**EX LEGE** = from the law
**EX OFFICIO** = by virtue of the office
**EX PARTE** = on behalf of one side only

**FACIO UT DES** = I do that you may give; a contract
**FACIO UT FACIAS** = I do that you may do; a contract
**FIAT JUSTITIA** = let justice be done

**GARNISHMENT** = court order requiring a third party to withhold property of a debtor
**GRAND JURY** = not less than 12 nor more than 23 jurors to hear evidence and decide whether to INDICT; federal grand jury has not less than 16

**GRATIS DICTUM** = an assertion

**HABEAS CORPUS** = writ requiring that a person be produced before the court with reasons for detention
**HAC LEGE** = under this law or condition
**HORRIBILE DICTU** = horrible to relate
**HORRIBILE VISU** = horrible to see
**HUNG JURY** = undecided after due deliberation

**IGNORANTIA JURIS NON EXCUSAT** = ignorance of the law does not excuse
**IMPEACH** = to challenge testimony or a witness; to demonstrate that a witness has lied
**IN ARTICULO MORTIS** = at the moment of death
**IN CAMERA** = in chambers; not in open court
**IN CURIA** = in open court
**IN CUSTODIA LEGIS** = in the custody of the law
**INDEMNITY** = legal exemption
**INDICT** = accuse
**INDICTMENT** = formal written accusation which must be proved by trial
**IN DUBIO** = in doubt
**IN FACIE CURIAE** = before the court
**IN FLAGRANTE DELICTO** = in the act of committing a crime; caught red-handed
**INJUNCTION** = court order requiring specific action
**IN LOCO PARENTIS** = in place of a parent
**IN MORA** = in default
**IN PERPETUUM** = forever
**IN PERSONA** = in person
**IN PERSONAM** = against a person
**IN PLENO** = in full
**IN RE** = in the matter of

**IN REM** = against a thing; an action against property
**IN SE** = in itself
**IN SITU** = in place
**IN STATU QUO** = in the same state as before
**IN TENEBRIS** = in doubt
**INTER** = between or among
**IN TERMINIS** = definitely
**IN TOTO** = entirely
**IN VACUO** = in a vacuum
**IN VENTRE** = in the womb
**IPSO FACTO** = by that very fact

**JURE** = by right
**JURE HUMANO** = by the will of the people
**JURE MARITI** = by a husband's right
**JURE NON DONO** = by right and not by gift
**JURE PROPINQUITATUS** = by right of relationship
**JURE SANGUINIS** = by right of blood
**JURIS PERITUS** = skilled in the law
**JURISPRUDENCE** = legal philosophy
**JUS** = law
**JUS CIVILE** = civil law
**JUS COMMUNE** = common law
**JUS PROPRIETATIS** = right of property

**LACHES** = negligence or unreasonable delay in pursuing a claim (from the French)
**LEGALIS HOMO** = a man with full legal rights
**LIS PENDENS** = pending suit
**LITE PENDENTE** = during the trial
**LITIGATION** = taking a case to court
**LIVOR MORTIS** = dark area on the dependent part of a cadaver

**LOCUS** = a place or location
**LOCUS CRIMINIS** = scene of the crime
**LOCUS DELICTI** = scene of the crime
**LOCUS STANDI** = place of standing; right to be heard by a court
**LOWER COURT** = court that tries a case

**MALUM IN SE** = evil or unlawful in itself
**MALUM PROHIBITUM** = prohibited evil or wrong
**MAN ONE** = manslaughter one; voluntary homicide
**MAN TWO** = manslaughter two; involuntary homicide
**MENSA ET TORO** = from bed and board
**MENS LEGIS** = spirit of the law
**MENS REA** = criminal intent
**MODUS OPERANDI** = manner of working
**MQS** = motion to quash subpoena
**MURDER 1** = murder in the 1st degree; premeditated and intentional
**MURDER 2** = murder in the 2nd degree; intentional without deliberation

**NIHIL DEBIT** = he owes nothing
**NIJ** = National Institute of Justice
**NO BILL** = no indictment; see TRUE BILL
**NOLLE PROSEQUI** = unwilling to pursue or prosecute
**NOLO** = *nolo contendere*
**NOLO CONTENDERE** = no contest; guilty without the admission of guilt
**NON LIQUET** = not clear; not proven
**NON OBSTANTE VERDICTO** = judgment for the plaintiff setting aside the verdict for the defendant
**NON PROSEQUITUR** = judgment where the plaintiff does not appear

NULLA BONA = no goods

ONUS PROBANDI = burden of proof

PAROLE = release on condition of good behavior; word of honor
PARS ADVERSA = the opposite party
PARTICEPS CRIMINIS = criminal accomplice
PC = penal code
PENDENTE LITE = pending litigation
PER CURIAM = by the court
PER DIEM = by the day
PER EUNDEM = by the same; by the same judge
PER INTERIM = in the meantime
PER PARES = by one's peers
PER SE = in itself
PER TOTAM CURIAM = by the whole court; unanimously
PLF = plaintiff
POST LITEM MOTAM = after litigation starts
POST MORTEM = after death; autopsy
POWER OF ATTORNEY = legal authorization to act for another
PPA = per power of attorney
PRIMA FACIE = on the face of it
PROBATE = establishing validity of a will
PROBATIVE = serving to prove
PRO BONO = for the public good; from *pro bono publico*
PRO CONFESSO = as if confessed
PROFFER = written offer of proof
PRO FORMA = in form
PRO NUNC = for now
PRO TEM = temporarily; from *pro tempore*

**QUID PRO QUO** = something for something

**REDACT** = edit out
**RES** = thing, cause, affair, case
**RES ADJUDICATA** = decided case
**RES GESTAE** = the facts
**RES IPSA LOQUITUR** = the thing speaks for itself; rule of evidence in which negligence may be inferred from the accident
**RESPONDEAT SUPERIOR** = let the superior answer (for his representative)
**RE VERA** = in truth
**RUBRIC** = title of a statute

**SCI FA** = show cause; from *scire facias*
**SDT** = SUBPOENA DUCES TECUM
**SEC LEG** = according to law; from *secundum legem*
**SEQUESTRATION** = seizure of assets until final judgment
**SINE DIE** = without a day; indefinitely adjourned
**SUB COLORE JURIS** = under color of law
**SUB JUDICE** = under deliberation by the court
**SUBPOENA** = under penalty; court order to appear and give evidence
**SUBPEONA DUCES TECUM** = court order to show up and bring documents
**SUI GENERIS** = of its own kind; unique
**SUI JURIS** = in one's own legal right
**SUMMUM JUS** = the highest law
**SUPREME COURT** = court of last resort

**TORT** = breach or violation of civil law
**TRUE BILL** = indictment; see NO BILL

**ULTRA VIRES** = beyond legal powers
**USCA** = US Court of Appeals
**USUFRUCT** = use of another's property as long as it remains undamaged

**VIS MAJOR** = superior force; inevitable accident
**VOIR DIRE** = oath by a witness to tell the truth (French for, to say the truth); usually used in reference to interviewing prospective jurors

**WRIT** = court order requiring specific action
**WRIT OF CERTIORARI** = court order calling up records of a lower court

# *COP TALK*

**AAFS** = American Academy of Forensic Scientists
**A&B** = assault and battery
**ACP** = automatic Colt pistol
     = cartridge for automatic Colt pistols
**ADA** = assistant district attorney
**ADW** = assault with a deadly weapon
**AFIS** = automatic fingerprint identification system
**AFLP** = amplified fragment length polymerase; for DNA analysis
**AK-47** = Soviet assault rifle; KALASHNIKOV, after the designer
**ALGOR MORTIS** = the chill of death; a way to calculate time of death
**AMMO** = ammunition
**ANFO** = ammonium nitrate and fuel oil; homemade explosive
**AP** = armor piercing, as in bullet
**APB** = all points bulletin
**APC** = armored personnel carrier
**AR-15** = civilian version of M-16 rifle
**ASCLD** = American Society of Crime Laboratory Directors
**ATF** = Bureau of Alcohol, Tobacco and Firearms; also BATF (US)
**AUTO** = misnomer for semiautomatic pistol
     = gun that fires continuously as long as the trigger is held back

**BAC** = blood alcohol content
**BAR** = Browning automatic rifle
**BATF** = Bureau of Alcohol, Tobacco and Firearms; also ATF (US)
**B&E** = breaking and entering

**BFA** = black female American
**BLACK & WHITE** = black and white police car; usually LAPD
**BLUE & WHITE** = blue and white police car; usually NYPD
**BMA** = black male American

**C-4** = plastic explosives
**CCW** = carrying a concealed weapon
      = permit to carry a concealed weapon
**CHP** = California Highway Patrol
**CID** = criminal investigation division or department
**CI** = confidential informant
   = counterintelligence
**CLIS** = Criminalistics Laboratory Information System (DOJ)
**CODE 1** = routine response
**CODE 2** = urgent, no siren or flashing lights
**CODE 3** = urgent, siren and flashing lights
**CODE BLACK** = disaster
**CON** = convict; prisoner
     = swindle (from confidence man or scheme)
     = confidence
**CON MAN** = confidence man; swindler
**CRIMINALIST** = one who collects and analyzes evidence
**CRIMINOLOGIST** = one who studies crime and criminals
**CSA** = Controlled Substances Act (US)
**CSU** = crime scene unit
**CS GAS** = tear gas, after inventors B.B. Corson and R.W. Stoughton

**DA** = district attorney
    = double-action; a handgun that may be fired by pulling the trigger or by cocking the hammer and then pulling the trigger (see SA, DAO)
**DAO** = double action only; a handgun that may be fired only by pulling the trigger (see SA, DA)

**DA/SA** = double action/single action; a pistol that offers both capabilities
**DB** = dead body
**DCM** = Director of Civilian Marksmanship (US)
**D&D** = drunk and disorderly
**DEA** = US Drug Enforcement Administration
**DEP** = deputy
**DEWAT** = deactivated war trophy, like a machine gun or grenade
**DIF** = death in family
**DL** = driver's license
**DMV** = department of motor vehicles
**DNA** = deoxyyriboneucleic acid; genetic "fingerprint"
**DOA** = dead on arrival
**DOB** = date of birth
**DOJ** = Department of Justice
**DUI** = driving under the influence
**DUIL** = driving under the influence of liquor
**DUM-DUM** = bullet with a truncated, flattened or deformed nose
**DWI** = driving while intoxicated

**EAP** = erythrocite/acid phosphatase, enzyme blood analysis
**ECU** = evidence control unit
**EDTA** = ethylenediaminetetraacetic acid; blood preservative
**ELECTROPHORESIS** = blood analysis to determine blood type through charged particles
**EMS** = emergency medical service
**EMT** = emergency medical technician
**EOW** = end of watch
**ERT** = emergency response team
**ET** = estimated time

**ETA** = estimated time of arrival
**ETD** = estimated time of departure
**EX CON** = former convict

**FBI** = Federal Bureau of Investigation
**FED** = federal
**FED's** = representatives of the federal government
**FLETC** = Federal Law Enforcement Training Center in Glynco, Georgia
**FLIR** = forward-looking infrared
**FMJ** = full metal jacket cartridge; military cartridge
**FORENSIC** = of the law; legal
**FORENSIC MEDICINE** = medicine in relation to the law
**FTA** = failure to appear
**FTIR** = Fourier transformed infrared spectroscopy
**FTP** = failure to pay
**FYI** = for your information

**GC/MS** = gas chromatography/mass spectrometry; testing of urine for drugs
**GLOCK** = pistol made primarily of lightweight plastic
**G-MAN** = government man; federal agent, usually FBI
**GSW** = gunshot wound
**GTA** = grand theft auto

**H** = heroin
**HBD** = has been drinking
**HOLLOW-POINT** = bullet with a concave nose
**HOOK** = tow truck
**HORN** = radio
**HP** = highway patrol

**IAAI** = International Association of Arson Investigators
**IACP** = International Association of Chiefs of Police
**IAWP** = International Association of Women Police
**ID** = identification
**IGB** = Prohibition of Illegal Gambling Business (US)
**INS** = Immigration & Naturalization Service (US)
**INTERPOL** = International Criminal Police Organization; worldwide consortium of 135 countries

**J** = judge
  = justice
**JA** = judge advocate
**JAG** = judge advocate general
**JAWS** = jaws of life; powerful prying tool
**JHP** = jacketed hollow-point cartridge
**JP** = justice of the peace
**JUV** = juvenile

**K** = kilo; thousand (metric system)
  = kilometer; thousand meters
**K-9** = canine
**KILO** = kilogram; thousand grams or 2.2 lbs.
**KALASHNIKOV** = AK-47 Soviet assault rifle
**KEVLAR** = bullet-resistant fiber
**KEVLAR JACKET** = bullet-resistant vest
**KEY** = kilogram; thousand grams or 2.2 lbs
**KLEPTO** = kleptomaniac; addicted to stealing

**LACERATION** = irregular tear of the flesh
**LAPD** = Los Angeles Police Department
**LD** = lethal dose
**LEAA** = Law Enforcement Alliance of America
**LH TWIST** = left-hand twist; direction of the rifling in a gun barrel

**LIVOR MORTIS** = dark area on the down part of a cadaver
**LSD** = lysergic acid diethylamide; "acid;" synthetic hallucinogenic drug made from fungus growing on wet grass or grain

**M-1** = WW II US Army rifle or carbine; also the designation for various military equipment
**M-14** = US Army rifle
**M-16** = light army rifle
**MAC-9** = 9mm submachine gun
**MACE** = methylchloroform chloroacetophenone; toxic chemical compound once used for riot control
**MAN ONE** = manslaughter one; voluntary homicide
**MAN TWO** = manslaughter two; involuntary homicide
**ME** = medical examiner
**MG** = machine gun
**MLC** = Money Laundering Control Act (US)
**MO** = method of operation (Latin: *modus operandi*)
**MOB** = mobile
**MOR** = manually operated rifle
**MP** = mounted police
   = missing person
**MURDER 1** = murder in the 1st degree; premeditated and intentional
**MURDER 2** = murder in the 2nd degree; intentional without deliberation
**MVA** = motor-vehicle accident
**MVT** = motor vehicle theft
   = Motor Vehicle Theft Law Enforcement Act (US)
**NAME** = National Association of Medical Examiners
**NAPO** = National Association of Police Officers
**NARC** = narcotics officer
   = DEA officer

**NAS&FP** = National Asset Seizure and Forfeiture Program (US)

**NCIC** = National Crime Information Center

**NCJRS** = National Criminal Justice Referral System

**NCMEC** = National Center for Missing and Exploited Children

**NFD** = no further details

**NILECJ** = National Institute of Law Enforcement and Criminal Justice

**NSA** = National Sheriffs Association

**NYPD** = New York Police Department

**OAH** = Outstanding American Handgunner

**OAHAF** = Outstanding American Handgunner Awards Foundation

**OD** = overdose

**OUI** = operating under the influence; driving a car after using alcohol or narcotics

**+P** = extra powerful ammunition

**PAL** = Police Athletic League

**PB** = parabellum; for war or combat

**PCP** = phencyclidine; a street drug; "angel dust"

**PCR** = polymerase chain reaction, used in DNA testing when there is not enough DNA for RFLP or when DNA is degraded; the process amplifies or copies and recopies what fragments there are

**PC** = penal code
  = precinct
  = police constable

**PD** = police department

**PERF** = Police Executive Research Forum

**PERP** = perpetrator

**PF** = Police Foundation
**PI** = private investigator
= personal injury
**PIO** = public information officer
**PM** = post-mortem; autopsy
**PMG** = Prison-Made Goods Statute (US)
**PR** = person reporting (an incident)
**PRO** = public relations officer

**RCMP** = Royal Canadian Mounted Police
**RH TWIST** = right-hand twist; direction of the rifling in a gun barrel
**RIGOR MORTIS** = stiffening of muscles after death
**RFLP** = restriction fragment length polymorphism, used in DNA testing; requires 20 times as much DNA as PCR but delivers genetic fingerprint
**RICO** = Racketeer Influenced and Corrupt Organizations (US statute)

**SA** = single action; a handgun that can be fired only after the hammer has been cocked
**SAAMI** = Sporting Arms and Ammunition Manufacturers' Institute
**S&W** = Smith & Wesson
**SBF** = single black female
**SBM** = single black male
**SEC** = Sexual Exploitation of Children (US)
**SEMI-AUTO** = semiautomatic; gun that fires once and reloads when trigger is pulled
**SEROLOGY** = scientific study of blood serum
**SLIM JIM** = flat metal piece for unlocking car doors
**SMG** = submachine gun
**SOP** = standard operating procedure

**SP** = state police
**SS** = US Secret Service
**SWAT** = special weapons and tactics
**SWAT TEAM** = police officers specially trained for dangerous armed confrontations
**SWF** = single white female
**SWM** = single white male

**T-MAN** = treasury agent
**TA** = traffic accident
**TAC** = tactical
**TAG** = license plate
**TAKE DOWN** = seize a suspect
**TC** = traffic collision
**TEC-9** = 9mm submachine gun
**TNT** = trinitrotoluene; a powerful explosive
**TOC** = tactical operations center

**UBF** = unidentified black female
**UBM** = unidentified black male
**UC** = undercover
**USC** = United States Code
**USPCA** = US Police Canine Association
**USMS** = US Marshals Service
**UTL** = unable to locate
**UWF** = unidentified white female
**UWM** = unidentified white male
**UXB** = unexploded bomb
**UZI** = 9mm submachine gun

**VEST** = bullet-resistant chest protector
**VIN** = vehicle identification number

**WC** = watch commander
**WFA** = white female American
**WIRE** = transmitter, usually concealed
**WMA** = white male American

## *GENERAL 10-CODES*
(not consistent in all localities)

**10-0** = caution
**10-1** = message not understood
**10-2** = signal strong
**10-3** = stop transmitting
**10-4** = messaged received; OK
**10-5** = relay message
**10-6** = busy
**10-7** = out of service
**10-8** = in service
**10-9** = repeat
**10-10** = fight in progress
**10-11** = animal problem
**10-12** = stand by
**10-13** = report conditions
**10-14** = prowler report
**10-15** = civil disturbance
**10-16** = domestic problem
**10-17** = meet complainant
**10-18** = urgent
**10-19** = return to station
**10-20** = location
**10-21** = contact someone by telephone
**10-22** = disregard

10-23 = on scene
10-24 = assignment completed
10-25 = contact someone
10-26 = detaining subject
10-27 = driver's license information
10-28 = vehicle registration information
10-29 = check for wanted
10-30 = unauthorized use of radio
10-31 = crime in progress
10-32 = person with gun
10-33 = emergency
10-34 = riot
10-35 = major crime alert
10-36 = correct time
10-37 = suspicious vehicle
10-38 = stop suspicious vehicle
10-39 = Code 3; siren and flashing lights
10-40 = Code 2; no siren or flashing lights
10-41 = beginning shift
10-42 = ending shift
10-43 = information
10-44 = permission to change locations
10-45 = dead animal
10-46 = assist motorist
10-47 = emergency road repair
10-48 = traffic control
10-49 = accident with injuries
10-50 = traffic accident
10-51 = request tow truck
10-52 = request ambulance
10-53 = road blocked
10-54 = livestock on road
10-55 = intoxicated driver

10-56 = intoxicated pedestrian
10-57 = hit and run accident
10-58 = direct traffic
10-59 = escort
10-60 = check area
10-61 = personnel in vicinity
10-62 = reply
10-63 = copy
10-64 = local message
10-65 = network message
10-66 = cancel message
10-67 = clear for message
10-68 = send information
10-69 = message received
10-70 = fire alarm
10-71 = advise nature of fire
10-72 = report progress of fire
10-73 = smoke report
10-74 = negative
10-75 = in contact with someone
10-76 = en route
10-77 = estimated time of arrival
10-78 = request assistance
10-79 = notify coroner
10-80 = pursuit in progress
10-81 = breathalyzer report
10-82 = make reservations
10-83 = school crossing assignment
10-84 = advise estimated time of arrival
10-85 = arrival delayed
10-86 = officer/operator on duty
10-87 = pick up
10-88 = advise telephone number

10-89 = bomb threat
10-90 = bank alarm
10-91 = pick up subject
10-92 = vehicle illegally parked
10-93 = blockade
10-94 = drag racing
10-95 = subject in custody
10-96 = detain subject
10-97 = test radio signal
10-98 = escaped prisoner
10-99 = shots fired, request backup
     = wanted

# *BUZZWORDS FROM CYBERSPACE*

**AAMOF** = as a matter of fact

**A:** = A-drive; disk or floppy drive

**ACCESS PROVIDER** = institution on the Internet that provides online access such as *AOL*, *CompuServe* and *Prodigy*

**ACL** = access control lists

**A-D** = analog to digital

**ADB** = Apple desktop bus; interface standard for connecting keyboards, mice and other input devices to Macintosh computers

**ADI** = Autodesk Device Interface

**A-DRIVE** = primary external floppy disk or diskette

**AI** = artificial intelligence

**AIX** = operating system; version of Unix developed by IBM

**ALGOL** = algorithmic oriented language; arithmetic language for PC'S

**ALGORITHM** = set of instructions

**ANS** = Advanced Network Services

**ANSI** = American National Standards Institute; principle standards board in the US on how programming languages should work

**AOL** = *America Online*; online system for retrieving information

**API** = application program interface; defines how programs work with menus, dialogue boxes and windows

**APP** = application or software

**ARC** = data compression program

**.ARC** = compressed files (file extension)

**ARCHIE** = file locating system on the Internet

**ARCHITECTURE** = the way computer equipment is designed

**ARCNET** = network protocol or transmission method that is inexpensive to implement

**ARPA** = Advanced Research Projects Administration; also DARPA (DOD)

**ARPANET** = Department of Defense nationwide computer network now integrated into the Internet

**ASCII** = American Standard Code for Information Interchange; standard way of representing characters on a computer; "askey"

**AT** = Advanced Technology, as in IBM AT personal computer

**ATM** = asynchronous transfer mode; fast network featuring fiber optic data transmission

**AUI** = attachment unit interface, to attach Ethernet cable to PC port

**AUP** = acceptable use policy; network rules

**.AVI** = audio video interleaved format (file extension)

**B:** = B-drive; disk or floppy drive

**BACAS** = Business Analysis and Customer Approval System

**BACKUP** = copy of a program or file for safekeeping
= program to make a copy of a file

**BAK** = back at keyboard

**.BAK** = backup file (file extension)

**BANG** = exclamation mark

**BASIC** = Beginner's Algorithmic System of Instructional Coding; form of English used in computer programming for beginners

**.BAT** = batch file; a sequence of commands (file extension)

**BAUD** = unit that measures a modem's speed; the number of times a signal changes state in one second

**BBFN** = bye bye for now; also TTFN

**BBS** = bulletin board system or service

**BCD** = binary coded decimal, used for accuracy in financial calculations

**B-DRIVE** = secondary external floppy disk or diskette
**BERNOULLI BOX** = removable data storage system
**.BIN** = file containing binary data (file extension)
**BIOS** = basic input/output system
**BIS** = suffix for international communication protocols meaning second revision (French for encore)
**BIT** = binary digit; smallest unit of data recognized by a computer
**BITMAP** = map or picture made up of dots or pixels that can be stored in a PC file
**BITNET** = network of mostly IBM mainframes connected to the Internet
**BMF** = bit-mapped font; type font made of dots or bits
**BMP** = bitmap
**.BMP** = bit-mapped graphics files (file extension)
**BOOT** = start up
**BPS** = bits per second
**BRB** = be right back
**BTW** = by the way
**BURN IN** = leaving a new PC on for at least 48 hours to allow faulty components to fail
**BUS** = carries information from one PC component to another
 = network where PC'S connect to a common line or bus
**BYTE** = amount of memory needed to store one character; eight bits

**C** = programming language
**C++** = improved version of C
**C:** = hard drive; internal main disk dive
**CAD** = computer aided design
 = computer aided dispatching (mobile communications)
**CAD/CAM** = computer aided design/computer aided manufacturing

**CAD/CAE** = computer aided design/computer aided engineering

**CAE** = computer aided engineering

**CARD** = circuit board or adapter for a PC, as in "sound card"

**CCD** = charge couple device; scanner device that changes light into electrical signals to the computer

**CD** = compact disc

**CD+** = CD enhanced format

**CDPD** = cellular digital packet data

**CD-ROM** = compact disc—read only memory

**CGA** = color graphics adapter; the original standard for IBM PC'S

**CGA MONITOR** = early color monitor

**CHIP** = array of millions of transistors on a small silicon wafer

**CISC** = complex instruction set computing; type of CPU that can process lots of instructions (see RISC)

**CIX** = Commercial Internet Exchange

**CLIENT** = computer that uses the services of another computer

**CLIENT/SERVER** = network of client PC'S connected to a bigger central computer or server that handles storage and data sharing

**CLONE** = almost identical copy of an IBM PC

**CMIIW** = correct me if I'm wrong

**CMOS** = complementary metal-oxide semiconductor; circuit that consumes very little power; "see-moss"

**COBOL** = common business oriented language for programming computers

**CODASYL** = Conference of Data Systems Languages

**CODEC ALGORITHM** = compression-decompression of video for PC'S

**COM** = serial interface identifier or port for accessories, as COM2

**.COM** = small, simple executable file (file extension)

**COMDEX** = Computer Dealers Exposition

**CON** = console; the keyboard and monitor

**COSMIC** = Computer Software Management and Information Center (NASA)

**CPS** = characters per second

**CPU** = central processing unit; the microprocessor, or computer's brain

**CRASH** = any major system failure
          = head assembly bears down on media that carries PC'S data, rendering it useless

**CRT** = cathode ray tube; the computer screen

**CRYPTO** = cryptography; encoding and decoding messages

**CSMA/CD** = carrier sense multiple access/collision detect; Ethernet network protocol for transferring information to the server.

**CTI** = computer telephone integration; also TAPI

**CUA** = common user access; IBM guidelines for computer programs

**CUL** = see you later

**CYBER** = cyberspace

**CYBERSPACE** = where the Internet resides, among other things

**D:** = D-drive; artificial partitioning of the hard drive
     = second hard drive
     = CD drive

**D-A** = digital to analog

**DAC** = digital-to-analog converter

**DARPA** = Defense Advanced Research Projects Administration (DOD)

**DAT** = digital audio tape; used for large backups

**DAUGHTERBOARD** = optional circuit board that connects to the MOTHERBOARD

**DB** = database; organized flat files; also DBASE

**DBASE** = database; trade name of early industry leader

**DBMS** = database management system

**DCE** = Data Communication Equipment

**DD** = double-density, disk or diskette

**DDE** = dynamic data exchange; links two application programs to share data

**DDS** = digital data storage

      = Dataphone Digital Service; first private digital line service

**DEC** = Digital Equipment Corporation

**DEFAULT** = predetermined function unless otherwise specified

**DES** = Data Encryption Standard; an NSA code, considered unbreakable

**DINGBAT** = asterisk

**DIP** = dual in-line package

**DIP SWITCH** = dual in-line package switch

              = manual switch for various ports

**DISK** = usually the hard disk inside a PC

      = compact disk or CD

**DISKETTE** = usually the 3.5-inch flexible information disk encased in hard plastic; see FLOPPY and HARD DISC

**.DLL** = dynamic link library file containing routines common to other files (file extension)

**DMA** = direct memory access

**.DOC** = document file (file extension)

**DOMAIN** = network

**DOMAIN NAME SERVER** = computer linking a network to the Internet

**DOS** = disc operating system; program that operates a PC

**DOT** = period

**DOWNLOAD** = transfer a program into a computer usually via modem

**DPI** = dots per inch
**DRAM** = dynamic random-access memory
**DRIVER** = PC program that runs or drives an accessory such as a printer
**DS/DD** = double-sided double-density, disk or diskette
**DSP** = digital signal processing
**DTE** = data terminal equipment interface
**DTP** = desk-top publishing
**DTR** = data terminal ready; computer signal to a modem that it's ready to receive information
**DUAL BOOT** = PC that boots offering choice of two operating systems
**DVD** = digital video disk
**DVP** = digital video producer; video-editing software
**DWIM** = do what I mean (not what I say)

**EBCDIC** = extended binary-coded decimal interchange code, like ASCII
**EDI** = electronic data interchange, via modem
**EDO** = extended data out; RAM chip that boosts performance
**EEPROM** = electronically erasable programmable read-only memory
**EGA** = enhanced graphics adapter, once used on IBM PC'S
**EGA MONITOR** = color monitor employing enhanced graphics adapter
**EIDE** = enhanced IDE
**EISA** = Enhanced Industry Standard Architecture; proposed standard for IBM compatible computers; "ee-sa"
**EISA BUS** = transfers information two to four times as fast as an ISA BUS
**E-MAIL** = electronic mail or messages sent between PC'S
**EMB** = extended memory block
**EMBED** = include something into a file or program
**EMF** = electromagnetic field

**EMF/ELF METER** = electromagnetic field/extreme low frequency meter; gauges level of radiation from video terminals, fans, power lines

**EMM** = expanded memory manager

**EMS** = expanded memory specification

**EOF** = end of file

**EOL** = end of line

**EPP** = enhanced parallel port

**EPROM** = erasable programmable read-only memory

**ESD** = electrostatic discharge

**ESDI** = enhanced small device interface; interface standard for hard disks

**ESRB** = Entertainment Software Ratings Board; ratings board for video games

**ETHERNET** = LAN network using radio signals over coaxial cables

= cable that connects PC'S in a network

**.EXE** = program files that run programs (file extension)

**EXPANSION CARD** = add-on circuit board that expands PC functions

**FAT** = file allocation table; a hidden table containing the location of files on a hard disk

**FATBITS** = pixels magnified on the screen

**FAX** = facsimile transmittal by telephone line

**FAX-MODEM** = FAX capability in a PC

**FDC** = floppy disk controller

**FED** = field emitter display

**FFT** = fast Fourier transform; math function used in image processing

**FITB** = fill in the blank

**FLOPS** = floating point operations per second

**FLOPPY** = 5.25" or 3.5" flexible plastic information disk

**FORTRAN** = formula translator; algebraic language for computers

**FPD** = flat-panel display, such as LCD

**FREENET** = free online system

**FTP** = file-transfer protocol; method of transferring files between two computers

**F2F** = face to face

**FUD** = fear, uncertainty and dread

**FYA** = for your amusement

**FYI** = for your information

**GATEWAY** = computer that connects one network to another

**GIF** = graphics interchange format

**.GIF** = compressed graphics files (file extension)

**GIGA** = billion

**GIGABIT** = billion bits

**GIGABYTE** = billion bytes

**GIGAFLOPS** = billion floating point operations per second

**GIGO** = garbage in, garbage out

**GOPHER** = retrieval tool for access to Internet data

**GPF** = general protection fault; warning that access to protected section of memory has been denied

**GUI** = graphical user interface; picture or icon commands instead of words; "gooey"

**HACK** = to break into a program and change it

**HACKER** = computer trespasser or burglar, usually via networks

**HANDSHAKE** = acknowledgment by two computers that they're ready to exchange information

**HARD DISK** = permanent hard-plastic information disk inside a PC

**HARD DRIVE** = operates the HARD DISC or disks; usually C-drive
**HD** = high density
**HDCD** = high-density compact disk
**HFS** = hierarchical file system
**HHOK** = ha ha, only kidding
**HIMEM** = high memory
**HMA** = high memory area
**HOTKEY** = key that allows switching between programs
**HOYEW** = hanging on your every word
**HTML** = hypertext markup language; programming language for WEB documents
**HTTP** = hypertext transfer protocol; enables WEB users to access and display documents
**HYPERLINK** = icon link between documents on WWW
**HYPERMEDIA** = like hypertext with video, music and animation
**HYPERTEXT** = text that includes codes that allow for retrieval of additional information

**IAC** = in any case
**ICMP** = Internet control message protocol
**ICON** = picture representing a function or a program
**IDE** = integrated drive electronics, for controlling hard disks
**IKWUM** = I know what you mean
**IMHO** = in my humble opinion
**IMNSHO** = in my not-so-humble opinion
**INTERNET** = worldwide computer network of universities, government facilities and individuals; 35 million PC's in 43,000 networks in 81 countries linked informally by telephone lines using a shared computer language
**INTERNIC** = Internet Network Information Center
**I/O** = input/output

_Buzzwords from Cyberspace_

**I/O ADDRESS** = input/output address allocated to each of a PC's devices
**IOW** = in other words
**IP** = Internet protocol
**IPX/SPX:** = Internet packet exchange/sequenced packet exchange; network protocol that allows PC's talk to one another; used in Novell NetWare environments
**IRC** = internet relay chat; real-time conversations on an open line which others can monitor; like an old-fashioned telephone party line
**IRQ** = interrupt request, by components for service from the CPU
**IS** = information systems
**ISA** = Industry Standard Architecture, based on the original IBM PC; "eye-sa"
**ISA BUS** = older but inexpensive technology (see EISA BUS)
**ISA/VESA** = ISA/Video Electronics Standards Association
**ISAM** = indexed sequential access method; technique for storing data
**ISDN** = Integrated Services Digital Network; digital phone line for faster connections between PC's, as for video conferences
**ISO** = International Organization for Standardization (for some strange reason not IOS)
**ITU** = International Telecommunications Union

**JMSC** = Japan MIDI Standards Committee
**.JPG** = picture files (file extension)

**KB** = kilobyte; one thousand bytes (actually 1,024)
**KWIM?** = Know what I mean?

**LAN** = local-area network; network of computers in a limited area such as one office building; see WAN

**LAPTOP** = small portable PC

**LCD** = liquid crystal display

**LED** = light-emitting diode

**LOL** = laughing out loud

**LPT** = parallel interface identifier; line printer

**M1** = super-fast CPU, like the PENTIUM

**MAC** = MACINTOSH

**MACTCP** = Macintosh TCP/IP

**MACRO** = group of keystrokes for repeating tasks

**MAU** = multi-port access unit; connection point between a PC and a file server in a Token-Ring environment

**MB** = megabytes; million bytes of memory (actually 1,048,576 bytes)

**MCA** = Micro Channel Architecture; a standard created by IBM for PC'S

**MCGA** = monochrome/color graphics adapter

**MDA** = monochrome display adapter

**MDA MONITOR** = one-color monitor such as yellow on a black screen

**MDSP** = microwave DSP

**MEG** = million bytes of memory

**MEGA** = million

**MENU-DRIVEN** = programs that can be started by highlighting them from a list or menu

**MHZ** = megahertz; one million cycles per second

**.MID** = musical files (file extension)

**MIDI** = musical instrument digital interface; allows computer communication with musical instruments

**MIMD** = multiple-instruction multiple-data stream computers; "mimdee"

**MIME** = multipurpose Internet mail extensions
**MIPS** = million instructions per second
**MMA** = MIDI Manufacturers Association
**MODEM** = modulator/demodulator; telephone-line connection for a PC
**MOTHERBOARD** = computer's main circuit board
**MOUSE** = hand-held pointing device
**MPC** = multimedia PC
**MPEG** = Motion Picture Experts Group; compression video
**.MPG** = movie files (file extension)
**MPS** = megabits per second
**MTBF** = mean time between failure; average life of a device
**MUD** = multi-user dungeon; a surrealistic place in computer games
**MULTITASKING** = running more than one computer program at a time
**MULTITHREADING** = group of concurrent instructions
**MULTIMEDIA SYSTEM** = computer presentation that includes sound, video, graphics and animation

**NCSA** = National Center for Supercomputing Applications
= National Computer Security Association
**NEI** = not elsewhere included
**NERSC** = National Energy Research Supercomputer Center
**NET** = INTERNET
**NETBIOS** = network basic input-output system
**NETBEUI** = netbios enhanced user interface; "net-buoy"
**NETCRUISE** = browse the Internet, usually via WWW; also "SURF"
**NETIQUETTE** = informal Internet rules
**NETSURF** = browse the Internet, usually via WWW; also "SURF"
**NETWORK** = two or more PC'S connected by phone lines via modem or cable

251

**NEWBIE** = new Internet user

**NEWSGROUP** = discussion forum on Internet's USENET

**NIC** = network interface card; assists in connecting PC'S and file servers to the network

**NII** = National Information Infrastructure; the Information Superhighway

**NIMH** = nickel metal-hydride battery

**NLQ** = near-letter quality

**NMI** = non-maskable interrupt

**NNTP** = network news transfer protocol

**NOP** = not operating properly

**NOS** = network operating system

**NOTEBOOK COMPUTER** = portable note-book-size PC; also laptop

**NREN** = National Research and Education Network

**NTN** = Nationwide Trivia Network

**OCR** = optical character recognition
= optical character reader

**ODBC** = open database connectivity

**OIC** = oh, I see!

**OLE** = object linking and embedding; inserting into documents, graphics or sound that stay linked so a change in one changes all

**OLTP** = online transaction processing

**ONLINE** = connected to a computer, as a printer
= connected to the Internet via an access provider

**ONLINE SERVICES** = commercial bulletin board systems: *America Online, CumpuServe, Prodigy*, etc.

**OOBE** = out-of-box experience; setting-up new equipment

**OOP** = object-oriented programming

**OS** = operating system

**OS/2** = IBM operating system for PC'S that uses a GUI with networking capabilities

**OSF** = Open Software Foundation
**OSI** = open systems interconnect
**OTOH** = on the other hand

**P6** = ultra-fast CPU; twice as fast as the PENTIUM chip
**PACKET** = basic unit of network data transmission; messages broken down into sending packets
**PARALLEL** = simultaneous function; see SERIAL
**PCI** = processor connection interface
**PCL** = printer control language; used to control specific printers
**PC/MCIA** = Personal Computer Memory Card International Association; sets standards for credit-card-size circuit boards or PC/MCIA cards
**.PCX** = Windows Paintbrush files (file extension)
**PDA** = personal digital assistant
**PDL** = page description language; codes for the printer
**PEER-TO-PEER** = network where all PC'S are equal and have equal access
**PEN-BASED COMPUTER** = accepts handwritten information from a special pen or stylus
**PENTIUM** = super-fast CPU
**PERSONAL HOMEPAGE** = WEB SITE set up by a single user
**PGP** = Pretty Good Privacy; freeware cryptography program
**PIF** = program information file
**PIM** = personal information manager
**.PIX** = graphics files (file extension)
**PIXEL** = picture element; the dot that forms the picture on the screen
**PLUG-AND-PLAY** = components that can be plugged into a PC and used without special programming
**PMMU** = paged memory management unit; chip enabling use of virtual memory

**PNCAH** = please, no cussing allowed here
**POINT-AND-CLICK** = PC with a mouse, tracking ball or track pad that lets you point an arrow at an item and select it by clicking
**PORT** = slot for adding peripheral hardware to a PC, like modems or printers
**POSIX** = Portable Operating System Interface for Unix
**POST** = power-on self test; tests of computer components and installed memory when on-switch is activated
**PPP** = point-to-point protocol; modem access to WEB via WEB BROWSERS
**PRE-EMPTIVE MULTITASKING** = allows computer to prioritize CPU use for maximum efficiency
**PROLOG** = programming in logic; programming language
**PROM** = programmable read-only memory
**PROTOCOL** = set of rules governing etiquette or methods of operation
**PTMM** = please tell me more

**QIC** = quarter-inch cassette used by tape backup drives
**.QTW** = movie files in Quick Time for Windows (file extension)

**RAW** = read after write
**RDBMS** = relational database management system
**RDOS** = real-time disk operating system
**README** = last-minute news that can be read by accessing the file
**RGB** = red, green and blue; early color monitor
**RING** = network where PC'S are connected in a circle
**RIP** = raster image processor; minicomputer in a printer
= routing information protocol; dynamic table used to determine which path to take to move data in TCP/IP environment

**RISC** = reduced instruction set computing; a type of CPU that can use and process limited instructions very quickly (see CISC)

**.RLE** = picture files (file extension)

**ROM** = read only memory; cannot be recorded upon

**ROTFL** = rolling on the floor laughing

**RSAC** = Recreational Software Advisory Council; ratings board for computer games (see ESRB)

**RLE** = run-length encoding

**ROUTER** = stores and sends data between LAN'S and WAN'S

**SAA** = systems application architecture; IBM guidelines for computers

**SCROLL** = continuous flow of information up or down the screen

**SCSI** = small computer system interface, for connecting computers to external devices such as a CD-ROM or printer; "scuzzy"

**SERIAL** = one function after another or one at a time; see PARALLEL

**SGML** = standard general markup language, for preparing documents for translation to print or CD

**SHAREWARE** = copyrighted program distributed free, but usually requiring payment for the instruction manual or a permanent license

**SHELL** = menu that lists programs to access by highlighting

**SIG** = special interest group

**SIMD** = single-instruction multiple-data stream computers; "simdee"

**SIMM** = single in-line memory module; circuit board holding memory chips

**SIP** = single in-line processor; type of memory expansion card

**SLN** = Science Learning Network

**SMTP** = simple mail transfer protocol; how E-mail gets delivered

**SNMP** = simple network management protocol

**SOFTWARE** = computer program, as distinguished from computer hardware

**SPA** = Software Publishers Association

**SPAM** = garbage or junk information

**SPLAT** = asterisk

**SPREADSHEET** = program made up of columns and rows

**SQL** = structured query language; database access language

**STAR** = network where PC'S are connected via a central PC or hub

**STYLUS** = special electronic pen for transmitting handwritten information to a pen-based computer

**SUPERSCALAR** = technology that allows CPU's to move data through two parallel pipelines

**SURF THE INTERNET** = browse the Internet

**SURGE** = uneven flow of electricity that could damage a computer

**SVGA** = super video graphics array

**SVGA MONITOR** = monitor with superior color characteristics and resolution

**SWG** = survey working group

**SYS** = system

**SYSOP** = system operator; the supervisor of a bulletin board

**SYSTEM 7** = Macintosh operating system


**TAPI** = telephony application programming interface; also CTI

**TCP** = tape carrier package
    = transmission control protocol

**TCP/IP** = transmission control protocol/Internet protocol; protocol (or language) used to connect PC'S and networks to the Internet

**TELEPHONY** = use of the modem as an answering machine or speaker phone

**TELNET** = ability to log into a remote computer and run it

**TERA** = trillion

**TERAFLOPS** = trillion floating point operations per second

**TFT** = thin-film transistor

**TFT-LCD** = thin film transistor liquid crystal display

**THREAD** = sequence of related instructions or messages

**TIA** = thanks in advance

**TIC** = tongue in cheek

**TIFF** = tagged image file format, of high-resolution dot images

**TNTL** = trying not to laugh

**TNX** = thanks

**TOKEN RING** = ring network that requires receipt of a "token" before a computer can "speak"

**TOPOLOGY** = how PC'S are connected, such as BUS, STAR or RING

**TRACKBALL** = sphere that controls a computer the way a mouse does

**TSR** = terminate-and-stay-resident program; designed to remain in memory after termination so it can be used again

**TT** = TrueType font

**TTFN** = ta ta for now; also BBFN

**TTKSF** = trying to keep a straight face

**TTY** = teletype

**TWAIN** = user interface for input devices like scanners

**.TXT** = text file containing only ASCII characters (file extension)

**TYVM** = thank you very much

**UAE** = unrecoverable application error; now GPF
**UART** = universal asynchronous reverse transmitter, for serial I/O
**UMA** = upper memory area
**UMB** = upper memory block
**UNC** = Universal Naming Convention
**UNIX** = operating system used on PC'S and mainframes
**UPS** = uninterruptible power supply; automatic backup power
**URL** = uniform resource locator of Internet addresses
**USENET** = network of Internet discussion groups; NEWSGROUPS
**USERID** = user identification
**USR** = user
**UTP** = unshielded twisted pair; cable used to attach PC to network
**UUENCODE/DECODE** = encrypts binary files as text in mail messages

**V.32** = modem
**V.32bis** = faster modem
**VDISK** = virtual disk; section of RAM set up as disk drive
**VDU** = visual display unit; the screen
**VESA** = Video Electronics Standards Association; standard for high-resolution video devices like monitors
**VESA DPMS** = VESA display power management system
**VGA** = video graphics array
**VGA MONITOR** = enhanced EGA color monitor (see SVGA)
**VIRUS** = self-starting, self-replicating program designed to erase data or merely display a harmless but unwanted message
**VL-BUS** = VESA local bus
**VLSI** = very large scale integration, of semiconductor chips to accommodate lots of transistors

.VOC = sound files (file extension)
**VRAM** = video RAM; faster than DRAM
**VRML** = virtual reality modeling language
**VRRV** = virtual reality roving vehicle

**WAIS** = wide area information servers; document search system; "waze"
**WAN** = wide-area network, of PC's connected by modem
.WAV = sound files (file extension)
**WDC** = Winchester disk controller; hard drive controller
**WEB** = WorldWide Web (see WWW)
**WEB BROWSER** = software for using the WWW and INTERNET, like *Mosaic* or *Netscape*
**WEB PAGE** = WWW site where specific information is located
**WEB SITE** = location of information and menu
**WEB SPEAK** = computer terms used on the WWW
**WIN** = *Windows*; PC operating system
**WINCHESTER DISK**: hard drive
**WORM** = write once, read many
**WP** = Word Perfect word processor
**WRT** = with respect to
**WTGP?** = want to go private?
**WWW** = WorldWide Web; graphical way to access or surf the internet
**WYSIWYG** = what you see is what you get; printer prints what's on screen; "wizzy-wig"

**XA** = extended architecture, for CD-ROM drives
**XENIX** = version of Unix operating system for PC's
**XMS** = extended memory specification
**XT** = Extended Technology, as in IBM XT; first IBM PC with a built-in hard disk

**YIU** = yes, I understand
**YIWGP** = yes, I will go private

**ZIF** = zero insertion force; a type of socket
**ZIP** = compressed file or type of compression
**.ZIP** = compressed files (file extension)

# *MEDICAL MUMBO JUMBO*

**A** = blood type; 40 % of the population (see AB, B and O)
**AAGP** = American Academy of General Practice
**AAD** = American Academy of Dermatologists
**A&D** = ointment; anhydrous lanolin, for irritated skin
**AAO** = American Academy of Ophthalmology
**AAP** = American Academy of Pediatrics
**AB** = blood type; 5 % of the population (see A, B and O)
**ABC** = airway, breathing and circulation; major components of CPR
**ABG** = arterial blood gas
**AC** = adrenal cortex; outer layer of the adrenal gland which secretes hormones
  = before meals (Latin: *ante cibum*)
**ACE** = angiotensin converting enzyme inhibitors; for treating high blood pressure and congestive heart failure
**ACLS** = advanced cardiac life support
**ACOG** = American College of Obstetricians and Gynecologists
**ACTH** = adrenocorticotropic hormone; essential to the growth, development and function of the adrenal cortex; chronic deficiency is Addison's disease
**AD** = Alzheimer's disease
**ADD** = attention deficit disorder; also ADHD
**ADH** = antidiuretic hormone; lessens secretion of urine
**ADHD** = attention deficit hyperactive disorder; also ADD
**ADP** = adenosine diphosphate; enzyme produced during muscle contraction
**ADR** = adverse drug reaction
**AEB** = atrial ectopic beat; offbeat beat of the upper heart chambers
**AF** = atrial fibrillation; chaotic beat of the upper heart chambers

261

**AG** = antigen; induces formation of antibodies which eliminate or counteract foreign substances in the body

**AHA** = American Hospital Association

**AIDS** = acquired immune deficiency syndrome; opportunistic infections resulting from HIV infection

**AIH** = artificial insemination by husband

**AIN** = acute interstitial nephritis; inflammation and swelling of the kidneys, usually from drug abuse

**ALL** = acute lymphocytic leukemia; most common in children

**ALS** = amyotrophic lateral sclerosis; Lou Gehrig's disease; progressive degeneration of nerve cells

**AML** = acute myelogenic leukemia; occurs primarily in adults; rapid onset, can be fatal in weeks if untreated

**ANS** = autonomic nervous system; controls involuntary functions

**AOA** = American Optometric Association

**APA** = American Pharmaceutical Association

**APC** = aspirin, phenacetin and caffeine

**ARC** = AIDS-related complex; a pre-AIDS condition not ill enough to be designated as AIDS

**ARDS** = acute respiratory distress syndrome; caused by injury to or infection of the lungs

**ARF** = acute renal failure; failure of one or both kidneys

**ARV** = AIDS-related virus

**AS** = anabolic steroids

**ASLM** = American Society of Law and Medicine

**ASTMH** = American Society of Tropical Medicine and Hygiene

**ASFV** = African swine fever virus

**ASO** = antistreptolysin O; antibody stimulated by infection with various streptococcus organisms

**AST** = aspartate aminotransferase; test for injury of liver or heart

AT = atrial tachycardia; rapid beat of the upper heart chambers

ATA = atmospheres absolute; measure of air pressure

ATL = adult T-cell leukemia

ATLV = adult T-cell leukemia virus

AUA = American Urological Association

AV = atrioventricular; A-V node: gateway to the heart's ventricles

AZT = azidothymidine (now called ZDU) treatment for AIDS as it inhibits replication of HIV


B = blood type; 10 % of the population (see A, AB and O)

BAL = British anti-lewisite; dimercaprol; an antidote in heavy-metal poisoning

B-CELL = part of the immune system; produces antibodies that attack invading agents

BCG = Bacillus Calmette-Guerin; vaccine used as a preventative of human tuberculosis

BID = 2 times a day

BLS = basic life support

BLV = bovine leukemia virus

BMR = basal metabolic rate; energy expended in the morning shortly after arising and 14 hours after the last meal

BP = blood pressure

BPD = bronchopulmonary dysplasia; primarily an infants' disease as a result of the lungs being treated with oxygen or ventilators

BPH = benign prostate hyperplasia (or hypertrophy); enlarged prostate

BSA = body surface area

BSR = basal skin resistance

BUN = blood urea nitrogen; nitrogen in the blood; a rough estimate of kidney function

**BVMD** = bag-valve-mask device; resuscitator bag

**C1-7** = seven cervical vertebrae at the top of the spine
**CAD** = coronary artery disease
**CAT SCAN** = computerized axial tomography scan; see CT SCAN
**CBC** = complete blood count
**C-COLLAR** = cervical collar; collar to immobilize the neck
**CCU** = coronary care unit; heart care
**CD4** = lymphocytes; best single predictors of onset of infections that define AIDS; T-helper cells
**CD8** = T-suppressor cells, call off the attack
**CF** = complement fixation; basis of tests for syphilis and infectious diseases
**CFS** = chronic fatigue syndrome
**CHF** = congestive heart failure
**CID** = combined immunodeficiency
**CL** = chloride; chlorine
**CLL** = chronic lymphocytic leukemia; from defective white blood cells mostly after age 60
**CM** = *chirurgiae magister*; Master in Surgery
   = centimeter
   = tomorrow morning (Latin: *cras mane*)
**CML** = chronic myelogenous leukemia; occurs primarily and insidiously in men 20-60
**CMV** = cytomegalovirus; a usually harmless herpes virus that can be sexually transmitted
**CN** = tomorrow night (Latin: *cras nocte*)
**CNS** = central nervous system
**CO** = cardiac output
   = carbon monoxide
**$CO_2$** = carbon dioxide
**CODE BLUE** = rush to resuscitate

COGTT = cortisone oral glucose tolerance test
COLD = chronic obstructive lung disease
CONTRA = contraindication; not indicated
COPD = chronic obstructive pulmonary disease; lung disease
COU = coronary observation unit (see CCU)
CP = cor pulmonale; heart enlargement due to lung failur
= cerebral palsy; paralysis resulting from defects in the brain
CPK = creatine phosphokinase; levels increase shortly after heart attack
CPR = cardiopulmonary resuscitation; massaging the chest to pump blood through the heart
CRASH = die
CRASH CART = emergency resuscitation equipment
CSD = cat-scratch disease
CSF = cerebrospinal fluid
CT = computerized axial tomography
CTS = carpal tunnel syndrome
CT SCAN = series of X-rays transformed by a computer into a two-dimensional image that resembles an anatomic slice; also CAT SCAN
CV = tomorrow night (Latin: *cras vespere*)
CVA = cerebrovascular accident; stroke
CVL = central venous line; CENTRAL LINE
CVP = central venous pressure
CVS = cardiovascular system
= chorionic villus sampling; early pregnancy test for damaged chromosomes
CWP = coal workers' pneumoconiosis; black lung disease

DAN = Divers Alert Network at Duke University, for sudden decompression
D&C = DILATION and CURETTAGE, usually of the uterus

**DIC** = disseminated intravascular coagulation; overactive blood clotting

**DDI** = dideooxyinosine; for treatment of AIDS infections

**DECON** = decontaminate

**DEFIB** = defibrilation

**DES** = diethylstilbestrol; synthetic estrogen to prevent pregnancy in women who have been raped; also the "morning-after pill"

**DIC** = disseminated intravascular coagulation; diffuse bleeding as well as excess clotting

**DNA** = deoxyribonucleic acid; chemical basis of heredity; the "double-helix" molecule

**DOT** = directly observed therapy

**DRG's** = diagnosis-related groups

**DTP** = diphtheria and tetanus toxoids with pertussis vaccine

**DT** = diphtheria
    = delirium tremens; hallucinations due to excessive alcohol use

**DVT** = deep venous thrombosis; blood clot in a vein

**D/W** = dextrose in water


**EBV** = Epstein-Barr virus
    = herpes-like virus which may be involved in mono and Burkitt's lymphoma

**ECC** = external cardiac compression; external heart massage or CPR

**ECF** = extracellular fluid

**ECG** = electrocardiogram; tracking of electrical impulses of the heart; also EKG

**ECT** = electroconvulsive therapy; shock treatment

**ED** = effective dose

**EDTA** = ethylenediaminetetraacetic acid; anticoagulant

**EEG** = electroencephalogram; tracking of electrical impulses of the brain

EF = ejection fraction: measure of pumping capacity of the heart

EKC = epidemic keratoconjunctivitus; infectious disease caused by an adenovirus; widespread in Japan, rare in US

EKG = electrocardiogram; see ECG

ELISA = enzyme-linked immunosorbent assay; detects antibodies to HIV proteins

EMB = ethambutol; antimicrobial drug used in treatment of TB

EMG = electromyography; diagnoses diseases that affect muscles, nerves and spinal cord

ENT = eye, nose and throat

EPT = early pregnancy test

ERCP = endoscopic retrograde cholangiopancreatography; x-ray visualization used to diagnose stones or tumors in the pancreas and gallbladder

ES = electric shock

ESR = erythrocyte sedimentation rate

EST = electro-shock treatment
= electrical-stimulating treatment


FA= first aid

FACD = Fellow of the American College of Dentists

FACP = Fellow of the American College of Physicians

FACS = Fellow of the American College of Dentists
= fluorescence activated cell sorter

F&R = force and rhythm, of pulse

FAS = fetal alcohol syndrome

FD = fatal dose

FeLV = feline leukemia virus

FEV = forced expirator volume

FR = French (catheter size)

FUO = fever of unknown origin

**G6PD** = glucose-6-phosphate dehydrogenase
**GAS** = general adaptation syndrome; response to stress
**GFR** = glomerular filtration rate
**GI** = gastrointestinal
**GP** = general practitioner
**GRID** = gay-related immunodeficiency disease
**GSW** = gunshot wound
**GU** = genitourinary
**GVHD** = graft-vs-host disease; a major problem in transplants

**HA** = hemagglutination; clumping together of red blood corpuscles
**HAE** = hereditary angioedema; a rare form of hives
**HB** = hemoglobin
    = hepatitus B
**HBO THERAPY** = hyperbaric oxygen therapy; pressure chamber providing 100% oxygen
**HCL** = hydrochloric acid
**HCO$_3$** = bicarbonate
**HCT** = hematocrit; amount of blood cells per total blood volume
**HDL** = high-density lipoproteins; "good cholesterol;" (see LDL)
**HF** = heart failure
**Hg** = mercury
**HGB** = hemoglobin concentration; amount of hemoglobin in a given amount of blood
**HI** = hemagglutination-inhibition
**HIB** = haemophilus influenzae type b; vaccine which prevents serious infant bacterial infection
**HIV** = human immunodeficiency virus
**HIV1** = causes most cases of AIDS
**HIV2** = less virulent form of HIV found in West Africa

HLA = human leukocyte group Λ; a group of tissue antigens
HLA B27 = an antigen which causes unusual reactions to common infections
HN = tonight (Latin: *hoc nocte*)
HPV = human papilloma virus; source of venereal or genital warts
HSV = herpes simplex virus
HTLV = human T-cell leukemia virus
HYPER = hyperactive; abnormally active
HYPO = hypodermic syringe; "needle"

IABP = intra-aortic balloon counterpulsation; assists blood circulation
I&O = intake and output
IBS = irritable bowel syndrome
ICF = intracellular fluid
    = intermediate care facilities
ICU = intensive care unit
IFN = interferon
IGA = immunoglobulin A
IH = infectious hepatitus
IL = interleukin
IM = intramuscular
IND = investigational new drug; a drug undergoing testing
    = indications
INH = Isoniazid; antimicrobial drug used in treatment of TB
IPPB = intermittent positive pressure breathing; assisted breathing
IPPV = intermittent positive pressure ventilation; assisted breathing
IPV = inactivated poliovirus vaccine
IU = international unit, for measuring out vitamins, hormones, enzymes, vaccines, etc.; specific biological quantity that produces a particular biological effect

**IUCD** = intrauterine contraceptive device
**IUD** = intrauterine device; a contraceptive
**IV** = intravenous
**IVDU** = intravenous drug user
**IVF** = in vitro fertilization; extracting an egg from a woman and fertilizing it "in glass," in a laboratory
**IVF BABY** = after IVF, the egg is re-implanted into the womb for natural gestation and birth
**IVP** = intravenous pyelography; contrast x-ray procedure allows looking into kidneys, bladder and ereters
**IV PUSH** = intravenous administration of medicine by quick and forcible injection
**IVU** = intravenous urography

**JRA** = juvenile rheumatoid arthritis

**KS** = Kaposi's sarcoma; skin tumors often associated with AIDS

**L1-5** = five lumbar vertebrae at the base of the spine
**LD** = Lyme disease
**LDH** = lactic dehydrogenase
**LDL** = low-density lipoproteins; "bad cholesterol;" (see HDL)
**LE** = lupus erythematosus
**LLQ** = left lower quadrant, of the abdomen
**LP** = lumbar puncture; tapping spinal fluid for neurological diagnosis
**LUQ** = left upper quadrant of the abdomen
**LVH** = left ventricular hypertrophy; enlargement of the left ventricle of the heart

**MAC** = maximum allowable concentration
**MAST** = medical anti-shock trousers

MBD = minimal brain dysfunction
MCH = mean corpuscular hemoglobin
MCHC = mean corpuscular hemoglobin concentration
MCV = mean corpuscular volume
MDR-TB = multiply drug-resistant tuberculosis
MED = minimal erythemal dose; how long it takes sunlight to turn one's skin pink
    = minimum effective dose
MFD = minimum fatal dose
MG = milligram
    = magnesium
MI = myocardial infarction; heart attack
MIC = minimum inhibitory concentration
MLD = minimum lethal dose; smallest quantity capable of producing death
MMR = measles, mumps, rubella vaccine
MONO = mononucleosis
MR = mental retardation
MRI = magnetic resonance imaging; used instead of radiation to examine head, CNS, spine, tumors and various abnormalities
MRSA = methicillin-resistant *Staphylococcus aureus;* staph germ resistant to antibiotics
MRT = mean residence time; average time a drug molecule resides within the body after rapid IV dose
MS = multiple sclerosis
MVA = motor-vehicle accident
MVP = mitral valve prolapse; bulging of one or both mitral heart valves

NAD = no appreciable disease
NIAID = National Institute of Allergy and Infectious Diseases

NICU = neonatal intensive care unit; care of newborns
NP = narcotic poisoning
   = nursing procedure
NPH = neutral-protamine-Hagedorn; intermediate-acting insulin
NSAID = nonsteroidal anti-inflammatory drug; eg, aspirin or ibuprofin

O = blood type; 45 % of the population (see A, AB and B)
OB = obstetrics; pregnancy, childbirth and care of newborns
OCD = obsessive-compulsive disorder
OD = doctor of optometry
ON = orthopedic nurse
ONP = operating nurse procedure
OPC = outpatient clinic
OPD = outpatient department
OPV = oral poliovirus vaccine
OR = operating room
ORT = operating room technician
OT = occupational therapy
OTC = over the counter (pharmaceuticals)
OTD = organ tolerance dose, of particular tissue

P = phosphorus
   = pressure
P&A = percussion and ausculation; thumping the chest and listening to it with a stethoscope
PAP TEST = Papanicolaou smear test for cancer of the cervix or uterus
PATH = pathology
PBI = protein-bound iodine
PC = after eating (Latin: *post cibum*)
PCK = polycystic kidney disease; cysts in the kidneys

**PCP** = pneumocystis carinii pneumonia; rare form usually common in AIDS

**PCR** = polymerase chain reaction; a test for viral nucleic acids

**PD** = doctor of pharmacy

**PDR** = Physicians' Desk Reference

**PE** = pulmonary embolism

**PEL** = permissible exposure limits

**PET** = positron emission tomography (see PETT)

**PETT** = positron emission transaxial tomography; similar to CT scanning

**PH** = hydrogen-ion concentration

**PHYS** = physiology

**PID** = pelvic inflammatory disease

**PKU** = phenylketoneuria; hereditary disease which can result in brain damage

**PMN** = polymorphonuclear leukocyte

**PMS** = premenstrual syndrome; premenstrual tension

**PO** = orally

**POLIO** = poliomyelitis

**POSSUM** = patient operated selector mechanism; permits the disabled to operate telephons and typewriters by breathing on controls

**POST-OP** = postoperative

**POTTS FRACTURE** = fracture of the lower part of the leg so foot is displaced

**PPD** = purified protein derivative; tuberculin; used to determine the presence of tuberculosis

**PPH** = primary pulmonary hypertension

**PPM** = parts per million

**PPNG** = penicillinase producing neisseria gonorrhea; strain of gonorrhea resistant to penicillin

**PPO** = Preferred Provider Organization

**PREEMIE** = premature baby

**PRF** = pulse recurrence frequency

**PRN** = as needed (Latin: *pro re nata*)
**PROG** = prognosis
**PROMED** = Program for Monitoring Emerging Diseases
**PSA** = prostate specific antigen; blood test for presence of antigens that could indicate prostate cancer
**PSP** = phenolsulfonphthalein; used to test kidney function
**PSRO** = Professional Standards Review Organization
**PSS** = progressive systemic scleroderma; thickening of the skin
**PT** = prothrombin time; a test of clotting time
**PTA** = percutaneous transluminal angioplasty; dilating or widening a diseased artery by inserting a plastic balloon
**PZA** = pyrazinamide; antimicrobial drug used in treatment of TB

**Q** = every
**Q4H** = every 4 hours
**QID** = 4 times a day
**QRS COMPLEX** = Q,R and S waves of an ECG
**QRST COMPLEX** = Q, R, S and T waves of an ECG
**QS** = as much as needed (Latin: *quantum sufficiat*)

**RA** = rheumatoid arthritis
**RAST** = radioallergosorbent test; for allergies
**RBC** = red blood cell
= red blood count
**RDS** = respiratory distress syndrome, usually in newborns
**RES** = reticuloendothelial system; defense cells that eliminate worn-out cells, invading agents and that repair tissue
**RF** = rheumatoid fever
= rheumatoid factor; helpful in diagnosing rheumatoid arthritis
**RH** = Rhesus factor in blood; serious complications can occur if Rh-negative mother conceives an Rh-positive baby

**RICE** = rest, ice, compression, elevation; treatment for athletic injuries

**RIG** = rabies immune globulin, for treatment of rabies

**RK** = radial keratotomy; incisions in the cornea of the eye

**RLQ** = right lower quadrant, of the abdomen

**RMP** = rifampin; antimicrobial drug used in treatment of TB

**RNA** = ribonucleic acid

**RPI** = Retinitis Pigmentosa International

**RQ** = respiratory quotient

**RU-486** = French abortion pill

**RUQ** = right upper quadrant, of the abdomen

**RVH** = right ventricular hypertrophy; enlargement of the right ventricle of the heart

**SAD** = seasonal affected disorder

**SAIDS** = simian AIDS

**SAO$_2$** = arterial oxygen saturation

**SBE** = subacute bacterial endocarditis; strep infection of the lining membrane of the heart

**SC** = subcutaneously; under the skin

**SCCM** = Society of Critical Care Medicine

**SCD** = sudden cardiac death

**SD** = sudden death

**SEM** = scanning electron microscope

**SIADH** = syndrome of inappropriate ADH secretion

**SLE** = systemic lupus erythematosus; lupus; a chronic and usually fatal systemic disease

**SM** = streptomycin; anti microbial drug used in treatment of TB

**SNF** = skilled nursing facilities

**SOLN** = solution

**SOS** = if necessary (Latin: *si opus sit*)

**SPECT** = single photon emission computed tomography
**STAPH** = STAPHYLOCOCCI bacteria
**STAT** = immediately (Latin: *statim*)
**STD** = sexually transmitted disease
    = skin test dose
**STP** = standard temperature and pressure
**STPD** = standard temperature and pressure dry
**STREP** = STREPTOCOCCI bacteria
**STS** = serologic test for syphilis
**SYM** = symptoms

**T** = temperature
**T1-12** = twelve thoracic vertebrae
**TAT** = tetanus antitoxin
**TB** = tuberculosis
**TBW** = total body water
**TC** = total cholesterol
**T-CELL** = from the thymus; part of the immune system; identifies invading agents and signals immune system to take defensive action (see B-CELL)
**TCR** = T-CELL receptor
**TENS** = transcutaneous electrical nerve stimulator; used to relieve pain by electrical impulse
**TIA** = transient ischemic attack; temporary interference of blood flow to the brain
**TID** = three times a day
**TMJ** = temperomandibular joint disorder; mis-aligned bite
**TNM** = tumor, nodes, metastases; method of classifying cancer
**TOPV** = trivalent oral polio vaccine
**TPA** = tissue plasminogen activator; expensive new bio-engineered drug that dissolves blood clots that cause heart attacks
**TPR** = temperature, pulse, respiration
**TRUS** = trans-rectal ultrasound

TSH = thyroid-stimulating hormone
TSLS = toxic shock-like syndrome
TSS = toxic shock syndrome
TT = transit time, of blood through heart and lungs

UAO = upper airway obstruction
URI = upper respiratory infection
US = ultrasonography; ultrasound
USP = United States Pharmacopoeia
UTI = urinary tract infection
UV = ultraviolet
UVA = ultraviolet rays that can pass through glass and penetrate deeply into the skin, aging it
UVB = ultraviolet rays that cause sunburn and skin cancer but cannot pass through glass

VD = venereal disease
VDH = valvular disease of the heart
VDRL = Venereal Disease Research Laboratory
VEB = ventricular ectopic beats; offbeat beat of the lower heart chambers
VH = viral hepatitis
VITALS = vital signs: breathing, pulse, blood pressure and temperature
VLDL = very low density lipoproteins
VNA = Visiting Nurses Association
VPC = ventricular premature complex; possible warning sign of heart disease
VT = ventricular tachycardia; rapid beat of the lower heart chambers

WAS = Wiskott-Aldrich Syndrome; a disorder of male infants characterized by eczema and recurrent infection

**WBC** = white blood cell
        = whole blood count
**WMA** = World Medical Association

**Z**= contraction (German: *zeckung*)
**ZDU** = zidovudine; formerly AZT; treatment for AIDS
that inhibits replication of HIV
**ZYG POINT** = zygomaxillary point; a point on the face
**ZZZ** = increasing contractions

## SOME COMMON MEDICAL TERMS

**ABSCESS** = buildup of pus
**ACIDOSIS** = too much acid
**ALIMENTARY** = of the digestive tract, from mouth to
anus
**ALZHEIMER'S DISEASE** = senile dementia; disorien-
tation, loss of memory and physical coordination
**AMENORRHEA** = failure to menstruate
**AMNIOCENTESIS** = analysis of the fluid around the
fetus to determine sex and possible disorders
**AMPHETAMINE** = drug that stimulates the CNS
**AMYL NITRATE** = a drug used to relax blood vessels
especially for angina; sexual stimulant called "poppers"
**ANABOLIC STEROIDS** = synthetic derivatives of
testosterone that enhance muscle bulk and strength
often with erratic mood swings; see STEROID RAGE
**ANAEROBIC BACTERIA** = able to live without air
**ANALEPTIC** = drug used to stimulate CNS especially
after barbiturate overdose
**ANALGESIC** = pain killer

**ANEURISM** = bulge in a vein or artery

**ANGINA** = intense chest pain usually the result of oxygen starvation of the heart (angina pectoris)

**ANGIOCARDIOGRAPHY** = x-ray examination of arteries, veins and heart

**ANGIOGRAPHY** = x-ray examination of blood vessels

**ANGIOPLASTY** = plastic surgery of blood vessels

= percutaneous transluminal angioplasty or PTA; dilating or widening a diseased artery by inserting a plastic balloon

**ANODYNE** = pain reliever

**ANOREXIA** = loss of appetite

**ANOREXIA NERVOSA** = loss of appetite as a symptom of mental illness

**ANOXIA** = oxygen deficiency

**ANTENATAL** = before birth

**ANTEPARTUM** = before onset of labor

**ANTERIOR** = before or in front of

**ANTIBIOTIC** = medicine for bacterial infections

**ANTIBODY** = attaches itself to an antigen and renders it harmless

**ANTICOAGULANT** = drug that prevents blood from clotting

**ANTIDOTE** = neutralizes poisons or their effects

**ANTIGEN** = substance in the body or introduced into the body which causes antibodies to form

**ANTIHISTAMINE** = drug for allergies

**ANTIHYPERTENSIVE** = drug that lowers blood pressure

**ANTIPYRETIC** = drug that lowers fever

**ANTITOXIN** = antibody capable of neutralizing a specific toxin or poison; an antidote

**ANTITUSSIVE** = drug that treats cough

**ANURIA** = failure of kidney function, urination

**AORTIC** = of the body's main artery

**APHASIA** = loss of ability to speak or understand due to brain damage

**APNEA** = absence of breathing

**APOPLEXY** = sudden loss of consciousness; shock or stroke

**AREFLEXIA** = absence of reflexes

**ARRHYTHMIA** = irregular heartbeat

**ARTERIOSCLEROSIS** = hardening of the arteries

**ARTERY** = blood vessel that carries oxygen-bearing blood away from the heart to the body

**ASCITES** = fluid in the abdominal cavity

**ASPHYXIA** = decrease in oxygen, increase in carbon dioxide in the body due to interference with breathing

**ASPIRATION** = removal of fluids by suction or siphoning

**ATAXIA** = irregularity; lack of muscular coordination

**ATHEROSCLEROSIS** = hardening of the arteries plus plaque inside

**ATRIAL** = of the upper chambers of the heart

**ATRIAL FIBRILLATION** = chaotic twitching of the upper heart chambers

**ATRIAL FLUTTER** = extremely rapid contractions of the upper heart chambers

**ATROPHY** = wasting away

**ATTENDING** = attending physician or surgeon, serving on staff in a teaching hospital

**AUSCULTATION** = listening for sounds with a stethoscope, especially from the chest and abdomen

**AUTOIMMUNE DISEASE** = the body tries to destroy some of its own tissue

**AUTONOMIC NERVOUS SYSTEM** = controls involuntary bodily functions such as glands and heart

**AXILLARY** = of the armpit

**BACTERIAL INFECTION** = can usually be treated with antibiotics

**BARBITURATE** = sedative

**BASAL CELL CARCINOMA** = cancer on the surface of the skin with low incidence of malignancy

**BELL'S PALSY** = paralysis of the face muscles

**BENIGN** = harmless

**BETA BLOCKER** = drug for anxiety or hypertension

**BEZOAR** = hard mass in the stomach or intestine, like a hair ball

**BIOPSY** = examination of a small tissue sample, usually for cancer

**BLASTOMYCOSIS** = fungous disease usually affecting the lungs

**BLOOD COUNT** = number of red and white cells

**BLOOD GASES** = the amount of oxygen, carbon dioxide and acidity in the blood

**BLOOD PLASMA** = the liquid part

**BLOOD SERUM** = the liquid left after blood clots

**BOUCHUT'S TUBE** = used for intubation

**BOUGIE** = for exploring and dilating canals like the male urethra

**BOUTONNIERE** = buttonhole-like opening in a membrane

**BREECH DELIVERY** = feet or butt first instead of head first

**BRONCHITIS** = inflammation of the bronchial tubes of the lungs

**BRONCHOSCOPY** = visual examination of the larynx and bronchial tubes

**BULIMIA** = overeating and vomiting

**BURKITT'S LYMPHOMA** = cancer of the lymph system

**BURSITIS** = inflammation of the joints; tennis elbow or housemaid's knee

**CANDIDA ALBICANS** = fungus; called thrush when in the mouth or vagina

**CANDIDIASIS** = yeast infection

**CARCINOGEN** = substance capable of causing cancer

**CARCINOMA** = cancer of the glands, skin and mucous membranes

**CARDIAC** = of the heart

**CARDIAC ARREST** = stopping of the heart

**CARDIOLOGIST** = heart specialist

**CARDIOPULMONARY** = of the heart and lungs

**CARDIOVASCULAR** = of the heart and blood vessels

**CARDIOVERTER** = electrical device for administering shocks to the heart

**CARDITIS** = inflammation of the heart

**CAROTID ARTERIES** = on either side of the neck which deliver blood to the head (see JUGULAR VEINS)

**CATHARTIC** = a substance that stimulates the bowels to evacuate

**CATHETER** = small flexible tube for evacuating or injecting fluids

**CATHETERIZATION** = insertion of a small flexible tube into the body

**CAUTERIZATION** = burning away tissue with electricity or chemicals

**CENTESIS** = puncture of a cavity

**CENTRAL LINE** = central venous line; a catheter through the chest into the principle vein emptying into the heart, for drawing blood or introducing medicine or nutrition

**CEREBELLUM** = movement-coordinating part of the brain

**CEREBRAL** = of the brain

**CEREBRAL CORTEX** = outer surface of the brain

**CEREBRUM** = largest part of the brain encompassing both sides and the cortex

**CERVICAL** = of the neck

**CERVIX** = neck-like part of the uterus

**CESAREAN SECTION** = surgical delivery of a baby through the abdomen

**CHANCRE** = ulcerated sore; first sign of syphilis

**CHEMO** = chemotherapy; use of chemicals to treat disease

**CHOLECYSTITIS** = inflammation of the gallbladder

**CHOLESTASIS** = impaired bile flow; obstructive jaundice

**CHOREA** = disease of the nervous system characterized by jerky movements; "SAINT VITUS' DANCE"

**CIRRHOSIS** = inflammation and hardening of an organ, as in liver disease

**CLONIC** = alternate contracting and relaxing of muscles

**COCCIDIOIDOMYCOSIS** = St. Joaquin fever; infectious fungous disease of the skin, lymph nodes, spleen, liver, bones, kidneys and brain, associated with AIDS

**COLIC** = pain in the abdomen

**COLITIS** = inflammation of the colon or large intestine

**COLOSTOMY** = surgery to create an artificial anus in the abdomen

**COMA** = abnormal deep stupor from which the patient cannot be aroused by external stimulus

**COMMINUTED FRACTURE** = crushed bone

**COMMUNICABLE** = infectious

**CONCUSSION** = jolt to the brain

**CONGENITAL** = from birth

**CONGESTION** = excessive blood or fluid in an organ or tissue

**CONJUNCTIVITIS** = inflammation of the eyeball

**CONTAGIOUS** = spread by physical contact

**CONTUSION** = bruise

**CONVULSION** = involuntary muscular contractions

**COR** = the heart

**CORONARY** = of the heart artery

**CORONARY THROMBOSIS** = heart attack caused by a blood clot in the heart artery

**COR PULMONALE** = enlargement of part of the heart due to lung failure

**CRANIAL** = of the skull

**CREPITUS** = noise of gas discharged from the intestines

**CROHN'S DISEASE** = inflammation of the lower intestine; ileitis

**CRYPTOCOCCOSIS** = infectious fungous disease of the lung which spreads to the meninges, kidneys, bone and skin; associated with AIDS

**CURETTAGE** = scraping out of tissue from an organ, usually the uterus

**CUTDOWN** = venous cutdown; an incision into the skin to locate a vein

**CYANOSIS** = bluish skin due to oxygen starvation

**CYANOTIC** = affected with CYANOSIS

**CYST** = abnormal sac containing fluid or solid material

**CYSTIC FIBROSIS** = hereditary respiratory disease; a buildup of mucus in the lungs

**CYSTITIS** = bladder infection

**CYSTOSCOPY** = examination of the bladder through the urethra

**DEBRIDEMENT** = removal of foreign material and damaged tissue in a wound or serious burn

**DECONGESTANT** = drug that dries up blocked nasal passages

**DECUB** = *decubitis*; Latin for lying down

**DEFIBRILLATION** = stopping the chaotic twitching of the heart muscles by electric shock or drugs

**DEHYDRATION** = when output of water exceeds intake

**DELIRIUM** = disorientation, usually with hallucinations

**DELIRIUM TREMENS** = hallucinations due to excessive alcohol use

**DEMENTIA** = deterioration of mental faculties

**DEMENTIA PRAECOX** = schizophrenia

**DEMULCENT** = something soothing for mucous membranes: lanolin, olive oil

**DERMATITIS** = inflammation of the skin

**DERMATOPHYTOSIS** = ringworm; fungous infection of hair, scalp and skin, as in athlete's foot

**DETOX** = detoxify; remove poisonous properties of a substance

**DEXTROSE** = simple sugar, highly soluble in water; GLUCOSE

**DIABETES MELLITUS** = too much blood sugar due to lack of INSULIN

**DIALYSIS** = separation of waste products from the blood, as in kidney failure

**DIASTOLIC PRESSURE** = blood pressure reading when the heart relaxes (see SYSTOLIC PRESSURE)

**DICK TEST** = for susceptibility to scarlet fever

**DICUMAROL** = anticoagulant

**DIGITALIS** = drug that increases the force of the heart beat

**DILANTIN** = anti-convulsant drug used especially in epilepsy

**DILATION** = enlargement or expansion

**DIPLOPIA** = double vision

**DIPSOMANIA** = alcohol addiction

**DISSECT** = to separate tissue or parts for study

**DIURESIS** = secretion of abnormal amounts of urine

**DIURETIC** = drug that stimulates the excretion of urine or body fluids

**DIVERTICULITIS** = inflammation in the intestine

**DORSAL** = of the back, as in dorsal vertebrae; also THORACIC

**DOWN'S SYNDROME** = mongolism; may include mental retardation

**DUODENUM** = small intestine below the stomach

**DURA MATTER** = membrane covering the brain and spinal cord

**DYSCHEZIA** = difficulty defecating due to loss of muscle coordination

**DYSCRASIA** = disease, as in blood dyscrasia; blood disease

**DYSLEXIA** = tendency to reverse characters when reading

**DYSMENORRHEA** = painful menstruation or cramps

**DYSPEPSIA** = indigestion

**DYSPHAGIA** = difficulty swallowing

**DYSPNEA** = difficulty breathing

**DYSTROPHY** = wasting

**DYSURIA** = painful urination

**EBOLA FEVER** = deadly hemorrhagic disease caused by newly isolated virus, after a river in Africa near where it first appeared

**ECCHYMOSIS** = bruise-like discoloration of the skin due to blood seepage

**ECHOCARDIOGRAPHY** = diagnosis of the heart with ultrasound

**ECLAMPSIA** = blood poisoning of pregnancy

**E COLI** = *escherichia coli* bacteria present in the alimentary canal; outside, it can cause infections

**ECTOPIC PREGNANCY** = outside the uterus, usually in the Fallopian tubes

**EDEMA** = swelling of tissue from a buildup of fluid

**ELECTROLYTE** = a solution which conducts electricity; acids, bases and salts

**EMBOLISM** = blocking of a blood vessel by a clot, fat globules or air bubbles

**EMBRYO** = unborn baby from second to eighth week (see FETUS)

**EMESIS** = vomiting

**EMETIC** = drug that induces vomiting in treatment for poisoning

**EMPHYSEMA** = respiratory disease causing difficulty in breathing; commonly caused by smoking

**ENCEPHALITIS** = inflammation of the brain

**ENCEPHALOPATHY** = dysfunction of the brain

**ENDOCARDITIS** = inflammation usually of the outer heart membrane (see PERICARDITIS)

**ENDOCRANIAL** = inside the skull

**ENDOMETRIOSIS** = a disease of the uterus

**ENDOSCOPY** = examination of a body cavity with an optical instrument

**ENDOTRACHEAL CUFF** = inflatable tube that provides airway through the trachea and prevents inhalation of foreign material

**ENTERITIS** = inflammation of the intestine

**EPIDEMIC** = infectious disease attacking many people at the same time

**EPIDERMIS** = outer layer of the skin

**EPILEPSY** = disease of the nervous system causing seizures

**EPINEPHRINE** = drug that constricts blood vessels, stimulates the heart and relaxes air passages in the lungs

**EPISIOTOMY** = incision to ease birth

**EPITHELIUM** = layer of cells forming the EPIDERMIS

**EPSTEIN-BARR VIRUS** = herpes-like virus which may be involved in MONO and BURKITT'S LYMPHOMA

**EROTOMANIC** = delusion of being loved by another, usually a celebrity

**ERYTHROCYTE** = red blood cell
**ESTROGEN** = female sex hormones that stimulate periods
**ETIOLOGY** = cause of a disease
**EUTHANASIA** = mercy killing
**EXAM** = examination
**EXCISION** = cutting away or taking out
**EXPECTORANT** = drug that helps remove phlegm from airways

**FACTITIOUS DISORDER** = self-inflicted or feigned illness; MÜNCHHAUSEN SYNDROME
**FEBRILE** = of fever
**FEMORAL** = of the thigh bone or femur
**FEMORAL ARTERY** = artery in the thigh
**FETAL** = of the FETUS
**FETUS** = unborn baby from third month to birth (see EMBRYO)
**FEVER** = body temperature above normal, usually 98.6° F or 37° C
**FIBRILLATION** = chaotic twitching of the heart muscles
**FILOVIRUS** = threadlike virus, such as the EBOLA
**FISTULA** = abnormal tubelike opening
**FLATLINE** = death or suspended animation, from no movement on instruments measuring life signs
**FLEXION** = bending or being bent
**FOLEY CATHETER** = a water balloon keeps it in place in the bladder
**FORCEPS** = various types of pincers
**FORENSIC MEDICINE** = medicine in relation to the law
**FRACTURE** = broken bone
**FURUNCLE** = a boil

**GANGRENE** = dead tissue due to blood starvation

**GAS GANGRENE** = GANGRENE in a wound infected by gas bacillus

**GASTRECTOMY** = removal of all or part of the stomach

**GASTRIC** = of the stomach

**GASTRITIS** = inflammation of the stomach

**GASTROENTERITIS** = inflammation of the stomach and intestines

**GERIATRICS** = diseases of the aged

**GLAUCOMA** = increased pressure within the eyeball that damages the retina and optic nerve

**GLOBUS SENSATION** = lump in the throat

**GLOSSITIS** = inflammation of the tongue

**GLOTTIC** = of the tongue

**GLUCOSE** = DEXTROSE sugar

**GOITER** = enlargement of the thyroid gland

**GOOD SAMARITAN LAW** = protects physicians who give emergency aid against malpractice

**GOUT** = acute arthritis and inflammation of joints in foot or knee caused by excess uric acid deposits

**GRANULOMA** = granular tumor or growth, as in leprosy

**GRAVE'S DISEASE** = overactive thyroid gland

**GRAY MATTER** = gray portions of the CNS including the brain

**GREENSTICK FRACTURE** = part of the bone

**GYNECOLOGY** = study of female diseases

**GYNECOMASTIA** = male breast reduction

**HALITOSIS** = bad breath

**HARE LIP** = vertical cleft in the upper lip

**HEARTBURN** = rising stomach acid causing burning sensation in the chest

**HEAVES** = vomiting

**HEIMLICH MANEUVER** = abdominal thrust; sudden compression of the upper abdomen to expel object blocking airway

**HEMATEMESIS** = vomiting blood

**HEMATOMA** = swelling caused by ruptured blood vessels

**HEMOCCULT TEST** = for hidden blood in stool; used to detect colon cancer

**HEMOLYSIS** = destruction of red blood cells with loss of hemoglobin through the kidneys, making the urine red

**HEMOPHILIA** = hereditary disease in which blood fails to clot

**HEMOPTYSIS** = coughing up blood from the respiratory tract

**HEMORRHAGE** = abnormal bleeding

**HEMORRHOIDS** = varicose veins in the rectum; "piles"

**HEMOSTAT** = clamp for a blood vessel

**HEPARIN** = anticoagulant to prevent blood clots

**HEPATIC** = of the liver

**HEPATITIS** = inflammation of the liver caused by viruses, alcohol, drugs, bacteria, funguses or parasites

**HEPATITIS A** = caused by a virus usually spread by contaminated food; a less serious form resolved without treatment or by bed rest

**HEPATITIS B** = caused by a virus spread by direct blood contact; a more serious form that may evolve into liver failure

**HEPATOMA** = tumor of the liver

**HEPATOMEGALY** = enlargement of the liver

**HERNIA** = abnormal protrusion of a muscle or organ

**HERNIATED DISK** = bulging of the gelatinous cushion between vertebrae causing pressure on nerves in the spinal column

**HERPES SIMIAE** = monkey virus almost always fatal in man; B virus

**HERPES SIMPLEX** = recurring infection caused by herpes virus; type 1: cold sores and fever blisters; type 2: genital sores
**HERPES VIRUS** = family of viruses which cause herpes simplex, herpes zoster and chicken pox
**HERPES ZOSTER** = shingles; inflammation of the spinal or cranial nerves from latent chicken-pox virus
**HIPPOCRATIC OATH** = oath exacted of medical students by Hippocrates in Ancient Greece, only part of which is still observed
**HIRSUTE** = hairy
**HISTOPLASMOSIS** = respiratory disease caused by a parasitic fungus; associated with AIDS
**HIVES** = itchy swellings on the skin
**HODGKIN'S DISEASE** = cancer of the lymph system
**HUMECTANT** = moistening agent
**HUMOR** = bodily fluid
**HUNTINGTON'S CHOREA** = inherited disease of the CNS resulting in DEMENTIA and bizarre involuntary movements
**HYDROCEPHALUS** = water on the brain
**HYDROPHOBIA** = fear of water; RABIES: deadly viral disease of the CNS
**HYPERALGESIA** = excessive sensitivity to pain
**HYPEREXTENSION** = extreme extension or stretching out
**HYPERGLYCEMIA** = excessive blood sugar
**HYPERPNEA** = increased rate of breathing
**HYPERPYREXIA** = fever above 106º F or 41.1º C
**HYPERTENSION** = high blood tension
**HYPERTROPHY** = increase in size of an organ or tissue not due to a tumor
**HYPERVENTILATION** = breathing faster than normal
**HYPOGLYCEMIA** = low blood pressure

**HYPOPROTHROMBINEMIA** = deficiency of blood clotting factor

**HYPOTENSION** = low blood pressure

**HYPOTHYROID** = insufficient thyroid output

**HYPOXEMIA** = insufficient oxygen in the blood

**HYSTERECTOMY** = removal of the uterus

**IATROGENIC DISORDER** = condition induced by treatment for something else

**ICTERUS** = yellowing of tissues; jaundice

**IDIOPATHY** = disease without apparent cause

**ILEITIS** = inflammation of the lower intestine; CROHN'S DISEASE

**IMMUNOASSAY** = test of body fluids to detect specific organisms

**IMPACTED** = pressed together so as to be immovable

**IMPETIGO** = inflammatory skin disease caused by STAPH, STREP or both

**INCONTINENCE** = inability to control bowel or bladder

**INCUBATION** = interval between exposure to infection and appearance of first symptom

**INDEX PATIENT** = first patient exposed to an epidemic

**INDURATION** = hardening of tissue

**INFARCT** = dead tissue as a result of a blockage of blood supply

**INFLUENZA** = acute, contagious respiratory infection caused by viruses and therefore not treatable with antibiotics

**INSULIN** = hormone essential for proper metabolism of blood sugar

**INSULIN SHOCK** = overdose of insulin resulting in reduced blood sugar

**INTERFERON** = protein formed when cells are exposed to viruses; protects cells against viral infection
**INTERN** = medical school graduate taking a year's training in hospital
**INTERNIST** = specialist in diseases not usually treated surgically
**INTESTINAL FLORA** = bacteria normally present in the intestines
**INTRAVENOUS** = into a vein
**INTRAVENOUS FEEDING** = introducing nutrients via special fluids
**INTUBATE** = insert a tube, especially into the windpipe
**IN VITRO** = in the test tube or laboratory (Latin: *in glass*)
**ISCHEMIA** = localized blood deficiency

**JAUNDICE** = yellow skin and eyes caused by bile pigments in the blood
**JUGULAR VEINS** = on either side of the neck which return blood from the head (see CARTOID ARTERIES)

**KERATITUS** = inflammation of the cornea
**KERATOTOMY** = incision of the cornea
**KINESIA** = motion sickness
**KNAPP'S FORCEPS** = forceps with roller-like blades

**LABIA** = lips
**LACERATION** = irregular tear of the flesh
**LACTATE** = salt derived from lactic acid
**LARYNGITIS** = inflammation of the LARYNX or voice box; hoarseness or loss of voice
**LARYNX** = upper part of the windpipe
**LASSA FEVER** = deadly disease caused by newly isolated virus, after a city in Africa where it first appeared

**LATENT** = hidden; not active

**LATERAL** = to the side

**LAVAGE** = washing out; irrigation

**LAXATIVE** = drug that eases constipation

**L-DOPA** = drug that treats Parkinson's disease

**LESION** = wound or sore

**LEUKEMIA** = excess white blood cells; a form of cancer

**LEUKOCYTE** = white blood cell that destroys foreign bodies

**LEUKOPENIA** = deficiency of white blood cells

**LIGATURE** = thread used to tie blood vessels

**LIPEDEMA** = painful fat syndrome; fatty, tender legs

**LIPOSUCTION** = suction out fat cells

**LITHIASIS** = formation of stones in the kidney or gall-bladder

**LITHOLAPAXY** = crushing and removal of stones from the bladder

**LOBOTOMY** = severing nerve tracts in frontal lobe of the brain

**LOU GEHRIG'S DISEASE** = amyotrophic lateral sclerosis, or ALS; progressive degeneration of nerve cells

**LUMBAGO** = lower back pain

**LUMBAR** = lower back between ribs and pelvis

**LUPUS** = skin disease

**LYMPHADENITIS** = inflammation of the lymph nodes

**LYMPH NODES** = produce lymphocytes, monocytes and act as blood filters

**LYMPHOCYTE** = cell that creates antibodies for the immune system

**LYMPHOMA** = growth in the lymph system, not necessarily malignant

**LYMPHOSARCOMA** = malignant tumor of the lymphatic tissue

**LYSIS** = gradual decline of fever or disease

**MACROPHAGE** = large white blood cell that destroys foreign bodies

**MACULA** = discolored skin

**MALIGNANT** = harmful; uncontrolled spreading; cancerous

**MANIA** = madness characterized by excessive excitement

**MASTECTOMY** = removal of breast tissue (see RADICAL MASTECTOMY)

**McBURNEY'S INCISION** = placement of incision used in appendectomy

**McBURNEY'S POINT** = location of tenderness in acute appendicitis

**MEDULLA** = marrow; inner portion of an organ

**MELANOMA** = skin cancer; malignant melanoma is the leading cause of death from skin disease

**MENINGES** = membrane covering brain and spinal cord

**MENINGITIS** = inflammation of the brain membrane

**METASTASIS** = spread of a disease through the body

**METHEMOGLOBINEMIA** = oxidized hemoglobin incapable of transporting oxygen

**MICTURITION** = urination

**MONONUCLEOSIS** = infectious glandular fever caused by a virus; "MONO"

**MORBID** = diseased

**MORIBUND** = dying

**MUCOUS MEMBRANE** = membrane lining passages that open to the air

**MUCUS** = fluid secreted by mucous membranes and glands

**MULTIPLE SCLEROSIS** = degenerative disease of the CNS and brain

**MÜNCHHAUSEN BY PROXY** = false illness claimed by one person for another

**MÜNCHHAUSEN SYNDROME** = self-inflicted or feigned illness; FACTITIOUS DISORDER
**MYALGIA** = tenderness or pain in the muscles
**MYASTHENIA GRAVIS** = weakness of muscles, especially the eyelids
**MYCOSIS** = fungous disease
**MYDRIASIS** = abnormal dilation of the pupil of the eyes
**MYELITIS** = inflammation of the spinal cord or bone marrow
**MYOCARDIAL INFARCT** = heart attack
**MYOCARDIAL INFARCTION** = heart attack due to a blood clot
**MYOCARDIAL ISCHEMIC PAIN** = pressing pain in the heart muscle
**MYOCARDIUM** = heart muscle
**MYOSIS** = contraction of the pupil of the eye
**MYOSITIS** = inflammation of muscle tissue
**MYOTONIA** = temporary rigidity of a muscle

**NARCOLEPSY** = sleeping sickness
**NARCOMANIA** = drug addiction
**NAUSEA** = sickness in the stomach occasionally followed by vomiting
**NECROTIZING FASCIITIS** = disease caused by flesh-eating bacteria
**NEONATAL** = pertaining to newborn infants less than one-month old
**NEOPLASM** = new, abnormal growth
**NEPHRECTOMY** = removal of the kidney
**NEPHRITIS** = inflammation of the kidney
**NEURALGIA** = sharp pain along a nerve
**NEURITIS** = inflammation of a nerve
**NEURO** = of the nerves or nervous system

**NEUROLOGICAL** = pertaining to the study of the nervous system

**NEUROSURGEON** = surgeon of the brain, spinal cord and nerves

**NITROGLYCERINE** = a vasodilator, especially for anginal pain

**NITROUS OXIDE** = anesthetic gas; "laughing gas"

**NONINVASIVE** = without surgery

**NOREPINEPHRINE** = drug for shock

**NOSOCOMIAL INFECTION** = acquired in a hospital; (see IATROGENIC)

**OBSTETRICS** = pregnancy, childbirth and care of newborns

**OCCIPITAL** = of the back of the head

**OCCLUSION** = blocking of ducts or blood vessels

**OCULAR** = of the eye

**OLFACTORY** = of smell

**ONCOLOGY** = study of tumors

**OPHTHALMITIS** = inflammation of the eye

**OPHTHALMOLOGIST** = eye specialist

**OPIATE** = narcotic derived from opium; pain killer or sedative

**ORTHOPEDIC SURGEON** = bone doctor

**OSTEITIS** = inflammation of the bone

**OSTEOCHONDRITIS** = inflammation of the bone and cartilage

**OSTEOLOGIST** = specialist in bone disease

**OSTEOMA** = tumor of the bone

**OSTEOMYELITIS** = inflammation of the bone, especially the marrow

**OSTEOPATH** = therapist skilled in manipulating bones, especially the spine

**OSTEOPLASTY** = bone surgery or grafting; plastic repair of bones

**OSTEOPOROSIS** = brittleness or weakening of the bones

**OTITIS** = inflammation of the ear

**OTORHINOLARYNGOLOGIST** = ear, nose and throat specialist

**OVARIECTOMY** = removal of an ovary

**PACEMAKER** = implanted battery-operated device to regulate heartbeat

**PALLIATIVE** = drug that relieves symptoms without curing

**PALLOR** = paleness

**PALPATE** = examine by touch

**PALPITATION** = rapid heartbeat

**PALSY** = paralysis

**PANCARDITIS** = inflammation of the entire heart

**PANCREATITIS** = inflammation of the pancreas

**PANDEMIC** = epidemic on a grand scale

**PAPANICOLAOU SMEAR TEST** = PAP TEST: for cancer of the cervix or uterus

**PAPILLOMA** = tumor of the skin or mucous membrane, usually benign

**PAPULE** = red raised area on the skin

**PARANOIA** = unfounded mistrust and suspicion

**PARAPLEGIA** = paralysis affecting both legs

**PARAPRAXIA** = disturbed mental process characterized by forgetfulness

**PAREGORIC** = opium derivative that eases intestinal cramps or diarrhea

**PARENTERAL** = injection into the bloodstream

**PARESIS** = slight paralysis

**PARKINSON'S DISEASE** = tremors, stiffness and slowness

**PAROTITIS** = mumps

**PAROXYSM** = sudden temporary attack

**PATHOGEN** = disease-causing agent

**PATHOGENIC** = causing disease

**PATHOGNOMONIC** = indicative of a disease, especially its symptoms

**PATHOLOGICAL** = diseased

**PATHOLOGIST** = specialist in diagnosing tissues in postmortems

**PATHOLOGY** = science of disease; condition produced by a disease

**PEDIATRICS** = pertaining to children's diseases

**PEDICULOSIS** = infestation of lice

**PELLAGRA** = disease due to lack of vitamin B2

**PEPTIC ULCER** = due to gastric juices in the stomach, duodenum or esophagus

**PERICARDIAL PAIN** = burning or stabbing pain due to inflammation of the pericardium

**PERICARDITIS** = inflammation of the membranes covering the heart

**PERICARDIUM** = the double membrane covering the heart

**PERISTALSIS** = involuntary wave motion, especially of the digestive tract

**PERITONEUM** = membrane lining the abdominal organs

**PERITONITIS** = inflammation of the membrane lining the abdominal organs

**PERNICIOUS** = life threatening

**PERNICIOUS ANEMIA** = deficiency of vitamin B12

**PERTUSSIS** = whooping cough

**PETECHIAE** = small purplish blood spots on the skin, as in typhus fever

**PHARYNGITIS** = sore throat

**PHARYNX** = common passageway from nose to larynx and mouth to esophagus

**PHLEBECTOMY** = removal of a vein

**PHLEBITIS** = inflammation of a vein

**PHLEBOTOMY** = surgical opening of a vein to withdraw blood

**PHOBIA** = irrational fear

**PLACEBO** = innocuous pill or medicine used in tests

**PLACENTA** = organ that contains the fetus during pregnancy

**PLANTAR** = of the sole of the foot

**PLASMA** = fluid part of the blood, watery and colorless

**PLEURA** = membrane covering the lungs

**PLEURISY** = inflammation of the membrane covering the lungs

**PNEUMOCOCCI** = bacteria responsible for pneumonia and meningitis

**PNEUMONIA** = infection of the lungs

**POLIOMYELITIS** = viral disease often resulting in paralysis; "polio" and "infantile paralysis"

**POLYP** = usually benign tumor that grows on mucous membranes, as in the lower intestine

**POSTERIOR** = behind or coming after

**POSTPARTUM** = after childbirth

**POTASSIUM** = mineral element essential for normal heart muscle function and conductivity of nerve impulses

**PRIAPISM** = abnormal persistent erection

**PROCTITIS** = inflammation of the rectum

**PROCTOLOGY** = diseases of the colon, rectum and anus

**PROCTOSCOPE** = instrument for examining interior of the rectum

**PROGESTERONE** = female sex hormone

**PROGNOSIS** = prediction or forecast

**PROLAPSE** = downward shift of a organ

**PROPHYLACTIC** = protecting against disease
$\qquad\qquad\qquad\;\;$ = condom

**PROSTATE** = male sex gland at the base of the bladder
**PROSTATECTOMY** = removal of all or part of the prostate
**PROSTATITIS** = inflammation of the prostate
**PROSTHESIS** = artificial limb or body part
**PRURIGO** = itchy skin disease
**PRURITIS** = itchiness
**PSITTACOSIS** = disease similar to pneumonia transmitted by birds; "parrot fever"
**PSORIASIS** = chronic skin disease characterized by scaly lesions
**PSYCH** = of the mind
**PSYCHOSOMATIC** = diseases caused by psychological factors
**PUERPERIUM** = the time after childbirth
**PULMONARY** = of the lungs
**PULMONARY EMBOLISM** = obstructing blood clot in a lung artery
**PURGATIVE** = cathartic or laxative
**PURULENT** = containing pus
**PYLORIC** = pertaining to the opening between stomach and duodenum
**PYREXIA** = fever
**PYROSIS** = heartburn

**QUADRIPLEGIA** = paralysis of the arms and legs
**QUINSY** = acute inflammation of the tonsils

**RABIES** = HYDROPHOBIA; deadly viral disease of the CNS
**RADICAL MASTECTOMY** = removal of the entire breast and surrounding tissue
**RADIOLOGY** = where x-rays are taken
= diagnosis and treatment with radioactive substances

**REMISSION** = easing or disappearance of symptoms or disease

**REN** = kidney

**RENAL** = of the kidney

**RESECTION** = removal of part of an organ or tissue

**RESERVOIR** = reservoir of infection; source of an infectious agent or disease

**RESIDENT** = physician who continues training in hospital after internship

**RETICULUM** = network

**RETINITIS** = inflammation of the retina of the eye

**RETINITIS PIGMENTOSA** = degeneration of the eye with pigmentary changes in the retina

**RETINOBLASTOMA** = malignant tumor of the retina, only in children

**RETRACTOR** = instrument to pull back edges of a wound or to separate the ribs or bones for surgery

**RHEUMATIC FEVER** = often followed by heart or kidney disease

**RH FACTOR** = common blood group raising problems if a pregnant RH-negative woman produces antibodies against her RH-positive fetus

**RHINO** = of the nose

**RHINOPLASTY** = plastic surgery of the nose

**RHINOVIRUS** = cold virus

**RHOGAM** = Rhesus gammaglobulin: given to prevent RH disease

**RICKETS** = improper development of bones and teeth due to lack of vitamin D

**RIFAMPIN** = antibiotic used to treat tuberculosis

**RIGOR MORTIS** = stiffening of the muscles after death

**ROCKY MOUNTAIN SPOTTED FEVER** = disease spread by ticks causing fever, rashes, headaches and muscle pain

**RUBELLA** = German measles
**RUBEOLA** = measles

**SACROILIAC** = joint connecting spine to hip bone
**SAINT VITUS' DANCE** = nervous disease with involuntary motions; CHOREA
**SALINE** = salt
**SALINE SOLUTION** = sodium chloride and distilled water; normally 0.85% salt
**SALMONELLA** = bacteria which cause food poisoning
**SARCOMA** = cancer of muscle, bone and other connective tissue
**SCABIES** = infection of parasites that burrow under the skin to lay eggs
**SCHICK TEST** = for susceptibility to diphtheria
**SCIATICA** = pain along the sciatic nerve from the base of the spine through the legs
**SCLEROSIS** = hardening or thickening of a tissue
**SCOLIOSIS** = curvature of the spine
**SCROFULA** = tuberculosis of the lymph nodes in the neck
**SCRUB NURSE** = operating room nurse who hands instruments to the surgeon
**SEBORRHEA** = greasiness of the skin
**SECTION** = cutting
**SEDATIVE** = drug that calms or relaxes
**SENESCENCE** = process of aging
**SENILITY** = deterioration associated with age
**SEPSIS** = infection from germs in blood or tissues
**SEPTICEMIA** = blood poisoning
**SEQUELA** = condition resulting from a disease
**SEROLOGY** = scientific study of blood serum
**SERUM** = fluid which moistens serous membranes, and the watery part of blood after coagulation

**SHOCK** = slowing of vital body processes

**SICKLE CELL ANEMIA** = hereditary anemia due to malformed red blood cells

**SIG** = Latin: *signum*; used on prescriptions to indicate "write [on the label]"

**SILICOSIS** = inflammation of the lungs associated with sand blasting and stone cutting

**SINOATRIAL NODE** = the heart's natural pacemaker

**SINUS** = hollow space in the bones of the face

**SINUSITIS** = inflammation of a sinus

**SOMNAMBULISM** = sleepwalking

**SOPORIFIC** = sleeping pill

**SPASM** = involuntary contraction of a muscle

**SPASTIC** = convulsive

**SPECULUM** = instrument to open vagina or cervix for examination

**SPHYGMOMANOMETER** = instrument for measuring blood pressure

**SPINA BIFIDA** = incomplete growth of vertebrae leaving spinal canal exposed

**SPINAL TAP** = withdrawal of fluid for analysis or to relieve pressure on the brain; lumbar puncture

**SPLENITIS** = inflammation of the spleen

**SPONDYLITIS** = inflammation of the spine

**SPUTUM** = mucus and saliva from the lungs and throat

**SQUAMOUS CELL CARCINOMA** = cancer on the surface of the skin than can spread but with low incidence of malignancy

**STAPHYLOCOCCI** = bacteria that cause food poisoning and skin infections

**STASIS** = standing still; stagnation of blood, urine or intestines

**STENOSIS** = narrowing; constriction

**STEROID RAGE** = irrational behavior and increased aggressiveness due to steroid abuse
**STEROIDS** = see ANABOLIC STEROIDS
**STETHOSCOPE** = instrument that amplifies the heart-beat and other body sounds
**STOMATITUS** = inflammation of the mouth
**STRABISMUS** = crossed-eyes
**STRANGURY** = painful interruption of urination due to spasms of urethra and bladder
**STREPTOCOCCI** = bacteria that cause scarlet fever and sore throat
**STRICTURE** = narrowing
**STROKE** = interruption of blood to the brain
**STUPOR** = unconsciousness; lethargy with suppressed feeling
**STYPTIC** = contracting a blood vessel; stopping bleeding
**SUBCLAVIAN** = under the clavicle or collarbone
**SUBCUTANEOUS** = under the skin
**SULFONAMIDES** = sulfa drugs; the first antibiotics
**SUPPURATION** = formation of pus
**SURGEON** = specialist in operating
**SUTTON'S LAW** = look for disease where it's most likely to be found, such as Alzheimer's in old people; after Willie Sutton who, when asked why he robbed banks, allegedly said, "That's where the money is."
**SUTURE** = sew together
= surgical thread
= line or seam
**SYNCOPE** = fainting
**SYNDROME** = group of related symptoms
**SYNOVIA** = lubricating fluid of the joints
**SYNTASIS** = stretching
**SYRIGMUS** = hissing or ringing in the ears

**SYRINGITIS** = inflammation of the eustachian tube
**SYRINGOMYELITIS** = inflammation and dilation of the spinal cord's central canal
**SYRINGOTOMY** = curing a FISTULA by cutting and closing
**SYSTOLIC PRESSURE** = blood pressure reading when the heart contracts or pumps (see DIASTOLIC)

**TACHYCARDIA** = abnormally rapid heartbeat
**TAY-SACHS DISEASE** = congenital disease of the brain characterized by disability, blindness and death
**TENDONITIS** = inflammation of a tendon
**TESTOSTERONE** = male sex hormone; natural steroid that stimulates tissue growth and blood flow
**TETANUS** = acute infection of a wound causing muscle stiffness or contractions; "lockjaw"
**TETRALOGY OF FALLOT** = four abnormalities of the heart
**THANATOID** = resembling death
**THORACENTESIS** = puncture of the chest to remove fluids
**THORACIC** = of the chest
**THORACOSCOPY** = examination of the lung membrane through a scope
**THORACOTOMY** = lung biopsy
**THORAX** = chest
**THROMBOSIS** = formation of a clot in the blood stream
**THROMBUS** = blood clot
**THRUSH** = fungus in the mouth or throat
**THYROIDECTOMY** = removal of the thyroid gland
**THYROID GLAND** = gland in the neck that regulates metabolism and growth
**TINEA** = ringworm; fungous infection of the skin; "barber's itch," "jock itch," "athlete's foot"
**TINE SKIN TEST** = for tuberculosis; (see PPD)

**TINNITUS** = buzzing or ringing in the ear
**TONIC** = muscular tension
**TONSILLECTOMY** = removal of the tonsils
**TONSILLITIS** = inflammation of the tonsils
**TONSILS** = lymphoid tissue at the back of the throat
**TORTICOLLIS** = stiff neck
**TOXEMIA** = blood poisoning
**TOXIC** = poisonous
**TOXICS** = poisons or drugs in the blood
**TOXIC SHOCK SYNDROME** = acute staph blood poisoning associated with use of tampons
**TOXIN** = poisonous substance produced by bacteria
**TOXOPLASMOSIS** = parasitic disease transmitted by animal feces or undercooked meat
**TRACHEA** = the windpipe
**TRACHEOTOMY** = surgical cut through throat to assist breathing
**TRACHOMA** = viral infection of the eye which could lead to blindness
**TRACTION** = drawing or pulling
**TRANQUILIZER** = drug that relieves stress
**TRAUMA** = shock or injury
**TREPAN** = bore into the skull to relieve pressure
= instrument for boring into the skull
**TRIAGE** = screening and classification of injured to determine priority of treatment
**TRICHINOSOS** = parasitic disease from under-cooked pork
**TRICHOMONIASIS** = parasitic inflammation of the vagina or male urethra
**TRISMUS** = contraction of the jaw muscles; "lockjaw"
**TUBAL LIGATION** = female sterilization in which the Fallopian tubes are tied or cut
**TUMEFACTION** = swelling

**TUMOR** = abnormal growth of tissue, harmless or cancerous

**TUSSIS** = cough

**TYPHOID FEVER** = bacterial infection spread by contaminated water, food, shellfish or human carriers; may result in dangerous intestinal hemorrhage

**TYPHUS** = disease spread by lice and characterized by high fever


**ULCER** = open sore

**ULCERATIVE COLITIS** = inflammation of the colon and rectum resulting in ulcers and blood in the stool

**ULTRASOUND** = VHF sound waves used to visualize internal organs or the fetus

**UREMIA** = retention in the blood of normally excreted toxins due to kidney failure

**URETER** = tube that connects the kidney to the bladder through which urine passes

**URETHRA** = tube from the bladder through which urine is voided

**URETHRITIS** = inflammation of the urethra

**UROGENITAL** = of the urinary and genital organs

**UROLOGY** = study of urogenital disorders

**URTICARIA** = HIVES; welts on the skin due to allergic reactions

**UTERUS** = womb


**VARICELLA** = chicken pox

**VARICOSE VEINS** = swollen veins due to weak valves in the veins (see HEMORRHOIDS)

**VARIOLA** = smallpox

**VASCULAR** = pertains usually to blood vessels

**VASCULITIS** = inflammation of the blood vessels

**VASECTOMY** = sterilization of the male by tying the tube in the penis

**VASOCONSTRICTOR** = causes blood vessels to narrow or contract

**VASODILATOR** = causes blood vessels to widen or enlarge

**VASOMOTOR** = of nerves having muscular control of the blood vessels

**VECTOR** = carrier or transmitter of a disease

**VEIN** = blood vessel carrying oxygen-depleted blood back to the heart

**VENEPUNCTURE** = puncturing a vein to withdraw blood

**VENEREAL DISEASES** = sexually transmitted diseases

**VENESECTION** = opening a vein to withdraw blood

**VENOUS** = of the veins

**VENTRAL** = of the front of the body: the abdomen

**VENTRICLE** = of the lower chambers of the heart

**VENTRICULAR FIBRILLATION** = chaotic twitching of the lower heart chambers

**VENTRICULAR TACHYCARDIA** = abnormally rapid beat of the lower heart chambers

**VERRUCA** = wart or tumor of the epidermis caused by a virus

**VERTEBRAE** = 33 bones of the spinal column; singular: vertebra

**VERTIGO** = dizziness; sensation of hovering in space

**VIRAL INFECTION** = cannot be treated with antibiotics; some can be prevented by vaccination

**VIREMIA** = viruses in the blood

**VIRULENT** = highly infectious

**VISCERA** = internal organs

**WASSERMAN TEST** = blood test for syphilis

**XERODERM** = dry skin
**XEROSIS** = abnormal dryness

**ZOONOSES** = diseases communicable from animals to man
**ZOOTOXIN** = poison produced by an animal, like snake venom
**ZYMOSIS** = fermentation

# MAJOR CITY AIRPORT CODES

Acapulco, Mexico .........................ACA
Albany, New York ........................ALB
Albuquerque, New Mexico .................ABQ
Anchorage, Alaska ........................ANC
Aruba, Aruba ............................AUA
Atlantic City International, New Jersey .........ACY
Atlanta, Georgia .........................ATL
Augusta, Georgia .........................AGS
Austin, Texas ...........................AUS

Baltimore, Maryland ......................BWI
Bakersfield, California ....................BFL
Bangor, Maine ..........................BGR
Baton Rouge, Louisiana ...................BTR
Bermuda ..............................BDA
Birmingham, Alabama ....................BHM
Billings, Montana ........................BIL
Bimini, Bahamas ........................BIM
Bismarck, North Dakota ...................BIS
Boise, Idaho ............................BOI
Boston, Massachusetts ....................BOS
Bridgeport, Connecticut ..................BDR
Buffalo, New York .......................BUF
Burbank, California ......................BUR
Butte, Montana .........................BTM

Calgary, Alberta .........................YYC
Cancun, Mexico .........................CUN
Casper, Wyoming ........................CPR
Cheyenne, Wyoming ......................CYS

Cedar Rapids/Iowa City ......................CID
Champaign, Illinois ..........................CMI
Charlotte, North Carolina .....................CLT
Charlottetown, Prince Edward Island .........YHG
Charleston, South Carolina ...................CHS
Chicago, Illinois — O'Hare ...................ORD
        — Midway .................MDW
Cincinnati, Ohio ............................CVG
Cleveland, Ohio .............................CLE
Colorado Springs, Colorado ..................COS
Columbia, South Carolina ....................CAE
Columbus, Georgia ..........................CSG
Columbus, Ohio .............................CMH
Cozumel, Mexico ...........................CZM

Dallas/Fort Worth, Texas — Intl. .............DFW
        — Love Field ........DAL
Decatur, Illinois ............................DEC
Denver, Colorado ...........................DEN
Des Moines, Iowa ...........................DSM
Detroit, Michigan — City ...................DET
        — Metro ..............DTW
Dubuque, Iowa .............................DBQ
Duluth, Minnesota ..........................DLH

Edmonton, Alberta .........................YEG
El Paso, Texas ..............................ELP
Evansville, Indiana ..........................EVV

Fairbanks, Alaska ...........................FAI
Fargo, North Dakota ........................FAR
Flagstaff, Arizona ...........................FLG
Flint, Michigan .............................FNT

Fort Lauderdale, Florida .......................FLL
Fort Myers, Florida ..........................RSW
Fort Smith, Arkansas ........................FSM
Fort Wayne, Indiana .........................FWA
Fresno, California ...........................FAT

Gander, Newfoundland .......................YQX
Goose Bay, Newfoundland ....................YYR
Grand Cayman, West Indies ..................GCM
Grand Forks, North Dakota ..................GFK
Grand Rapids, Michigan .....................GRR
Green Bay, Wisconsin .......................GRB
Greensboro/Winston-Salem, North Carolina .....INT
Greenville/Spartanburg, South Carolina .........GSP

Halifax, Nova Scotia .......................YHZ
Harrisburg, Pennsylvania ...................MDT
Hartford, Conn/Springfield, Massachusetts .....HFD
Havana, Cuba .............................HAV
Hilo, Hawaii ...............................ITO
Honolulu, Hawaii ..........................HNL
Houston, Texas International ................IAH
Huntsville, Alabama .......................HSV

Indianapolis, Indiana ......................IND

Jackson, Mississippi .......................JAN
Jacksonville, Florida .......................JAX
Juneau, Alaska .............................JNU

Kansas City, Missouri International............MCI
Kalamazoo, Michigan .......................AZO
Kingston, Jamaica...........................KIN

| | |
|---|---|
| Knoxville, Tennessee | TYS |
| Kona, Hawaii | KOA |
| | |
| Lansing, Michigan | LAN |
| Las Vegas, Nevada | LAS |
| Lexington, Kentucky | LEX |
| Lincoln, Nebraska | LNK |
| Little Rock, Arkansas | LIT |
| Long Beach, California | LGB |
| Los Angeles, California | LAX |
| Louisville, Kentucky | SDF |
| | |
| Macon, Georgia | MCN |
| Madison, Wisconsin | MSN |
| Memphis, Tennessee | MEM |
| Meridian, Mississippi | MEI |
| Mexico City, Mexico | MEX |
| Miami, Florida | MIA |
| Milwaukee, Wisconsin | MKE |
| Minneapolis/St. Paul, Minnesota | MSP |
| Mobile, Alabama | MOB |
| Moline, Illinois | MLI |
| Montgomery, Alabama | MGM |
| Montreal, Quebec | YMQ |
| | |
| Nashville, Tennessee | BNA |
| Nassau, Bahamas | NAS |
| New Orleans, Louisiana | MSY |
| New York, New York — Kennedy | JFK |
| — LaGuardia | LGA |
| — Newark | EWR |

Oakland, California . . . . . . . . . . . . . . . . . . . . . . . . . . .OAK
Oklahoma City, Oklahoma . . . . . . . . . . . . . . . . . . . .OKC
Omaha, Nebraska . . . . . . . . . . . . . . . . . . . . . . . . . . . .OMA
Orange County, California . . . . . . . . . . . . . . . . . . . .SNA
Orlando, Florida . . . . . . . . . . . . . . . . . . . . . . . . . . . .MCO
Ottawa, Ontario . . . . . . . . . . . . . . . . . . . . . . . . . . . .YOW

Palm Springs, California . . . . . . . . . . . . . . . . . . . . . .PSP
Pensacola, Florida . . . . . . . . . . . . . . . . . . . . . . . . . . .PNS
Philadelphia, Pennsylvania . . . . . . . . . . . . . . . . . . .PHL
Phoenix, Arizona . . . . . . . . . . . . . . . . . . . . . . . . . . .PHX
Pittsburgh, Pennsylvania . . . . . . . . . . . . . . . . . . . . .PIT
Pocatello, Idaho . . . . . . . . . . . . . . . . . . . . . . . . . . . .PIH
Providence, Rhode Island . . . . . . . . . . . . . . . . . . . .PVD

Quebec City, Quebec . . . . . . . . . . . . . . . . . . . . . . . .YQB
Raleigh/Durham, North Carolina . . . . . . . . . . . . . .RDU
Rapid City, South Dakota . . . . . . . . . . . . . . . . . . . .RAP
Regina, Saskatchewan . . . . . . . . . . . . . . . . . . . . . . .YQR
Reno, Nevada . . . . . . . . . . . . . . . . . . . . . . . . . . . . . .RNO
Rochester, New York . . . . . . . . . . . . . . . . . . . . . . . .ROC
Rockford, Illinois . . . . . . . . . . . . . . . . . . . . . . . . . . .RFD

Sacramento, California . . . . . . . . . . . . . . . . . . . . . . .SMF
Saginaw, Michigan . . . . . . . . . . . . . . . . . . . . . . . . . .MBS
Salt Lake City, Utah . . . . . . . . . . . . . . . . . . . . . . . . .SLC
San Antonio, Texas . . . . . . . . . . . . . . . . . . . . . . . . . .SAT
San Diego, California . . . . . . . . . . . . . . . . . . . . . . . .SAN
San Francisco, California . . . . . . . . . . . . . . . . . . . . .SFO
San Jose, California . . . . . . . . . . . . . . . . . . . . . . . . . .SJC
San Juan, Puerto Rico . . . . . . . . . . . . . . . . . . . . . . . .SJU
Santa Fe, New Mexico . . . . . . . . . . . . . . . . . . . . . . .SAF
Sarasota/Bradenton, Florida . . . . . . . . . . . . . . . . . .SRQ

Saskatoon, Saskatchewan . . . . . . . . . . . . . . . . . . . . . .YXE
Savannah, Georgia . . . . . . . . . . . . . . . . . . . . . . . . . . .SAV
Seattle/Tacoma, Washington . . . . . . . . . . . . . . . . . .SEA
Shreveport, Louisiana . . . . . . . . . . . . . . . . . . . . . . . .SHV
Sioux City, Iowa . . . . . . . . . . . . . . . . . . . . . . . . . . . .SUX
Sioux Falls, South Dakota . . . . . . . . . . . . . . . . . . . .FSD
South Bend, Indiana . . . . . . . . . . . . . . . . . . . . . . . . .SBN

Spokane, Washington . . . . . . . . . . . . . . . . . . . . . . . .GEG
Springfield, Illinois . . . . . . . . . . . . . . . . . . . . . . . . . . .SPI
Springfield, Missouri . . . . . . . . . . . . . . . . . . . . . . . . .SGF
St. John, New Brunswick . . . . . . . . . . . . . . . . . . . . . .YSJ
St. John's, Newfoundland . . . . . . . . . . . . . . . . . . . . .YYT
St. Louis, Missouri . . . . . . . . . . . . . . . . . . . . . . . . . . .STL
Syracuse, New York . . . . . . . . . . . . . . . . . . . . . . . . . .SYR

Tampa/St. Petersburg, Florida . . . . . . . . . . . . . . . . . .TPA
Topeka, Kansas . . . . . . . . . . . . . . . . . . . . . . . . . . . . .TOP
Toronto, Ontario . . . . . . . . . . . . . . . . . . . . . . . . . . . .YTO
Tucson, Arizona . . . . . . . . . . . . . . . . . . . . . . . . . . . . .TUS
Tulsa, Oklahoma . . . . . . . . . . . . . . . . . . . . . . . . . . . .TUL

Vancouver, British Columbia . . . . . . . . . . . . . . . . . .YVR

Washington, DC — National . . . . . . . . . . . . . . . . . .DCA
                    — Dulles . . . . . . . . . . . . . . . . . .IAD
West Palm Beach, Florida . . . . . . . . . . . . . . . . . . . . .PBI
Wichita, Kansas . . . . . . . . . . . . . . . . . . . . . . . . . . . . .ICT
Windsor, Ontario . . . . . . . . . . . . . . . . . . . . . . . . . . .YQG
Winnipeg, Manitoba . . . . . . . . . . . . . . . . . . . . . . . . .YWG

## POSTAL CODES
### FOR US STATES & TERRITORIES

| | |
|---|---|
| ALABAMA | AL |
| ALASKA | AK |
| ARIZONA | AZ |
| ARKANSAS | AR |
| CALIFORNIA | CA |
| COLORADO | CO |
| CONNECTICUT | CT |
| DELAWARE | DE |
| DC | DC |
| FLORIDA | FL |
| GEORGIA | GA |
| GUAM | GU |
| HAWAII | HI |
| IDAHO | ID |
| ILLINOIS | IL |
| INDIANA | IN |
| IOWA | IA |
| KANSAS | KS |
| KENTUCKY | KY |
| LOUISIANA | LA |
| MAINE | ME |
| MARYLAND | MD |
| MASSACHUSETTS | MA |
| MICHIGAN | MI |
| MINNESOTA | MN |
| MISSISSIPPI | MS |
| MISSOURI | MO |
| MONTANA | MT |
| NEBRASKA | NE |
| NEVADA | NV |

| | |
|---|---|
| NEW HAMPSHIRE | NH |
| NEW JERSEY | NJ |
| NEW MEXICO | NM |
| NEW YORK | NY |
| NORTH CAROLINA | NC |
| NORTH DAKOTA | ND |
| OHIO | OH |
| OKLAHOMA | OK |
| OREGON | OR |
| PENNSYLVANIA | PA |
| PUERTO RICO | PR |
| RHODE ISLAND | RI |
| SOUTH CAROLINA | SC |
| SOUTH DAKOTA | SD |
| TENNESSEE | TN |
| TEXAS | TX |
| UTAH | UT |
| VERMONT | VT |
| VIRGINIA | VA |
| VIRGIN ISLANDS | VI |
| WASHINGTON | WA |
| WEST VIRGINIA | WV |
| WISCONSIN | WI |
| WYOMING | WY |

## *POSTAL SYMBOLS FOR CANADIAN PROVINCES & TERRITORIES*

```
ALBERTA ...................................AB
BRITISH COLUMBIA ........................BC
MANITOBA .................................MB
NEW BRUNSWICK ...........................NB
NEWFOUNDLAND ..........................NF
NORTHWEST TERRITORIES ..................NT
NOVA SCOTIA ..............................NS
ONTARIO ..................................ON
PRINCE EDWARD ISLAND ..................PE
QUEBEC ...................................PQ
SASKATCHEWAN ...........................SK
YUKON TERRITORY .......................YT
```

# NUMERICAL NOMENCLATURE

**00** = standard buckshot-size designation (.33 inch); "double ought"

**007** = James Bond, fictional agent of MI-6 whose 00 designation is a license to kill

**1-A** = fit for military service

**1B** = first base (baseball)

= one-base hit, or single (baseball)

**1K** = one kilometer; a race of that length

**1LT** = first lieutenant

**2B** = second base (baseball)

= two-base hit, or double (baseball)

**2-BBL** = 2-barrel carburetor (automotive)

**2-D** = two dimensions

**2LT** = second lieutenant

**2x4** = standard piece of lumber, from its approximate width and thickness in inches

**2 1/2** = 2 1/2-ton truck; "deuce and a half" (military)

**3B** = third base (baseball)

= three-base hit, or triple (baseball)

**3C** = Third Cambridge Catalog of Radio Stars (astronomy)

**3-D** = three dimensions

**3M** = Minnesota Mining and Manufacturing; also MMM

**4x4** = four-wheel drive

**4-BBL** = four-barrel carburetor (automotive)

**4d** = four-penny nail, 1 1/2" long

**4-F** = unfit for military service

**4 WD** = four-wheel drive

**5W** = weight or thickness of motor oil; extremely thin

**5W-30** = from 5-weight to 30-weight; viscosity or thickness of motor oil—five being thin when cold, 30 being thick when hot

5W-40 = see 5W-30
5K = five kilometers; a race of that length
6d = six-penny nail, 2" long
6's and 7's = confused; "at sixes and sevens"
7.62 = pistol or rifle
       = caliber of ammunition in millimeters; "NATO"
8d = eight-penny nail, 2 1/2" long
9MM = nine millimeter pistol
       = caliber of ammunition in millimeters
10 = business-size envelope, 4 1/8" x 9 1/2"
10 GAUGE = shotgun
             = very large shotgun shell
10K = ten kilometers; a race of that length
10MM = ten millimeter pistol
         = caliber of ammunition in millimeters
10-SPEED = bicycle with ten speeds or gear changes
10W = weight or thickness of motor oil
10W-30 = see 5W-30
10W-40 = see 5W-30
10W-50 = see 5W-30
12d = twelve-penny nail, 3" long
12 GAUGE = shotgun
             = large shotgun shell
16d = sixteen-penny nail, 3 1/2" long
16 GAUGE = shotgun
             = medium shotgun shell
20d = twenty-penny nail, 4" long
20 GAUGE = shotgun
             = small shotgun shell
20W = weight or thickness of motor oil
20/20 = normal eyesight
21 = card game; blackjack

22 = rifle or pistol
   = caliber of ammunition in inches (.22)
25 = pistol
   = caliber of ammunition in inches (.25)
30 = newspaper symbol marking the end of a piece of copy
30/06 = rifle of .30 caliber, model 1906; "thirty ought six"
30-30 = rifle of .30 caliber, model 1930; "thirty thirty"
30W = weight or thickness of motor oil
32 = pistol
   = caliber of ammunition in inches (.32)
33 1/3 = long-playing record, from 33 1/3 rpm
38 = pistol or revolver
   = caliber of ammunition in inches (.38)
40W = weight or thickness of motor oil
44 = revolver
   = caliber of ammunition in inches (.44)
45 = record, from 45 rpm
   = pistol or revolver
   = caliber of ammunition in inches (.45)
**50 caliber** = heavy machine gun, after its caliber in inches (.50)
50W = viscosity or thickness of motor oil; extremely thick
50-50 = even split or even odds
55 = federal speed limit; "double nickel"
66 = US Route 66; old designation for famous highway from Chicago to LA
72 = usual par round in golf
73 = model of Winchester rifle or carbine, after 1873
75 = French artillery piece, after its caliber in millimeters; "French 75"
76 = 1776, as in Spirit of '76
78 = record, from 78 rpm
**82nd** = US Airborne Regiment

**86** = stop serving inebriated customer; bartender slang code
     = no more left; restaurant code
**88** = model of Oldsmobile
     = keys on a piano
     = German WW II antiaircraft gun, after its caliber in millimeters
**94** = model of Winchester rifle or carbine, after 1894
**98** = model of Oldsmobile
**100** = standard sprint race; one-hundred-yard dash
**101** = a basic class in college, as "Biology 101"
**101st** = US Airborne Regiment
**105** = artillery piece, after its caliber in millimeters
**144** = one gross; a dozen dozen
**201** = military personnel file; 201 file
**223** = caliber in inches of cartridge used in M-16 rifle (.223)
**225** = Buick Electra 225; "deuce and a quarter"
**300** = model of Chrysler
**303** = rifle (British)
     = caliber of ammunition in inches (.303)
**357** = magnum revolver or pistol
     = caliber of ammunition in inches (.357)
**380** = pistol
     = caliber of ammunition in inches (.380)
**401(k)** = defined contribution pension plan; after US tax code section
**403(b)** = defined contribution pension plan for employees of colleges, hospitals and some nonprofit institutions
**410** = very small shotgun gauge, actually .410 caliber; "four-ten"
**442** = heroic WW II Japanese-American regiment in US Army
     = Oldsmobile muscle car
**500** = usually the Indianapolis 500 automobile race

**666** = ancient designation for the devil or the antichrist
**880** = half-mile race, in yards
**911** = emergency telephone number for police, fire or medical assistance
**1040** = IRS tax-return form; "ten-forty"
**1911** = automatic pistol designated by date of adoption by military; also known as a "45"
**90210** = a ZIP code in Beverly Hills, California